Here's what's being about the Great Vacations With Your Kids series

"I can't imagine books that cover their subjects more thoroughly, clearly and honestly than the Great Vacations With Your Kids series. Dorothy Jordon truly knows everything that's worth knowing about family travel. For parents who want to explore the world with their children, these books are positively indispensable."

—Bill McCoy
Senior Editor, *Parents Magazine*

"Jordon's books are a must for families. Her descriptions of organizations, lodgings, outfitters and programs show parents the many ways they can enjoy vacations with their children. The wealth and variety of trips are impressive."

—Candyce Stapen
Contributing Editor, *FamilyFun*

"Dorothy Jordon is the den mother of family travel, so it's no wonder she's writing the ultimate get-up-and-go family vacation series. You'll love her insider tips, and the Booked for Travel reading lists, too."

—Susan Lapinski
Articles Editor, *Child Magazine*

"As far as family travel is concerned, Dorothy Jordon has been there and done that. *Great Vacations With Your Kids* are invaluable, extremely readable, totally knowledgeable resources for everyone, whether you idea of vacation involves roughing it or being pampered."

—Nancy Clark
Deputy Editor, *Family Circle*

"When it comes to traveling with children, Dorothy Jordon is the Pied Piper of tour guides. The next time I leave home with my daughters, I am going to one of these kid-friendly destinations."

Jack Bierman
Editor, *L.A. Parent* magazine

ACKNOWLEDGMENTS

Throughout this book I use the work "we" in lieu of "I." This is because this entire series could not have been created without the help and assistance of the many contributors to **Family Travel Times**®.

Specifically, I want to thank Joy Anderson for her fine editing and writing and her patience during the tenure of this project. I also want to thank my most avid supporters and contributors — my husband, David Ferber and my sons, Jordon and Russell Ferber — with whom I have shared many adventure vacations.

Thanks are also due Carol Eannarino, Debra Wishik Englander, Holly Reich, Claudia Lapin, Ann Banks, Candyce Stapen, Christine Loomis, Ronnie Mae Weiss and the numerous parents who have shared their travel experiences with us.

No book of this sort can be complete without the participation of our "test" children — Jordon Ferber, Russell Ferber, Victoria Anderson, Rachel Shapiro, Kate Petre, Jenny Jordon, Alissa Kempler, Jonah Sobel, Daniel Sobel, Dylan Kreitman, Jenna Kreitman, Elise Englander and Adrienne Bernhard.

And, I would like to thank my parents Sydelle and Charlie Jordon for instilling in me a sense of adventure and spirit that led me to explore the many options in this book.

About the author

Dorothy Jordon has been involved with the travel industry for 26 years. She is the founder and managing director of TWYCH, Travel With Your Children, the resource information center for parents and travel agents on family travel.

Dorothy Jordon is the leading spokesperson in the nation on family travel. Since 1984 she has published **Family Travel Times**®, a newsletter specializing in family travel. She was the contributing travel editor to *Family Circle* and was the travel editor for *Child Magazine*. Her family travel columns and articles have been published in *Parents Magazine*, *USA Today*, *The New York Times*, *Ladies Home Journal*, *Travel Weekly*, *The Los Angeles Times*, *Diversion*, *Travel/Holiday* magazine, *Cond Nast Traveler* and more. She has appeared on national television's Good Morning America, Live with Regis and Kathy Lee, The Today Show, ABC's Business World, CBS News, FOX News, CNN, Financial News Network, The Travel Channel and many more programs.

Dorothy is married and lives in New York City with her husband and two teenage sons. They all still enjoy family vacations together.

Great Adventure Vacations

With Your Kids

by Dorothy Jordon

World Leisure Corporation
Hampstead, NH • Boston, MA

Distributed to the trade in the USA by
LPC Group, Login Trade, 1436 West Randolph Street, Chicago, IL 60607
tel. (312) 733-8228; (800) 626-4330

Distributed to the trade in Canada by
E.A. Milley Enterprises, Inc., Locust Hill,, Ontario L0H 1J0, Canada; tel. (800) 399-6858

Mail Order, Catalog and Special Sales by
World Leisure Corporation, 177 Paris Street, Boston, MA 02128
tel. (617) 569-1966; fax: (617) 561-7654; e-mail: wleisure@aol.com

ISBN: 0-915009-48-X

*This is dedicated to the memory
of two individuals whose lives came to an end
during the writing of this book.*

*Susanne Jensen — who never lived to see her
dreams realized and filled the lives of those
who knew her with love and hope --*

and

*Frances Tyler, fondly known as Mrs. T.,
the matriarch of The Tyler Place, who shared
her dreams with hundreds of families every year.*

TABLE OF CONTENTS

INTRODUCTION

When we were young, adventure vacations as we know them today did not exist. Adventure travel was strictly for the skilled and daring independent adult traveler. This is not to say that families didn't hike, fish, canoe, camp and the like when they went off on vacation; they did. But how many went whitewater rafting, drove cattle or trekked in the Himalayas? In the past couple of decades, these adventures and many others have become as available to families as the cottage on the lake was to generations past. Whereas, formerly, exciting physical activity was just one element of the family vacation, on adventure vacations, the activity itself is now the focus of the experience. This book, **Great Adventure Vacations With Your Kids**, is for any of you who want to learn how, where and with whom to enjoy these experiences, whether you're traveling with a baby, toddler, school-age child or teen, if you're a two-parent family, a single parent, part of a multigenerational group or a grandparent with grandchildren in tow.

We have been writing about adventure (and other) vacations in our newsletter, Family Travel Times®, for more than a dozen years. Our goal throughout the years has always been the same: to help people take the type of vacation they want, bring along their children, and return having had a great time, anxious to head out as a family soon again. The selections in this book include organized trips, do-it-yourself possibilities, and a wide array of accommodations and destinations from which you can head out each day and explore the world around you.

WHAT IS AN ADVENTURE VACATION?

Adventure is a subjective experience. The identical activity can leave one person yawning with boredom while another's heart is pounding in terror. Broadly speaking, an adventure vacation offers physically challenging activity in an outdoor environment; coincidentally, this just happens to be what the majority of children crave most. There are so many different types of family adventures up for grabs — at all seasons, in every climate and all across the globe — that it's impossible to say which are the "best."

To begin, not all individuals (and by extension families) are equally active. We've seen families who had never ventured further than the deep end of a luxury resort's swimming pool have the time of their lives on a river rafting trip. One friend told us that her family's hot air balloon excursion over the Arizona desert, floating quietly and serenely through the sky, was her favorite family adventure. Some may not find this at all daring but, for our friend (who admits to a fear of heights) it took real courage.

We never cease to be amazed at how adventure travel has changed. A dozen years ago, any organized vacation outing that included children, almost without exception, automatically meant a camping trip. This is no longer the case, as you'll discover as you read on. Today, even those who believe that sleeping under the stars is directly related to the number of stars a hotel has garnered can take advantage of a wide range of adventurous fare.

Though you can choose to take many of these vacations on your own, we definitely prefer joining an organized trip, especially those where there will be youngsters in our children's age group. Perhaps the major advantage of doing so is that, in most instances, there will be experts to help with (or take over completely) the most arduous tasks. On the majority of our adventure vacation choices where camping is involved, you need not own any special gear (it will either be provided or may be rented). You'll awaken to the smell of fresh-brewed coffee and go to sleep at night without having to worry about putting out the fire. We even know of a rafting company that brings comfortable fold-up cots for participants to sleep on. Then, there are the more "civilized" trips, where you'll stay at country inns, lodges and cabins. But it's not just the pampering that makes organized trips so appealing; it's the camaraderie that builds day by day with fellow travelers and the good feeling that the expert guides accompanying you truly care about you and your kids.

There are plenty of more rugged excursions within these pages as well; but, remember, a "soft" adventure can still be a very exciting adventure.

WHO TAKES ADVENTURE VACATIONS?

Back in the 1950s and 60s, our family took many marvelous vacations, yet neither I, nor my sister or brother, can remember either of our parents doing any even remotely adventurous activity. We kids were an active bunch, and our folks always encouraged us to take on new challenges, by choosing holiday spots where we learned to canoe, hike or bike. However, our parents tended to watch us, rather than join us, which was pretty typical parent-behavior for that era.

Having developed a taste for the active, outdoor life, I guess you could say I was lucky to wind up with a man who shared my enthusiasm. When I first met my husband David, he had just returned from a nine-month journey that included trekking in Nepal. From the beginning, we took active vacations, so when our two boys came along, we just naturally expected to include them. It wasn't always easy (our boys are now 15 and 18 so we're talking about quite a number of years ago) but we discovered that, regardless of how old the boys were, we didn't have to give up anything we wanted to do. We often did it differently than we did before their arrival; we sometimes did less of it on vacation than we might have without them along, but the important thing was that we did it, brought them along and sparked their interest in active outdoor adventures at the same time. Our oldest son rode in a bike seat as soon as he could sit up comfortably; by strapping a baby carrier on one of our backs, we were able to get out into the woods and mountains which surrounded our house in Vermont. Having little kids didn't keep us from enjoying the water either (we used to joke that we owned the smallest life preserver ever made — goodness knows where and how we found it). Over the years, adventure holidays have become a way of life for our family. Though we've gone the rough and rugged camping-out route, for the most part, we've chosen to travel in a bit more comfort.

It should come as no surprise that today's adventure vacationers can include absolutely anyone — babies, senior citizens, even those with physical disabilities. While different tour operators and outfitters often have minimum age recommendations and regulations, there's something out there for everyone. There's much to be said for introducing children to these active, outdoors pursuits at an age when they're not afraid to use their bodies, have lots of physical energy and boundless enthusiasm for new things. The earlier something is learned, the more naturally it becomes part of one's self and the more pleasurable it will be during one's lifetime.

For those of you who have been active all of your lives, and haven't found parenthood any reason to change, this book ought to expand your horizons. For others, who need more direction and handholding, we'll just point out that on the majority of the family adventures we mention here, there's lots of help on hand in the form of experienced trip leaders, instruction, support vehicles, etc. Yes, you can still hike, bike and canoe with your kids without taking any special organized tour; but just think how much more fun it could be traveling side by side with other families similar to your own.

If you're uncertain whether your family is up to, or will really enjoy, an entire vacation devoted to an adventure such as river rafting or mountain biking, head for a place where you can try out the activity you're considering for a day, or even half a day. It makes all sorts of sense to test the waters before plunking down hard-earned dollars on a vacation you may not be so sure of. We did this last winter when we tried dog sledding for the first time, just for the day. We were amazed to discover how much we enjoyed it. A multigenerational family with grandparents and a nine-month old was also on our trip, and they were as enchanted as we were.

ARE ADVENTURE VACATIONS SAFE?

We'd be lying if we said that adventure travel is risk free. However, any potential problems will be substantially mitigated as long as all participants listen to and follow instructions from the guides, tour leaders or outfitters. It is imperative that you speak with your children about these risks in advance — whether they be poison ivy or falling overboard off a raft into whitewater. Don't frighten them, but make certain that they know they need to pay strict attention to the safety procedures. Try to find out if they have any concerns and, if you don't have the answers, query the outfitter or look for a book on the subject. Don't be shy about asking about safety, instruction, emergency procedures and like issues. Many operators can furnish you with the names of other families who have taken the trip you are considering. Don't hesitate to contact these references and encourage your kids to speak with their counterparts.

Most important is to be completely honest about both your own and your children's capabilities. Never, ever, lie to the outfitters just to be able to join an appealing-sounding trip. Conrad Fourney of Headwaters River Company (see page 53) is considering making his minimum age 14, with no exceptions, because more than once families have not been honest about a child's age and it has ruined the trip for others. Restrictions exist not just because of weight and strength but the ability of a child to comprehend the potential risks. While ages on many trips are generally flexible, no one knows your kids better than you do. What we hope for our kids is that the brash and daring ones will learn proper caution, while the reticent ones will gain enough confidence to try that which seems daunting.

You need not spend every day hip-to-hip with your kids to have a great vacation with them. On many of the trips we write about, there may be several daily options to accommodate the more intrepid members of the group. If you truly want to be challenged, you might split your family up for part of the day and hike the high trail or take the longer bike ride. If it works for the trip leader, go and enjoy yourself.

HOW THIS BOOK IS ORGANIZED

This book focuses on the active aspect of outdoor vacations, rather than on the glorious scenes and sights you're apt to discover in your journeys — which is the concentration of **Great Nature Vacations With Your Kids**. We've divided this book into six chapters:

CHAPTER 1: **Planning Your Family Adventure Vacation:** How to choose a vacation, know which questions to ask, prepare your kids, avoid the pitfalls — in short, all the tools you need to make your vacation happen.

CHAPTER 2: **Adventure Travel Companies:** This chapter lists a number of different types of adventure vacations and the outfitters and tour operators who welcome children on their trips. Since so many operators offer adventures where the activities overlap — such as a trip which features biking and hiking or rafting and horseback riding — we've put the companies into alphabetical order as opposed to category of adventure. Out of all the myriad possibilities, we've selected companies that have longtime experience with families and those that are well-established, but have only recently become family-friendly. Many of the resources we mention will steer you toward even more opportunities.

CHAPTER 3: Stay & Play: This chapter makes suggestions for vacation accommodations where families can enjoy a variety of adventures by day and come back to the same comfortable bed and bath each night. Some of the adventures you'll find are for the entire family to enjoy together; some are just for one or the other generation. From country inns to dude ranches, the common denominator of all of the write-ups in this chapter is the warm family welcome you'll receive.

CHAPTER 4: **Mountain Adventures:** The idea here is similar to *Stay & Play,* but since there are so many mountain locales where great family adventures abound, we gave these vacations their own chapter. All offer a wide variety of lodging options in a variety of price categories, from campgrounds to luxury resorts.

CHAPTER 5: **Tour Operators:** This compendium of tour companies describes organizations that include adventure travel among their many offerings. They include both commercial and non-profit organizations.

CHAPTER 6: **Camping:** This chapter is devoted to camping on-your-own. Advice on camping in general, selecting between RV or car-camping, finding a campground and much more are included.

Following the chapters are the appendices of what we consider to be **Best Bets For Those Traveling With** — *Babies, Toddlers, Teens, Multigenerational Groups, Single Parents* and so on. Even though listings throughout the chapters indicate minimum ages, you may decide to check out these appendices first.

Throughout this book you'll find **Booked for Travel** sidebars: short reviews of books on specific types of activities, books with listings of invaluable resources, even books to read to and with your children that enhance your vacation experience. Some of the books explore areas in your own backyard, while others will take you to the far corners of the earth. Not all of them are specifically travel-oriented, yet, in some way, each one can enrich your family adventure. You'll also find **Great Vacations Tips** which contain information on a variety of resource organizations and travel advice.

If the adventure you seek is not within these pages, you'll most likely find it in one of the other books in our series. Scuba diving and sailing, for example, are part of **Great Sports Vacations With Your Kids**, wildlife excursions are the focus of **Great Nature Vacations With Your Kids**, archaeological digs and visiting Native American sites are among the chapters in **Great Learning Vacations With Your Kids**, houseboating is covered in **Great Cruise Vacations With Your Kids**, while great places to snorkel is just one of the activities found in **Great Island Vacations With Your Kids**.

As parents with years of traveling with kids under our belts, we know that these types of vacations bring many rewards. Adventure travel has broad appeal to both mind and soul, not to mention its benefit to our bodies. Moreover, the shared experience of an adventure vacation strengthens family ties and brings a new kind of closeness with a special flavor all its own.

BOOKED FOR TRAVEL

"The outdoors is one giant, adventurous playground for children, full of fun and surprises around every corner." Positive and practical, Michael Hodgson's WILDERNESS WITH CHILDREN: *A Parent's Guide to __Fun__ Family Outings* has chapters on camping, cross-country skiing, canoeing, kayaking and biking, plus checklists, suppliers, first aid information — in short, just about everything you need to know before you head for an outdoors adventure with your children. Most chapters end with a list of *Tips in a Nutshell*. Hodgson is a father who practices what he preaches — his daughter Nikki went on her first camping trip at the age of one month. A very down-to-earth, useful resource. (Stackpole Books)

CHAPTER 1

PLANNING YOUR FAMILY ADVENTURE VACATION

Over the years we've noticed how family vacations seem to get a bad rap both from the people who don't take them and the ones who don't plan them properly. We've learned — sometimes the hard way — that just bundling up your kids and taking them along doesn't always work very well — unless you've done your homework. Though this is true for all types of vacations, it is perhaps even more key before embarking on the adventure vacations found in this book, where the respective physical abilities of participants play such a major role.

The planning process is not nearly as difficult as you might believe and the payoff is enormous. If you follow our step-by-step guidelines in this chapter, we guarantee that you'll return home from your next family adventure having all had a great time.

PLANNING FOR YOUR FAMILY'S NEEDS

This is the most important aspect of the planning process. If we've learned nothing else over the past 13 years of taking, talking up and writing about family vacations, we can say unequivocally that the criteria for a successful vacation are distinctly individual. The great trip your brother took, the outstanding resort your neighbor visited, the enticing journey you read about in a magazine or newspaper may not necessarily work for you. Therefore, it's imperative that you do an analysis of your family group before signing on the dotted line.

Begin with your youngest child and work your way up. Consider what each person's needs are and then try and see how you can blend them. Physical considerations come first. Many of the questions we advise you to ask (see page 11) address this issue.

CHOOSING THE ADVENTURE

The more experienced among you might want to skip ahead to the next section, as you most likely have already chosen a particular type of adventure. For novices who have absolutely no idea of where to begin, we understand that you may share some of the typical fears of first-time adventurers: "What if I don't like it?" "What if the kids are unhappy?" If this sounds like you, try what we call 'a taste of adventure' — sign up for a short outing that lasts no more than a day or two, and read the *Mountain Adventures* and *Stay & Play* chapters for more ideas.

On the other hand, if you've decided that the time has come for your family to strike out on a quest for adventure, begin by speaking first with the adults who will be joining your group. We always remind parents that vacation time is no time to be a martyr; choose the kind of vacation you want to take and then find a specific one where your kids will be happy too. Should you discover that more than one type of adventure receives high marks, remember that many operators found in this guide offer combination trips that may feature all the activities on your wish list. We direct your attention again to the *Stay & Play* and *Mountain Adventures* chapters, which are filled with numerous possibilities.

We ourselves are very tempted by all of the trips in this book, even though we haven't actually experienced all of them. Biking, for example, is something we've only done on day trips since, as city dwellers, it was quite a long time before both of our kids became capable riders. When we finally did reach that point, it turned out that our younger son honestly didn't enjoy being on a bike for a long period of time. On the other hand, we have done many, many of the adventures in this book and highly recommend you consider rafting, canoeing, hiking, dog sledding, camping, and horseback riding as integral features of your next vacation. Something special occurs between parent and child as you float down the river, hike through a world of wildflowers or saddle up for a day on the range. And, don't forget, the adventure need not be the entire vacation, just one special feature of your holiday.

BOOKED FOR TRAVEL

Christine Loomis' FAMILY ADVENTURES: *More Than 500 Great Trips for You and Your Kids of All Ages,* a first-rate resource, is jam-packed with terrific family adventure suggestions and expert advice. While easy to use, the book would have greatly benefited from a proper index; the one that is included is the book's only disappointment. We're in total agreement with Christine that "Adventure travel is for everybody ... You don't have to be a diehard daredevil or world-class athlete, you don't have to be young (though you can be) and you don't have to rough it unless you want to." Unlike our **Great Vacations with Your Kids** book series, where nature, adventure, learning, cruising and sport vacation possibilities are presented in individual volumes, this book encompasses all of the above activities in one work. Another distinctive difference is that Loomis' book focuses on the adventures, including schools and clinics, whereas this book only covers these facilities if they can be visited as part of a family vacation. We are good friends with Christine and her family and have shared several of our own family adventure vacations with them. Though our books are similar in focus, both will be of interest to families with a yen for adventure. (Fodor's)

ENABLING THE DISABLED

There may be physical impediments that preclude one type of vacation or another. Back problems, so common in this day and age, often frighten folks from considering a rafting trip (though my own positive experiences even after two back operations opens the possibility that this may be an unwarranted concern for other sufferers). If a member of your group (child or adult) has a physical disability, there's lots of help available. Society for the Advancement of Travel for the Handicapped (SATH), provides a wealth of travel information. A membership organization, you can call 212-447-SATH or write to SATH at 347 Fifth Avenue, New York, NY 10016. The Disability Bookshop in Vancouver, WA, carries a *Directory of Travel Agencies for the Disabled*, a wonderful resource for any family in which a member has any type of debilitating condition. Call the bookshop at 800-637-2256 or 206-694-2462 and ask for a complete listing of their offerings. The National Handicapped Sports Organization in Rockville, MD, has more than 85 chapters located throughout the United States. Call 800-966-4647 or 301-217-0960 for the address and phone number of the chapter closest to you.

Other useful organizations include: the National Sports Center for the Disabled in Winter Park, CO (970-726-5514); the Breckenridge Outdoor Education Center in Breckenridge, CO (970-453-6422); *Disabled Outdoor Magazine* (708-366-8526) and *Access to Recreation: Adaptive Equipment for the Physically Challenged* (800-634-4351).

DECIDING WHERE TO GO

In many instances the choice of where you adventure will be budget driven. Adventure vacations tend to be pricey — for several reasons. Most adventures require specialized equipment, and you never want to stint on the quality of gear. Reputable outfitters and tour operators need to be fully insured, another considerable expense. It's also necessary to invest in expert training in order to have qualified guides and instructors, who must then be remunerated fairly. The good news is that since terrific adventure vacations can usually be found close to home, there's no need to lay out money on expensive airfare for the three, four or more of you. For those of you who expect to travel by car, please read our *ABCs of Car Travel* at the end of this chapter. It will smooth the road to your destination.

Another piece of very important advice: Go only where you're wanted. Don't sign on with a group that states it welcomes "well-behaved" children. All parents want well-behaved kids but we all know that the behavior of our children is something we can only direct, not always control. This book only lists operators, properties and the like that really do welcome youngsters, though not each property or every trip a company operates may be appropriate for all configurations of families.

It's important that you listen carefully and follow the advice of the outfitters.

Be realistic in making your arrangements. Don't, for example, expect your children to be cheerful and raring to head out on a biking expedition after a full day of traveling. (They might be, but you can't count on it.) Add extra time to your trip (or conversely shorten your adventure by a day) to avoid stress of this nature.

Realistic expectations are also important. If you're anticipating perfection, you're immediately setting yourself up for disappointment. Choose carefully and be flexible. If the family trip you've signed on for doesn't include a peer for your youngster (we once took a trip on which there were half a dozen 10-year-olds and our one-and-only 7-year-old), turn it into an opportunity to get some one-on-one time with your child. Ask the trip leaders to integrate the group in a way that all the children can feel included.

Adventure vacations can work for many different family configurations. They tend to work well for single parents, for a variety of reasons, not the least of which is the group camaraderie that evolves — eating together, sharing challenges, and more. These trips tend to attract a mixed group of participants — from active singles to seniors — making them ideal for intergenerational and multigenerational groups as well.

INVOLVING YOUR KIDS

The next step is discussing your choices with your kids and getting their input. Even if you've made your final decision, it's important, especially when traveling with teenagers, to let them feel as if they have some control over this decision. The bottom line is that the more kids know and understand about an upcoming trip, the more cooperative they'll be on the journey itself. You'll not only be able to eliminate the "unknowns" that make youngsters uneasy, you'll also be able to spark their interest in a way that is certain to enhance the experience.

Once you've made your selection, explain as much as possible to your kids. Since the days ahead will be filled with new and exciting exploits, the more kids know, the easier and more carefree the trip will become. We also recommend that you ask for references from the tour company, preferably a family reference so that your kids can speak with another child who has already taken the trip you're planning. This will both pique your child's interest and help allay any fears he or she may harbor. Remember, enthusiasm is infectious.

Next, head to the bookstore or library to learn more about your trip — both for yourself and your kids. Throughout this book you'll find short reviews of books on pertinent adventures. You might select an instruction manual written for kids on the activity at hand or a short story in which the protagonists are enjoying the great outdoors.

A lesson often sticks best if it's introduced with humor and there's no doubt that WILLY WHITEFEATHER'S OUTDOOR SURVIVAL HANDBOOK FOR KIDS will bring many smiles to the faces of young readers even though it's about a serious subject. The quasi-comic book format contains drawings of dangers to avoid and ways to keep safe. Willy himself is a backwoods guide and the Honorary Chief of the Black Creek Cherokee of Florida and he wrote this book specifically for children so that they too will be able to survive outdoors. (Harbinger House)

QUESTIONS TO ASK

Regardless of the adventure you've chosen, there are specific questions you should ask of the outfitter or tour operator.

- **How long has the company been in business under the same ownership and what is the percentage of repeat business?**

New owners may be as terrific (or even better) than former ones, but if the original owners loved kids, you'll want to confirm that the same commitment to families has carried over into the new regime. One well-known adventure travel company, which recently changed hands, also changed its attitude and has severely limited its "family" trip options, so much so that we have not included it in this volume. The former owner, a parent, knew first-hand how special family adventure trips are. Repeat business is always a positive sign and one in which adventure travel companies take particular pride.

- **Does a company operate the trip you're interested in itself or does it subcontract the outfitting and/or guiding?**

It's far from a sin to subcontract; in fact, using local, on-site professionals to deal with the clientele may be the best way for some operators to go. On the other hand, when traveling with kids, you need to know with whom you are signing on in order to be sure that the guides' and instructors' attitudes toward your children are as positive as the policy of the company you've booked with.

- **What is the experience of the leader and how long has he or she been with the company?**

Because of the inherent risks of adventure travel, experience is more important than on other types of guided tours. Don't forget to ask if the leader has also had experience with family trips. We think that the longer a guide has been with a company, the more flexible he or she is likely to be in dealing with any changes that may have to be made en route. We like to hear that both members of the permanent staff and/or management also lead trips, especially if they are parents themselves. Ask if the guides are certified in their particular area of specialty.

- **What types of lodging are utilized?**

Because adventure travel groups tend to be small (which is a plus most of the time), operators sometimes house guests in places where accommodations are not large enough for family groups. One of the negatives here is that if your kids can't share your sleeping quarters with you, you may have to pay full price for them.

- **If the trip involves camping, where do you sleep and what are the facilities at the camp?**

How far is the campsite from the trail, the river, the road, etc.? We turned down the opportunity to take a trip that really turned us on when we learned that there was a hefty trek at the end of almost every day to reach the campsite. It sounded too grueling. Ask about what is offered in lieu of a bathroom. Some outfitters set up a toilet, some bring along solar-heated shower bags. Don't forget to explain the set-up to your kids in advance of your trip. This is no time for surprises.

- **What type of cuisine is featured?**

We're all for giving our kids healthy food — and lots of it — but we also want to make certain they'll eat on vacation. Our boys wouldn't touch fish when they were younger, so we always checked to be sure that an alternative was provided for them when there was fish on the menu. Child-friendly food should be relatively simple and offer some choices. Another important concern is snack food and refreshments during the day. Kids, as we know, need to eat and drink more frequently than adults. If no snacks and drinks are carried by the operator, include them on your bring-along list.

- **How is group size determined?**

This may be decided by someone other than the operator. In Minnesota, for example, rules for the number of persons in a party visiting the Boundary Waters is regulated by park authorities. Small groups offer a unique sense of intimacy but also limit the number of children who will be on hand for your children to play with. There should be an adequate number of guides for the number of participants. This figure varies between activities but, trust us, after speaking with two or three operators you'll get a good handle on what proper ratios are.

• **Can the company provide a reference?**

We've said it before and we'll say it again — ask for a reference of a family group similar to your own. Encourage the children to speak with each other. Have a list of your concerns ready before you make the call, but also allow the reference to give you information and details you may not have considered.

• **What is the company's policy on alcohol?**

You'd be surprised at how many companies permit unlimited beer drinking during the day. We never ceased to be amazed at the number of outright drunken rafters we've encountered along the river. Not only does this set a bad example for your kids, recreationers who need alcohol to enjoy themselves pose a potential danger for all.

• **What ages have worked best?**

Not all family trips work for all ages of children and tour outfitters should have a pretty good handle on which ages have had the most success on their trips. If you listen carefully enough, you'll most likely get a good sense of how flexible the company is in its attitude toward kids. We've noticed that the majority of family-friendly trips tend to be the less rigorous ones and think that's great — for families with young children and for first-timers. However, by the time your kids are teenagers, it's quite probable that they will derive greater pleasure from a more challenging itinerary.

• **How experienced do you need to be to participate?**

On many trips you need bring nothing more than your sense of adventure. On others, special skills are necessary. Many of the horseback trips in this book, for example, require a certain degree of riding expertise. Ask what, if any, instruction is provided on the trip. Normal healthy people can enjoy the majority of the organized trips described in this book.

• **What equipment is provided and what do you need to bring with you?**

Will you need special gear — hiking or riding boots, sleeping bags, bike helmets? Ask specifically if the equipment is properly sized for children your kids' ages (and weights) and if it's included in the cost or rented separately. Helmets should be worn by parents and kids on all bicycle trips and on many rafting trips. Bring your own if you've any doubts of fit or availability.

- **How are the days structured? Is there activity all day long?**

We prefer trips that strike a nice balance between vigorous activity and leisurely pursuit, combined with some degree of flexibility. On hiking/biking/walking trips participants often have the possibility of selecting daily distances, with options offered each day. Stops should include places kids will enjoy, such as the visit to a candy factory on one of Michigan Bicycle Touring's (see page 65) trips.

- **What support is offered en route?**

Many participants who take adventure vacations are far from Olympic hopefuls. Therefore, it's not surprising that many trips feature van support, also called "sag wagons" for those who for some reason or other want to take a break. This is especially good news for parents when their kids' energy flags. It is imperative, however, to understand the rules of these vehicles since many require that a parent ride along with the child. Though this is understandable for young children, it's a bit perplexing when your child is 17-years-old.

Another question to ask bicycle tour operators is about mechanical support. Some companies will assist you in the fixing of flat tires and have trip leaders who double as mobile repair shops, while others are strictly hands-off and only give you directions (and a ride) to the nearest bike shop.

Be specific about who carries what. When traveling with kids it's preferable to carry only a day pack and not have to worry about the rest of your gear. After all, that's one of the reasons for joining an organized group.

> **GREAT VACATIONS TIP:** Sunburns are a common hazard in the mountains, even in winter when the snow acts as a giant reflector allowing the sun to do extensive damage to your face. Be sure to bring along lots and lots of sunscreen for yourself and your kids. And make them use it (or ask the instructors as ski school to see that they do).

There are also questions specific to the type of adventure selected that you might want to ask. We address many of these in Chapter 2, Adventure Travel Companies.

BOOKED FOR TRAVEL

ADVENTURE VACATIONS is a compilation of 50 diverse adventures in our 50 states, an ambitious undertaking. Among the more unusual adventures are Airplane and Airship Adventures (e.g., fighter plane piloting and blimp rides) and *Caving and House-Building*. Author Stephanie Ocko has not attempted to write the definitive work on the subject. Rather, she gives a succinct description of each adventure, and includes a few names and addresses to get you started. Some will get turned on by an exciting-sounding possibility and then may feel let down when the specifics needed to turn your enthusiasm into a vacation aren't there. There are some good suggestions in the *Other Sources* sections, but families will have to do a lot more research. (Citadel)

A word about prices. As a general rule of thumb, all of the prices in this book are land-only and do not include taxes or gratuities. For the most part you'll have to make your own way to the meeting point, though on some trips airport transfers are included in the cost. Prices listed in this book are for 1996 unless otherwise noted.

BOOKED FOR TRAVEL

Mitch Kaplan's **52 NEW JERSEY WEEKENDS** contains a year's worth of seasonal outings in the Garden State. The suggested weekends are a blend of cultural, sporty, nature-oriented and active-outdoor getaways. In this latter category are chapters on *Biking the Back Roads, Playing on the Delaware River, Canoeing in the Pinelands, Yes, You Can Ski Here* and more. Since the author has tried out all 52 suggestions himself, many of them with his own kids, his accounts are all entertainingly personalized. As New Yorkers, we're especially grateful that Kaplan has lifted the veil on his home state's many unexpected treats. (Country Roads Press)

WHEN THINGS GO WRONG

We encourage you to voice any complaints you have while on a trip. Try, as best you can, to express yourself in a calm manner (no whining allowed) when explaining what you're experiencing and how it differs from what your expectations are. If you grin and bear it and complain only when you return from a so-called disastrous trip, no one wins. There's a definite art to communicating criticisms. Rather than yelling in front of other participants, having a word in private with the trip leader and describing the problem works best. Don't say — "We were promised . . ." Better to say, "It was my understanding that . . ." "My daughter thinks you don't like her" will be much more effective than "Why aren't you including my daughter in . . ." Accusations are rarely productive. Expression of valid misunderstandings and what may simply be a lack of communication between the parties is the route to take. Try not to become too anxious when things go wrong; anxiety is catching and if you lose control, the kids probably will too.

THE ABCs OF CAR TRAVEL

Our family took many car trips when we were young. My mother always had a seemingly unending supply of sandwiches and snacks and had the foresight to plan visits which would be fun for us kids, without giving up the agenda she and my father had in mind. There were the inevitable back-seat squabbles — each of us vying for window seats — yet my memories are all very positive.

Though all of the parenting books promised us that three-week-old Jordon (he's now 18) would be lulled to sleep by the motion of the car on our first family car trip, we learned early on that he hadn't read these volumes. From the George Washington Bridge almost all the way to our house in Vermont, he expressed his unhappiness in clear and vibrant terms. Almost three years later, Russell joined our family and he, too, had trouble acclimating to long trips in the car. By this time Jordon was asking if we were there yet as we approached 23rd Street (our starting point was 11th Street!). Patient as we thought we were, by the time we arrived at our destination, we were frazzled, already dreading the trip home. We wound up selling our house and, for a while, we avoided car trips like the plague. Sometimes we had no other choice but to travel by car, so we began listening to advice and tips from friends, relatives and even strangers. Eventually we became creative strategists ourselves. We've survived the stage of one of the boys weeping, "He's looking out my window!" Finally we have learned the knack of turning long journeys into fun and exciting family times — which we're delighted to share with you.

Always talk about the trip with your kids in advance of departure. You'll be surprised at how much even very young kids understand, particularly when put in familiar terms. For example you might tell a toddler that a two-hour drive is like watching two Sesame Street programs. For a longer trip, liken it to being at school for an entire day, in their seats!

Buckle up. It's a given that young children will be secured in car seats but parents need to set the example by always using seat belts. Bring along a towel to cover up the carseat and/or steering wheel, which can become extremely hot if you park your car on a sunny day.

Comfort is a high priority. We bring along pillows, sometimes blankets, so that the boys can cushion themselves for sleep. Children need to be able to see out of the car windows without difficulty.

Dress intelligently. Tight clothes, fancy garb and the like should be saved for arrival. Inevitably your child will get dirty if you anticipate looking fresh and clean at your destination. Better to find a bathroom a few miles from the end of your journey in which to change. Bring sweatshirts if you plan on turning the air-conditioning on high.

Each family member should pack toys, games and books to help entertain him or herself en route. Guidance from parents is important, but not as important as the children having some control over the selections. We've learned that children as young as 18 months have definite points of view, and even an understanding of which of their favorite items they can play with over and over again. Elicit their assistance.

BOOKED FOR TRAVEL

KIDS TRAVEL: *A Backseat Survival Kit, Complete With Everything We Could Possibly Think Of* is without a doubt the most comprehensive compendium of travel games and activities we've ever encountered. There's a pouch filled with markers, string for cat's cradle and embroidery floss for friendship bracelets and hair weaves; a book full of old favorites like license plates and classic board and travel games, plus instructions on palm reading, how to draw comic book superheroes, and more; a secret decoder and a 100-page pad of puzzles, mazes, etc. affixed to its own clipboard. Phew. Our advice — Don't leave home without it! (Klutz)

First-aid kits should be kept in the glove compartment and might include: Bandaids, antibacterial ointment, analgesics (e.g., Tylenol), insect repellent, sunscreen, thermometer, medical prescriptions, antidiarrheal, cotton swabs, gauze pads, adhesive tape and tweezers.

Games and toys should be placed where children have easy access to them without parental assistance. This is to not to discourage interaction, but to avoid frustration for the kids.

Humor goes a long way in changing the mood when cooped up in a car. Turn a complaint into a joke. Acknowledge that being in a car is unpleasant by poking fun at it. We've found our kids giggling through their tears when doing this.

Involve the kids as much as possible, even while en route. Bring along a map and highlighter, marking down your progress as you travel. We carried a "navigator's hat" when the kids were younger and had them participate in the reading of the map, determining where we would be stopping, etc.

BOOKED FOR TRAVEL

Is the l KID-YOU-NOT ROAD ATLAS: A Kids' Guide To The Land Of The Free And The Home Of The Strange! really "more fun than actually going on vacation" as it claims? Maybe not quite, but it sure is clever, funny and highly kid-pleasing (it's also pretty gross, but that's what keeps them amused). Chances are your kids will learn as much or more U.S. geography from this book than they will from a more standard atlas. You'll stave off backseat squabbling if you invest in a copy for each young passenger of reading age. (American Map Corp.)

J uice-in-a-box, we're convinced, was designed for traveling families. Just be careful when inserting the straw not to squeeze the box! Freeze several the night before taking off; these will keep other items cool for most of your trip. It will also provide refreshing drinks all day long. We've even used them to chill medication!

K now where you'll be staying by 5 p.m. This pre-dinner time, in addition to being when kids are often the crankiest, is when the barrage of questions from the backseat seems never-ending. More importantly, it's also when hotels and motels begin to fill up and *No Vacancy* signs begin to shine. Having a destination in mind will help you give the kids both a sense of security and something to focus on.

L og expenses, distances covered, sights visited, etc. and create a journal of your trip. Lots of folks like to do this because it involves interaction and creates memories. Kids old enough to add could take on the role of bookkeeper.

M usic, music, music. Whether you've got a CD or a cassette player, the options are limitless. There are tunes everyone can sing together or likes to hear. Stories and books on tape are great too. For those times when you can't agree, Walkman is there, but try not to let your teens stay plugged in, out of the family conversation.

N ever stay in an unpleasant situation you can avoid. Traffic is a prime example. If you can't get off the highway completely, pull over and jump rope, throw a ball around, have an impromptu picnic. Nothing is worse than being stuck in a car that's not going anywhere.

O rganize your belongings in a manner that works for your family, both inside the car and in the trunk. We like to put the kids' stuff on top, since somehow they always seem to need something.

Pack a day bag in the front of the trunk and, depending on the season, include swim suits, towels, rain ponchos, hats, mittens and a change of clothes for everyone. That way you'll be prepared for all emergencies.

Quiet time helps everyone. Don't entertain your kids every minute. Children who learn to amuse themselves develop valuable self-sufficiency skills which will serve them well in later life. Napping is fine too; kids are generally not as enraptured with the scenery as adults are.

Relax and retreat to a vacation state of mind. The phones aren't ringing; there are fewer time limitations; there's time to listen and hear what your kids have to say. Savor these moments; they disappear all too quickly.

Stop back seat bickering by consulting your kids in advance about how they think car disputes should be solved. Write down their solutions and when the first complaint rings out, whip out the pad with their responses and read their words back to them. This ploy really works!

Take along: A surprise game or toy; snack food that is not too salty or too sticky (fruit is a good choice); a shade to block the rays; an old blanket; extra pacifiers; flashlight and lots of extra batteries.

Underplan. Don't include too many must-dos or must-sees. Go with the flow.

Vary the types of roads you take, some highway, some backcountry roads. Change seats from time to time if your kids get real antsy. Play different kinds of music. Make an impromptu stop.

Wake any sleepers about 10 minutes before you plan to stop so they can re-enter the world with a minimum of grogginess (and get their shoes on).

X-pect the unexpected. Something unforeseen is sure to crop up — a too-good-to-pass-up street fair, a flat tire, a detour. Here's another occasion when a sense of humor and common sense can be tapped to advantage.

Young toddlers with excessive energy are the hardest to satisfy. Early communication, involvement and lots and lots of stops where they can release energy will work wonders.

Zippered or plastic bags are always handy to take along. Use them for garbage, special treats, wet towelettes, etc. They are also great repositories for the inevitable goodies children collect during your trip!

CHAPTER 2

ADVENTURE TRAVEL COMPANIES

In the pages that follow, you'll find descriptions of more than fifty companies that specialize in adventure vacations and also welcome families. In each write-up we've tried to give you the minimum age requirements, but remember, unless a company's liability insurance states a specific minimum age, the operators are usually quite flexible. Speak with them directly about your child's experience and ability and, above all, don't lie about your child's age.

In researching this book, we discovered so many companies that welcomed kids, that it even surprised us and we've been writing about outdoor vacations with kids for more than a dozen years. It was truly difficult to decide which to include, but we're confident that every one we've listed will be happy to hear from you. Not all of them will feature trips that can accommodate your children's ages or abilities. If not, there's a good chance they can refer you to another company that can help you. This is a very close-knit group.

Depending upon the type of adventure trip you select, you'll need to ask different questions when evaluating the different options. For example, if you're considering a hiking trip, ask how the operator rates the hikes: by distance covered or by the difficulty of the terrain? How does the distance covered translate into hours of activity? The main difference between hiking and walking is the terrain; the latter is generally described as smooth and gentle trails with few if any hills. Most hikers carry some sort of day or backpack and you'll want to be certain that your child can comfortably carry his or her own personal items. To check this out in advance, have the children march around the house or backyard with the pack at its heaviest (before the liquids are consumed). If it's too heavy, remove some of the non-essential items.

Kayakers will want to ascertain the types of craft available. Are there kid-sized boats or two- or three-person kayaks suitable for families? Will you need wetsuits? Most rafting companies have invested in updated craft, so you can be fairly certain that your raft will be a self-bailer. You might want to inquire as to whether there is a dry bag accessible during the day (dry bags are given to participants on overnight trips to store all gear in).

BOOKED FOR TRAVEL

PADDLE AMERICA: A Guide to Trips & Outfitters in All 50 States, by Nick and David Shears has gotten raves from canoeing and kayaking professionals nationwide. Outfitters are listed in each state where they run trips (making for multiple entries in many cases). There are good, brief descriptions of the trips, including mention, where applicable, of those which work for families. BUT, unless you want to read the book cover-to-cover, you're going to need to know the names of some likely family-friendly operators and/or in which states they're based — in other words there's no index and no appendices. Otherwise, we like this book. (Starfish)

When any specific equipment is involved it's imperative that you find out if kid-sized gear is provided. This could make the difference between your child feeling a true sense of accomplishment versus having a day (or more) of frustration. You also want to ask kayak and canoe trip operators if there are any portages during the trip (and how many and how long). Bear in mind also that kids may not be able to do quiet paddling for hours on end. Not only will they tire, they might also become quite bored. The peacefulness and beauty of the setting may be idyllic for the adults in your group but kids need and want some activity, trust us on this. If your trip involves camping, more and more outfitters provide tents, sleeping bags and air mattresses — but never assume that they will be included; often they are rented to participants for a fee.

In most cases, you'll want to be informed in advance about the type of support that's on hand. What happens if your child gets too tired to continue — whether you're hiking, biking, rafting or whatever? Most bike tour operators use "sag wagons" in such an instance and on a recent rafting vacation with Class VI River Runners (see page 43), several of the teenagers (including one of ours) were so tired from staying up late into the night that they were only too pleased to be passengers on the oar raft instead of paddlers.

While we list a number of bicycle tour operators, devout do-it-yourself types can easily plan their own itineraries and skip the packages by investing in a good bike book (there are several reviewed in this chapter), picking interesting routes that also offer some fun family stops along the way. Again, you'll need to know the stamina of your kids and how hilly or mountainous the terrain is. We've found that taking day bike trips is a good way to begin. Check out Chapter 3, *Stay & Play*, for suggestions. Burley-type carriers and the new trail-a-bikes are opening the world of biking to families who previously were left out because their children were either too small or not strong enough to participate in biking excursions. Several bike tour operators limit the use of this type of equipment; some not only rent them, they recommend them; others don't permit you even to attach your own child seat to one of their rental bikes. Never be shy about asking for the specifics and, by all means, don't forget about helmets — for yourself as well as your children.

We've been so busy writing these books that we haven't had time to explore the Internet, but have noticed that just about all of the outfitters have referenced their web pages for more information. If you're on line and have the time to surf the net, we highly recommend your doing so (better yet, get those computer-literate kids into the act). You can even e-mail some of the outfitters your list of questions, a real money-saver when there's no toll-free phone number.

> **GREAT VACATIONS TIP:** Trail-A-Bike, made in Canada, come in a variety of sizes and shapes and when attached to just about any adult bicycle turn it into a "child-friendly tandem." A Trail-A-Bike can even come equipped with a child's carrier. Some of the configurations can carry more than one child. The bikes are recommended for children between the ages of 2 and 10. Kids can pedal or coast, the choice is theirs. To find where to purchase as well as where you can rent (across the continent) an Adams Trail-A-Bike, call 888-TAKE-ME-2. We've used cycles with trail-a-bikes and think they're absolutely terrific. The latest models are sturdier and offer increased stability.

BOOKED FOR TRAVEL

THE SPECIALTY TRAVEL INDEX: *Directory of Special Interest Travel,* helps adventurers (and other travelers) zero in efficiently to find which tour operators go where to do what. Three indices: *Interest/Activity, Geographical* and *Tour Operator Listings* are both easy and fun to use (we challenge you not to get sidetracked by all the great-sounding trips you'll see listed). But wait, there's more. *Travelscope* contains first-hand stories of all kinds of adventures – a recent issue had *Kayaks, Castles & Kielbasa: Feasting & Festing in Poland, Monkey Watching in Costa Rica, Diving the Bay Islands in Honduras, Focus on Fiji* and more. Published twice a year, a subscription is a bargain at $10. (Specialty Travel Index, 305 San Anselmo Ave., San Anselmo, CA 94960)

ABOVE THE CLOUDS TREKKING (ATCT)
P.O. Box 398, Worcester, MA 01602-0398
Phone: 800-233-4499/508-799-4499
Fax: 508-797-4779

IN THEIR OWN WORDS: We have not only trekked and led expeditions throughout the country of Nepal, we have lived there. We maintain a full-time office in Kathmandu and guarantee every departure we list in our brochure. For 14 years we have helped travelers encounter new cultures, encouraging participants to respect the dignity of their hosts. Our relationship with Nepal goes far beyond the commercial, it is an affair of the heart and soul. Our specialty is taking people to those parts of Nepal where local people are going about their lives the way they always have. On our 16-day *Family Treks* we aim for as much interaction as possible between us and the Nepalis we meet en route. In Nepal, the family as a unit is one of the keys to understanding the mind and heart of the Nepali people. Our depth of experience both as trekkers and parents combined with our concern for quality is unmatched anywhere.

THE TRIPS: Steve Conlon, founder of ATCT, was among the first international adventure tour operators to offer family treks, initially visiting his wife's relatives as part of each excursion. Today, Conlon offers a handful of departure dates for ATCT's *Family Treks*, all of which are scheduled around traditional school holidays. These trips follow the route of one of the company's most popular excursions, *A Taste of Trekking*, and has been altered to fit the needs of families with children. Two extra days are added for the trekking portion of the trip, porters (sherpas) are on hand to carry children who are either too young or too tired to walk and special diets are provided for children throughout the journey. After a full day of sightseeing in Kathmandu and a flight to Biratnagar, trekkers head for the picturesque corner of eastern Nepal, visiting the villages of Gupha Pokhari, Nundhaki and Chainpur along the way. At each stop kids meet and play with local Nepali youngsters. All ages are welcome to join what Steve promises to be a unique and rewarding cultural and adventuresome experience. However, it is definitely his opinion that the trip is ideal for ages 5 to 14. "Younger than that, it's a fun experience but the kids don't necessarily bring home a lot of memories to draw from over time; older than that and they tend to get bored with the lack of cool things to do. The very best ages seem to be from 8 to 11, though it obviously varies with the kids." As parents who practice what they preach, the Conlon's young trekkers are now 10 and 14!

RATES: Family Trek costs $1,900/adult, $1,100/ages 8 to 15, $950/ages 2 to 7, $600/under age 2. There is a $300 single supplement that applies to a single parent who does not want to share accommodations with his or her kids. Airfare to/from Nepal and lunches and dinners while in Kathmandu are not included.

BOOKED FOR TRAVEL

Lonely Planet Press publishes guidebooks for independent, adventurous travelers — the kind of folks who don't think twice about including their kids in the party when they head out to trek the Himalayas or raft up the Amazon. **TRAVEL WITH CHILDREN**, now in its third edition, is written by Australian-based Maureen Wheeler and deserves a prominent place on your travel library shelf. Many of her family's overseas adventures have been in Asia. In addition to the Wheelers' personal reminiscences, various independent contributors share their first-person *Travel Stories* of foreign holidays with their own kids (one father wrote an amusing, quite cynical account of his family's visit to exotic Southern California). Even more germane for the parent contemplating a journey to an underdeveloped country with kids are the advice chapters, which are filled with invaluable information on preparation, getting to and around your destination, how best to cope with local conditions (where to stay, eat, etc.), health and safety considerations, and tips on traveling when you're pregnant. (Lonely Planet)

ADIRONDACK MOUNTAIN CLUB (ADK)
P.O. Box 867, Lake Placid, NY 12946
Phone: 518-523-3441

IN THEIR OWN WORDS: We are a non-profit organization committed to providing opportunities for environmentally responsible outdoor recreation through outings, outdoor programs and mountain facilities. Located in the midst of the Adirondack High Peaks, our wilderness lodges in unforgettable settings offer hiking opportunities like none other and have all the comforts of home with the luxury of homestyle meals, comfortable rooms and friendly staff eager to share their knowledge of the Adirondacks. Throughout the year our schedule of events provides dozens of opportunities to learn things from canoeing to rock climbing.

THE TRIPS: ADK could easily have also fit into our *Stay & Play* category as it offers both lodging and trip opportunities for families. Among the lodging options are its Adirondak Loj, a year-round outdoor center located on the shore of Heart Lake, accommodating up to 46 guests with family rooms, a large living room with a stone fireplace, and homecooked meals. For guests at the lodge, children's nature crafts, canoe rentals, the Nature Museum, and guided hikes are sponsored year-round. The Johns Brook Lodge, a three-and-a-half mile hike from the nearest road also features family rooms and is open during the spring (no meals), summer and fall seasons. Mountain cabins accessible by foot trails are also open year-round.

Summer and fall programs at ADK include a five-night *Adirondack Wilderness Family Camp* (welcoming children of all ages), two-night *Explore and Discover Days* (geared for families with children ages 6 to 12) and overnight *Introductory Rock Climbing* outings (for adults and youths ages 12 to 17). The two-and-a-half day *Paddling Adirondack Style* trip teaches the fundamentals of canoeing, followed by guided canoe day trips.

Come winter and continuing into spring, possibilities include a *Snowshoe Map & Compass* workshop, a *Family Telemark Skiing* weekend for those with children 12 and older, a *Winter Family Weekend* geared for ages 9 to 14, plus *Adirondack Ice Fishing* and *Adirondack Snowshoe Trek*.

All workshops welcome children accompanied by parents though certain courses and events require instructor permission. Kayak, canoe and rock climbing workshops are offered in addition to those mentioned above.

RATES: Rates are half price for children under 12 and free for children 2 and under at all ADK facilities. Loj family room rates begin at $32/night/adult with breakfast. Dinner is additional, as are trail lunches. Mid-week specials feature three meals/day and begin at $119/adult. Prices are slightly lower at the Johns Brook Lodge. Cabins for four persons begin at $75/night/adult. *Family Camp* costs $60/person; *Explore & Discover* is $150/adult, $70/child; *Rock Climbing* is $115/adult; *Paddling* is $100/adult; *Family Telemark Skiing* is $125/person; *Winter Family Weekend* is $160/adult, $80/child. The *Snowshoe Trek* is $236 and *Ice Fishing* is $40. Prices are lower for Club members. Membership is priced at $45/family.

ALLAGASH CANOE TRIPS
P.O. Box 713, Greenville, ME 04441
Phone: 207-695-3668
Fax: 207-695-2492

IN THEIR OWN WORDS: We welcome children between the ages of 5 and 12 on all of our trips except those for more advanced paddlers (which take place in Canada and along the St. John River in Maine). These are suitable for older children and teens with some experience. All of our trip leaders are registered guides with extensive first-aid training. They are also good cooks! Our trips vary in length and we encourage you to consider the longer excursions, which provide the best opportunity to experience the character of the vast woodlands and unwind from the stresses of the "civilized" world. While fishing opportunities are best in May and June, wildlife encounters are plentiful all season long. Our guided trips free you of the responsibility of planning, meal preparation and other camp chores plus provide knowledgeable companions who know the most special places in the area and will teach you about the north country in a way that books and maps cannot possibly accommodate. Guests have the opportunity to explore the region and have plenty of time for relaxation. Many of our trips are ideal for family and friends seeking quality outdoor time together, wanting to share the beauty and peacefulness of the north woods.

THE TRIPS: The most recommended-for-family trips include those along the Allagash Waterway or the West Branch Penobscot River, the Moose River Bow Trip, and a "less intense" adventure along the West Outlet of the Kennebec. The Canadian trips are for skilled canoeists and feature plenty of rapids and wilderness camping. They often have portages, some quite long. On most of these trips previous whitewater experience is required.

Scheduled trips vary in length from five to nine days; several are accessible only via floatplane. Custom trips can be designed to meet individual needs, often only three or four days long. Day and overnight trips can easily be arranged.

RATES: Any youngster age 18 or younger traveling with an adult is considered a "kid." *Allagash River Trips* cost from $625–$750/adult, $475–$495/kid. The five-day *West Branch Penobscot River trip* is $475/adult, $350/kid. Custom trips begin at $350/adult/three days, $225/kid, and may be slightly higher when fewer than four adults are in your group.

> *GREAT VACATIONS TIP:* Two organizations can be particularly helpful when you're planning a canoe or kayak trip. Both the American Canoe Association (7432 Alban Station Blvd., Springfield, VA 22150-2311; 703-451-0141) and the Professional Paddle Sports Association (formerly the National Association of Canoe Liveries and Outfitters, Box 248, Butler, KY 606-472-2202). Both offer consumer advice and have listings of useful publications and periodicals.

ARIZONA RAFT ADVENTURES (AzRA)
4050 E. Huntington Drive, Flagstaff, AZ 86004
Phone: 800-786-RAFT/520-526-8200
Fax: 520-526-8246

IN THEIR OWN WORDS: At the heart of the American Southwest, the San Juan River was the lifeblood of the ancient Anasazi cultures. Our trips on this river allow guests to be as relaxed or as energetic as they like. They are ideally suited to those interested in getting off the beaten path, exploring and learning. The river wanders from "four corners" country through ridges and plains and offers the best introduction to river running for families that we've ever seen. Parents, children and grandparents form timeless bonds during these special times. While we have been hosting whitewater rafting trips in the Grand Canyon for 30 years, our San Juan trips offer a family-friendly alternative to expensive and long river trips.

THE TRIPS: AzRA welcome kids 7 and older on all of its San Juan River rafting trips. Kids 5 and older with previous camping and swimming experience are also invited with their families. At various times AzRA has designated specific trips as *Family Fiesta Weeks* when inflatable kayak lessons, Navajo tales, wildlife tracking and other kid-pleasing activities are added to the agenda. Three- to seven-day trips are possible. Sleeping bags, pad, line and ground cloth are all provided, as are lifejackets. Two-person tents can be rented. During the "high flow" months of May and June, AzRA offers five- to eight-day San Juan River adventures, which feature hard-shelled kayak instruction and are open to ages 16 and older.

Additionally, AzRa leads trips along the mighty Colorado River through the Grand Canyon, with a choice of motorized or oar rafts. On motor trips, youngsters 10 and older can join small groups of 15 participants for an eight-day 225-mile journey from Lees Ferry to Diamond Creek in a single 32-foot raft. The oar or all-paddle options are components of the six- to 14-day *Hybrid Trips* (minimum age 12), where participants get to try their skill on either oar rafts or all-paddle rafts. The shorter trips require a rigorous 7.5 mile hike in or out of the Canyon. *All-Paddle* trips (minimum age 16) are suitable for those looking for a "physically challenging experience." AzRA is committed to making trips through the Grand Canyon possible for people with disabilities.

RATES: Family Fiesta trips have been priced at about $410/adult for three days to $800/adult for eight days. *Grand Canyon Trips* range in price from $1,080-$2,050/adult. Youngsters under 16 receive a 15 percent discount. *Kayak Instruction* is $1,088 for eight days with no youth discounts. For all trips, an additional $1/day contribution to conservation groups is added to the rates; payment is at your discretion.

BOOKED FOR TRAVEL

WHITEWATER RAFTING IN NORTH AMERICA: *The 200 Best Rafting Adventures in the United States, Canada, Mexico and Costa Rica,* by Lloyd Amstead, is a great book for families. At the beginning of each chapter is a river comparison chart which includes minimum age and recommended level of experience and in the back index there is a section on *Best Half-Day Trips for Beginners, Small Children and Seniors.* Once you have selected a likely river and/or outfitter, the book then gives you all the where/when/how much data you'll need. Another winner. (Globe Pequot)

BACKROADS
1516 Fifth Street, Berkeley, CA 94710-1740
Phone: 800-462-2848/510-527-1555
Fax: 510-527-1444

IN THEIR OWN WORDS: With a Backroads vacation, the journey truly is its own reward. Parents and children share a vacation built around activity — bicycling, walking or hiking —instead of seeing the world through the car windows. Together they take in natural wonders, culture and history at every turn and celebrate the exhilaration of meeting new challenges. A relaxed pace allows time to pause and watch two bear cub frolic; to exclaim in awe at bald eagles soaring above; and to see how cheese is made, glass is blown and how humans lived long ago. Backroads *Family Trips* offer several daily mileage choices, allowing everyone in the family to ride at their own pace, secure that the support van is never far away. Most of our family vacations offer carefree camping, with families recounting adventures around the campfires while Backroads' trip leaders prepare hearty meals and handle all of the camp chores. Sleeping beneath the stars in roomy tents is a perfect end to active days. Several family inn trips are also available.

THE TRIPS: Backroads has long offered biking trips to families with children of all ages. There is no minimum age — everyone is welcome. Initially, the company's special family departures were offered on camping trips within North America. We're pleased to report that Backroads has expanded its family options to include a number of inn-to-inn trips, as well as trips to Europe. A number of special family departures are tailor-made to accommodate a wide variety of abilities and designed with lots of options for additional recreational fun. Schedules are relaxed, a minimum of traffic is anticipated and all trips are accompanied by expert leaders who enjoy sharing these relaxing and exciting trips with families. Custom trips can also be arranged. Since Backroads' founder Tom Hale's daughter is just a toddler, we expect that more and more family-welcoming trips will continue to be featured in years to come.

Two- to eight-day inn or camping trips include: *California Weekends* (*Alexander Valley Camping* or *Point Reyes Camping* utilizing mountain bikes); *Canadian Rockies* with the choice of either camping or staying at inns; *Idaho Camping* (mountain bikes); *Maine Camping; Nova Scotia Camping; Vermont Camping;* and *Washington, Puget Sound*, camping or inn-to-inn. In Europe there are trips in the Czech Republic (inns), France (two, both camping) and Switzerland (inn). These family trips operate between May and August and each sounds more appealing than the next. Options on many of the trips include fishing, hiking, swimming, sea kayaking, canoeing and horseback riding. Several of the campgrounds have swimming pools; one even has a miniature golf course. Children (7 and older for camping trips, 13 and older on inn trips), are welcome on the trips not designated as family trips so long as the hotels and other lodgings utilized do not have age restrictions. On all trips, kids under 4 years old or less than 40 lbs. are required to be in a child's car seat (provided by the parent) while traveling in the van. Parents must accompany children under age 8 in the van. Burley trailers and kids' bikes are available for rent on the family departures.

Family departures are also integral to Backroads' *Walking & Hiking* trips. From Washington State's Olympic Peninsula to the Canadian Rockies and the province of Nova Scotia, both camping and inn trips are scheduled. Come winter, cross-country ski outings are on tap for Backroads participants — many of which welcome kids.

RATES: With a few exceptions, all meals are included. Children 6 and under (sharing accommodations with parents) get a 40 percent discount, ages 7 to 12/20 percent, 13 to 16/10 percent. If not sharing a room, on inn trips, ages 16 and under receive a 10 percent discount. On *Family Trips,* babies and toddlers up to age 2 get a 75 percent discount when sharing with two adults. Single parents receive a 10 percent discount for accompanying children 16 or younger. Five days Idaho: $749; six days Puget Sound: $749/camping, $1,298/inn; five days Canadian Rockies: $1,298/inn; six days Canadian Rockies: $749/camping; five days Maine Penobscot Bay: $698/camping, $,1245/inn; five days Southern Vermont: $698/camping, $1,298/inn; six days Nova Scotia $698/camping; six days Czech Republic: $1,798/inn; eight days France: $1,148/camping; six days France: $948/camping; six days Switzerland: $1,995/inn; California Weekends: $239/camping.

BOOKED FOR TRAVEL

In THE BICYCLE TOURING MANUAL, Rob van der Plas makes a powerful case for bike touring as the superior mode of exploring the great outdoors. He writes, "hikers and mountaineers, skiers and canoeists — all folks who are similarly self-propelled and closely in touch with nature . . . are mostly limited to a small region, characterized by one type of terrain . . . the cyclist travels at some speed through the vastness . . . getting the full experience of nature's variety." Since the author was taken on bicycle camping trips when he was a child, and has toured with his own kids as an adult, it is no surprise that he advocates bicycle touring as very much a family activity. His *Touring with*

Children chapter covers ways to carry a child, children's seats, children's bikes, riding with children, tandems and more. His advice is solid in every respect both on the specifics of cycling and on traveling with children in general. (Bicycle Books)

BATTENKILL CANOE, LTD. (BCL)
P.O. Box 65, Historic Route 7A, Arlington, VT 05250
Phone: 800-421-5268/802-362-2800
Fax: 802-362-0159

IN THEIR OWN WORDS: We offer a wide variety of trips from our home on the Batten Kill, one of America's finest rivers, plus trips which venture as far afield as Canada, Costa Rica and Great Britain. We know that canoeing is a great way for families to vacation together, and each year we review our schedule and select trips that are perfect for families with younger kids. On these trips we relax our pace, plan special activities, modify menus and hand pick guides who understand and support the needs of young travelers. Instruction and safety guidelines are integral to all of our trips, so parents needn't worry while on vacation.

THE TRIPS: Children 5 and older are welcome on the designated family trips. On all other trips, the minimum age is 13 (though special arrangements can be made for those 7 and older after speaking with BCL). Carolyn Parker, Director of Touring, particularly recommends the *St. Croix Voyageur*, a four-night camping trip along the border between Maine and New Brunswick, Canada, because it offers great paddling and spectacular scenery. With gentle yet challenging whitewater, you'll paddle past rolling wooded hills, wetlands and marshes, granite outcrops and glacial deposits. Another good choice is the nine-day/eight-night *Dumoine Whitewater*, another camping trip along "a sparkling jewel of a river deep within the wilds of rural Quebec." The pace is leisurely with time for fishing, hiking, swimming, sunning and relaxing. Both of these are considered family trips. In past years, family trips have included a number of rivers in Vermont and several in Costa Rica, BCL's winter home.

One-day trips on the Batten Kill are offered daily for both independent paddlers and for those who prefer to join a guided excursion.

RATES: When sharing accommodations with adults, children ages 5 to 10 receive a discount of 50 percent, ages 11 to 16, 25 percent. If not sharing, the discounts are 20 percent and 10 percent. The *St. Croix Voyageur* is $537/adult and the *Dumoine Whitewater* is $618 for the six-day trip, $738 for nine days. Trips to Costa Rica begin at $1,550/adult. On inn-based trips, meals (beginning with dinner on the first night through lunch on the last day), lodging, guide service, canoe equipment and transportation during the trip are included. On camping trips the canoe equipment, guide service and all camping gear save sleeping bags, which can be rented for $55/trip, are included.

At one end of the freshwater vacation possibility spectrum, **QUIET WATER CANOE GUIDE, NEW HAMPSHIRE, VERMONT:** *Best Paddling Lakes and Ponds for All Ages*, by Alex Wilson, is one of those books whose title sums it up. You'll discover not only the best bodies of water for canoeing, but also where to camp, what wildlife you may spot, and much more. This book, too, is part of a series so do ask about other titles. (Appalachian Mountain Club)

BEAR TRACK OUTFITTING CO.
P.O. Box 937, Grand Marais, MN 55604
Phone: 800-795-8068/218-387-1162
Fax: 218-387-1162

IN THEIR OWN WORDS: We and our five children invite you to experience a canoe adventure where our combination of Northern hospitality and professional experience as deluxe outfitters guarantees your vacation will be a success. You can depend on us to plan and pack a wilderness adventure that you will remember for years to come. We are a full-service outfitter and we pride ourselves on offering the finest quality equipment to make your trip safe and most comfortable. We work with you to route a trip especially suited to you and your kids. We look forward to introducing you and your family and friends to the Boundary Waters Canoe Area — an established protected wilderness area providing one of the most refreshing and interesting recreational opportunities anywhere.

THE TRIPS: David and Cathi Williams, in business for 24 years, outfit canoeists, kayakers, backpackers, mountain bikers, fly-fishers, cross-country skiers and winter campers. Generally speaking, most clients choose to travel unescorted, though guides may be hired to accompany any party for an additional fee (there are a few guided specialty trips too, but these are not necessarily suitable for families).

Bear Track provides everything: all equipment, the necessary wilderness permit (limited number available), and food for the journey. Meals include home-baked breads and offer a vegetarian option. You can canoe for one day or as many as you like. Instructional clinics are also scheduled throughout the season. There's no minimum age requirement, and life vests are provided for all participants. You can rent a canoe (and other equipment) by the day or opt for a fully outfitted trip. On the completely outfitted trips, guests receive free lodging in Bear Track's rustic cozy cabins at Bally Creek Camp the night before the trip. After a hearty breakfast, the Williams go over the equipment, the guidelines for safety and success, and review the route. Families are generally routed on trips with no difficult portages, where the campsites are convenient to fishing, swimming and easy hiking.

It should be noted that Boundary Waters' rules prohibit any one party from being more than nine persons or four watercraft. Larger groups need to understand that this means that they will not be able to camp together or congregate together. Bear Track altered its group rate policy when this change went into effect and now offers it to parties of nine.

RATES: Three-day outfitted trips begin at $180/person; seven-day trips begin at $340/person. Children 12 and under receive a 25 percent discount (one child per adult) and kids 4 and under go free. Cabin rentals at Bally Creek Camp are $55–$75/night. Private guides are approximately $150/day.

BOOKED FOR TRAVEL

CANOEING MADE EASY, by I. Herbert Gordon, and KAYAKING MADE EASY, by Dennis Stuhaug (both subtitled **A Manual for Beginners with Tips for the Experienced**), are part of a series of step-by-step outdoor recreation handbooks which contain absolutely everything one might wish to know about how to become competent and/or proficient in a particular sport. For us, Canoeing is more readable and easier to use. The problem with Kayaking is that there's more material to take in than can ever reasonably be expected to stick. Also, much of the prose is dry and the illustrations sparse, but if you read with highlighter in hand, the book should become more usable. On the plus side, both authors are fathers who obviously enjoy sharing their waterborne adventures with their own kids and stress that canoeing and kayaking are suitable for all ages. The chapter on Canoeing with Kids begins, "There aren't many times that we are closer to our children than when we take them canoeing with us...you and your kids are alone together, learning, teaching and sharing." And we love the advice in Taking Your Kids Kayaking, e.g., "A young child just out of the toddler stage is not going to be a significant motor on your voyages. That said, they'll only learn by doing. They need a paddle. What they don't need is an adult paddle..." and so on, describing what can be used, etc. The emphasis is on making the experience fun and confidence-building for the child. (Globe Pequot)

BICYCLE ADVENTURES, INC. (BAI)

P.O. Box 7875, Olympia, WA 98507
Phone: 800-443-6060/360-786-0989
Fax: 360-786-9661

IN THEIR OWN WORDS: Our trips are not only a lot of fun, they are a great value. We offer more trips in the Pacific Northwest than any other company, some of which we run as often as 25 times in one year. We feel that our selection of cycling routes, restaurants and inns can't be beat and focus our energy on knowing a lot about a small area rather than a little about a wide geographic area. While many companies' trips begin the first day with dinner and van back to the starting point after breakfast on the last day, our first and last days are full days. We know from the comments of prior guests that you will have a wonderful time on our trips, which are designed for those ready to experience an enjoyable, carefree, safe and secure vacation.

THE TRIPS: BAI trip leaders are thoroughly knowledgeable about their surroundings and each trip includes a *Head Guide* who is authorized to make spontaneous changes and additions to a trip to "enhance the group's pleasure." All trips allocate time for non-cycling activities. Although there are no trips specifically designed for families (and BAI's registration form doesn't even indicate that youngsters may participate), it is not unusual for children to accompany their parents on suitable-sounding trips.

Among the itineraries that BAI considers quite "doable," (i.e., easy enough) for younger riders 10 years and older are the *San Juan Islands*, the *Columbia Gorge*, the *Cascade Sampler*, the *Oregon Coast*, the *California Redwoods* and the *California Wine Country*. Tours last from four to six days and most include some daily hiking in addition to cycling. For example, the Columbia Gorge trip includes a full day of hiking, whitewater rafting, and biking on relatively flat terrain, with distances covered ranging from 19 to 32 miles each day. Some of the trips feature camping as well. Participants on *San Juan Islands - Camping* spend two nights by the shores of a scenic lake and two in a state park, enjoying a sea kayaking trip, hiking, and biking anywhere from 15 to 25 miles each day. The *Oregon Coast Camping* trip is considered ideal for beginner or younger cyclists, covering 130 miles in five days with only 20 percent of the terrain rated as hilly.

Custom trips are another possibility for families. If you're an experienced biking family, ask BAI about its *Oregon Cascades* itinerary and check out those on the Gulf Islands of British Columbia.

RATES: Young adults between the ages of 10 and 16 and sharing a room or tent with their parents receive 10 percent off trip fees. The *Columbia*

Gorge trip is $1,096/adult; *Cascades Sampler*: $772; *California Redwoods*: $1,242; *California Wine Country*: $854; *San Juan Islands*: $822/inn, $628/camping; *Oregon Coast Camping*: $598. On some trips airport transfers are included; on others there's an additional fee.

BIKE VERMONT
P.O. Box 207, Woodstock, VT 05091
Phone: 800-257-2226/802-457-3553
Fax: 802-457-1236

IN THEIR OWN WORDS: We are the only bicycle touring company to operate exclusively in Vermont and the Connecticut River Valley and we consciously limit the size of our groups, staying at small country inns. This results in a friendly, low-key, relaxed and wonderful biking experience. No matter what your biking skills or experience, we have a trip to meet your needs. Vermont is a world of back country roads, small villages, valleys, hills and mountains and our goal is to help you enjoy getting to know this wonderful area in a personal, intimate way.

THE TRIPS: Many kids have joined Bike Vermont during its 20 years of operation. As a general rule of thumb, youngsters should be at least 10 years old. Participants are encouraged to pedal at their own pace, selecting among the daily routes offered. Helmets, toe clips and gel seat covers are supplied at no extra charge. Among those tours which are recommended as "great for kids" are the five-day midweek tours of *Middlebury/Otter Creek Valley*, *Northfield/Woodstock*, and *Proctorsville/Five Rivers* — all featuring very different views of Vermont. Bike Vermont is one of the few bicycle touring operators that does not feel that the easy trips are the only ones which will please families, though a number of their trips do indicate easier terrain. Five-day midweek tours meet on Sunday evenings and end on Friday afternoons; six-day tours also begin on Sundays and terminate on Saturday afternoons; weekend trips meet on Friday evenings for dinner and end on Sunday afternoons.

RATES: The three-day midweek tours range from $390 to $465/adult; weekend trips $250 to $315; five-day trips $695 to $780. There is a 10 percent discount for the third and fourth person in the room.

BILL DVORAK'S KAYAK AND RAFTING EXPEDITIONS
17921-B US 285, Nathrop, CO 81236
Phone: 800-824-3795/719-539-6851
Fax: 719-539-3378

IN THEIR OWN WORDS: We invite you to join us for the adventure of a lifetime. Having guided river trips since 1969, we've watched our children grow up on the river and know that is has a powerfully moving effect on children as well as on adults. All of our trips make it easy for you to enjoy the best of whitewater beauty and adventure. We encourage families to participate and even offer kids free trips. We believe that part of the magic of a river trip is that it allows each individual to be in neutral territory to interact with the kid in all of us.

THE TRIPS: Jaci and Bill Dvorak generally use a combination of weight (50 lbs.) and varying minimum ages as the basis for which kids can come along on their more than 29 canyon trips on a total of 10 rivers: the Arkansas, Colorado, Dolores, Green, Gunnison, Middle Fork of the Salmon, North Platte, Rio Chama, Rio Grande and the Salt. The five- to six-day *Desolation & Gray Canyons* trip, 86 miles along the Green River, is considered an "excellent family trip" and welcomes children 5 and older. Participants explore Native American pictographs and abandoned homesteads during stops between the rapids encountered en route.

In Colorado, a number of two- and three-day trips along the Colorado River, into *Little Gore Canyon* and the North Platte River, depart from June through August. On these trips, prices are determined by how many family members participate, beginning with a family of three.

Other "great family trips" include two or three days along the Rio Charma in New Mexico and a seven-day excursion exploring the *Lower Canyons of the Rio Grande* along the Texas/Mexico border.

Half-day to three-day trips on the Arkansas River in Colorado can be combined with horseback riding, mountain biking, 4-wheel drive tours or an overnight horseback trip at the Upper Arkansas Recreation Area. Some sectors of this river are suitable for kids 5 and older. Though there are trips along the Colorado River for kids this young, trips into the Grand Canyon require kids to be 12 and older. Dvorak's brochure clearly notes the minimum ages on all of the river trips it offers.

Additionally, an unusual number of instructional seminars — kayak, canoe, raft, inflatable kayak — are offered on a variety of rivers, and range in length from a half day to 12 days. Size requirements and physical ability dictate whether or not these will be appropriate for your kids. There are also a number of fully-guided custom fishing trips; some use canoes, others utilize rafts.

RATES: Desolation/Gray Canyons (Green River, Utah) and *Ponderosa/ Slickrock Canyons* (Dolores River, Colorado) both feature a number of kids-go-free dates valid for one child under 13 per full fare adult. On other trips, youth prices are valid for kids under 13 and are approximately 10 percent lower than the adult rates. Adult rates on the *Desolation Canyon Trip* are $815/five days, $925/six days. *Rio Chama* is $265/two days, $390/three days; *Rio Grande* $870/seven days. The specially-priced family trips range in price from $585 for a family of three/two days to $1,565 for a family of six/three days. Expect prices to go up about five percent for 1997.

BOUNDARY COUNTRY TREKKING (BCT)
590 Gunflint Trail, Grand Marais, MN 55604
Phone: 800-322-8327/218-388-9972
Fax: 218-388-4487

IN THEIR OWN WORDS: Since 1978 we've specialized in providing exciting adventure vacations. In winter, dog sledding, Nordic skiing and snowshoeing trips take advantage of our unique lodging options: warm cozy cabins and yurts, 16-foot round canvas structures equipped with gas lights and cooking stove, fully outfitted kitchen and skylight (with a nearby outhouse). Several of our trips are well-suited for families, including the sled dog adventures and guided canoe trips in Minnesota's Boundary Waters Canoe Area Wilderness, without doubt the world's premier canoeing area. We're very excited by having more families know about us as we have found that those who travel with us often return year after year.

THE TRIPS: We were originally led to BCT through word of its extensive and varied winter sled dog adventure program. Open to children 9 and older, those over 12 actually have the opportunity to drive their own sled, while forging a bond with the teams of affectionate Alaskan huskies. The heavily dog-centered mushing program is run by Arleigh Jorgensen, one of North America's leading mushers, who believes that the best way to learn about mushing is to do it yourself. Two- to four- day adventures include all meals and lodging in yurts along the trail, modern cabins or a combination of both. A five-day expedition travels over 100 miles across the Boundary Waters from the Gunflint Trail and the U.S./Canadian border lakes along the historic "Voyager Highway." There are expeditions to the Canadian Arctic Northwest Territories and tent camping dog sled trips as well.

In the warmer seasons, BCT runs canoe trips, which are suitable for children as young as 6. The usual plan is to establish a base camp from which daily excursions may be taken. These camps are generally located near hiking trails, old historic sights and "other points of interest to children." BCT's three-day/four-night *Introductory Canoe Adventure* was specially designed for families and features lodging on the days of arrival and return, guided canoeing for three days with two nights of camping, instruction and all canoeing and camping gear. An advanced trip is also operated.

Also appealing are unique "off-the-beaten-path year-round vacation lodging" choices. The *Little Ollie Lake Cabin*, for example, is a two-bedroom cabin with a fully equipped kitchen, free-standing fireplace, full bath, sauna and, in summer, the free use of a canoe. Hiking trails are just out the door and mountain bike trails steps away. In winter, the cabin is snowbound in the center of the famed Gunflint Nordic Trail System so that guests must ski in and out for half a mile, though food and gear are taken in via snowmobile. Yurts also come equipped with canoes in the summer and are accessible via hiking, biking and skiing. Snowshoe and cross-country trails start right at the door.

Other programs from BCT are lodge-to-lodge hiking and/or skiing and guided mountain biking.

RATES: Dogsled Trips cost $520/person/two nights, $830/three nights, $1,090/four nights. Value season prices are about 25 percent less. A child sharing the dog sled with an adult pays 70 percent of the adult cost. *Introductory Canoe Adventure* is priced by the number of participants: $420/person for two to three people, $375/four to six people. The *Little Ollie Lake Cabin* in summer is $690/week for the first two people, $100/each additional person. Nightly rates are $110/midweek and $125/weekends with additional persons paying $20. Yurts cost $60/night plus $10/additional persons. Children under 6 are free, ages 6 to 12 pay 50 percent.

BROOKS COUNTRY CYCLING TOURS (BCCT)
140 West 83rd St., New York, NY 10024-5003
Phone: 212-874-5151
Fax: 212-874-5286

IN THEIR OWN WORDS: We are committed to high quality rides, great food and fine lodgings. A small, personal company, our enthusiastic professional guides have been leading our tours for some time. One of our goals is to make bicycling vacations as affordable as they once were. Quite a number of our tours include young people and we're always happy to steer parents towards the best possible experience for their family.

THE TRIPS: When we first began writing about family bicycle vacations, it was Arlene Brooks (whose husband Jerry is the proprietor of BCCT) who explained to us that bicycling trips are most difficult with children between the ages of 5 and 9, when they are too young to pedal under their own power for any substantial distance and too old to remain happily ensconced in a child's seat. With the advent of new equipment this has changed some.

Among BCCT's most recommended-for-family trips on the domestic front are: cycling in *Florida's Lake Country*; cycling in *Martha's Vineyard* and *Berkshire Camping* (both in Massachusetts); and weekend cycling trips to Cape May, New Jersey, the Maryland Shore, the Pennsylvania Dutch country and Rhode Island beaches. Day trips in the New York metropolitan area are also good possibilities. If you're local to the area, these trips may be just the ticket for determining if you'd like to take a longer family bike vacation. On several of these outings, the group stops for a swim; on others there's a picnic lunch in a park with a children's playground or a stop to do some fruit picking in season.

The Florida trips range from two to five days during February and March and can easily be combined with a trip to Orlando theme parks. The Lakeside Inn, listed on the National Register of Historic Places, is perched on the shore of Lake Dora and features a swimming pool, tennis courts and boating on the lake. The Berkshire trip is described as camping with a "touch of class." Spacious platformed tents complete with electricity, wooden cots and a campfire are featured. Optional extras include two half-day hikes and tickets to performances at Tanglewood. On the Eastern Maryland shore where the cycling is easy and visiting the beach part of the fun, you'll enjoy the comforts of the Great Oak Lodge. If you choose the Rhode Island weekend, it's recommended that you bring along your kites, since you'll be staying right on the beach,

Best choices for travels abroad are *Barging and Biking in Holland* and *Self-Guided Biking in England*; both are ideal for families. According to Arlene, "kids of all ages would love the Holland Barge Trip," as it is very informal, with small, cozy cabins and an eclectic international group. The terrain is flat and youth discounts are offered. Seven-night trips depart every Saturday between April and October. There are three itineraries offered on several dates from May to October in Britain: the Cotswolds (seven days), Devon (seven days) and East Anglia (five days). Everything's been planned in advance; all you have to do is follow the map.

RATES: The *Florida* trip is $89/day including hotel accommodations and breakfast; *Berkshire Camping:* $319; *Cape May Weekend,* $265; *Maryland Shore,* $279; *Rhode Island,* $265-$309; *Pennsylvania Dutch,* $297; day trips: $52 with van transfers, $28 without transfers. The *Holland* trip begins at $898/adult; *England* is $749/five days and $998/seven days. There is a five percent discount for the third family member under the age of 12, a 10 percent discount for the second child under 16 and a 25 percent discount for each subsequent child between the ages of 6 and 10 sharing accommodations with parents. There is a 50 percent discount for children under the age of 6 sharing accommodations with parents.

Membership Club Discounts offer a $5 discount on day trips with a 50 percent discount for every fifth trip, a five percent discount on any overnight tour and 50 percent discounts on van transfers for multi-day trips, a free BCCT tee-shirt and more. Membership costs $65/person and entitles all to the above discounts.

Norma Green retells **THE HOLE IN THE DIKE**, the ever-popular tale of the little Dutch boy who saves his country from flooding. Interestingly, this story was the invention of an American author, Mary Mapes Dodge and first appeared in her book **Hans Brinker** (or **The Silver Skates**) (another classic). Eric Carle did the illustrations and they are first rate. (Scholastic)

BUTTERFIELD & ROBINSON (B&R)
70 Bond Street, Toronto, Ont., Canada M5B 1X3 CANADA
Phone: 800-678-1147/416-864-1354
Fax: 416-864-0541

IN THEIR OWN WORDS: Our walking and biking trips are best described as celebrations of the past, an immersion in a region's cultural heritage. We pioneered bike trips in Europe back in 1966 and remain true to our founding philosophy: see the best of the world at your own pace. Our trips are meticulously researched, include deluxe accommodations, and have been refined to meet the highest of standards. We often stay in places for more than one night to minimize packing and unpacking and plan a wide array of diversions. None of our trips are endurance tests. Each year we select several biking and walking trips as family departures recommended for children ages 13 and over.

THE TRIPS: Among the trips B&R, a highly-respected biking and walking tour operator, has designated as family departures are: *Holland & Belgium*, *Morocco* and *Belize & Guatemala*, featuring both summer and Christmas vacation departure dates. Past destinations have included the Swiss Alps, Brittany, the Loire Valley and the Italian Veneto. Custom trips are also a possibility.

Holland & Belgium is an eight-day/seven-night biking trip which begins by barge to Utrecht, visits the fabled towns of Gouda and Oudewater, passing dikes and windmills, and terminates in Bruges, the jewel of Flanders and sometimes called the "Venice of the North."

"This isn't camping — it's Hollywood," said one dazzled traveler on B&R's Morocco itinerary. Over the course of nine days and eight nights, you'll visit Casablanca, travel through the desert by Land Rover, camel and bicycle and visit a luxurious former hunting lodge in the Atlas Mountains, where you'll explore by foot or horseback.

In Belize you'll discover Mayan ruins, snorkel the barrier reef and tread softly through the rain forest and explore the Guatemalan city of Antigua during the eight-day/seven-night journey.

All of B&R's trips fill up quickly and several are already booked through 1997 but it's always worth calling and seeing if there have been cancellations, new family departures added or additional destinations welcoming families. Young adults 18 and older are welcome on any scheduled B&R departure.

RATES: Holland & Belgium is $3,475/person. *Morocco Biking & Walking* is $3,495/person. *Belize & Guatemala* is $3,250/person. There are no discounts for youngsters unless triple rooms are possible at the utilized lodgings. Single supplements apply only to single rooms.

CANOE COUNTRY ESCAPES (CCE)
194 South Franklin Street, Denver, CO 80209
Phone: 303-722-6482

IN THEIR OWN WORDS: All of our traditional guided trips are moderately-paced, featuring experienced guides who enjoy sharing their love of the outdoors with participants. Our family trips don't just "allow" children, they're geared to families. The leisurely trip features a layover day every other day and no hard paddling. We've found that kids discover that paddling, portaging and helping with camp chores can actually be fun. We never realized the ground-level delights of this wilderness until we went with kids — frogs, crayfish, mushrooms, blueberries, spider webs, moose "nuggets"! This "back-to-basics" adventure in a gentle wilderness gives families a new appreciation for each other and shared memories that will last a lifetime.

THE TRIPS: Don't let the address fool you. Though coordinators Brooke and Eric Durland live in Colorado, their trips take place in the Minnesota-Ontario Boundary Waters. They offer three options for families: *Family Trips* with other family guests; custom-guided trips, for families with children of all ages, where you pick your own dates; and "straight outfitting," where you rent the equipment and purchase food while CCE provides the route planning. All feature great fishing, fun swimming, beautiful scenery and abundant wildlife. While the majority of the trips are camping trips, there are also lodge-to-lodge packages with comfortable accommodations (minimum age 8).

The *Family Trip* (six days/seven nights, minimum age 5) begins with an overnight at Gunflint Lodge (see page 52), which has "adopted" CCE trips into its program. A typical day includes about six to eight miles of paddling and several short portages, a long lunch break and intermittent swimming. Long before the sun sets it's time to find a campsite and pitch tents. The Forest Service has outfitted campsites with fire grates and latrines. Everyone participates in all of the chores, with guests taking turns at learning new skills. There are three traveling and three layover days. On the latter, time is spent exploring, fishing, swimming, canoeing, etc. The trip offers just the right balance of exercise and leisure time.

RATES: Both *Family Trips* and *Lodge-to-Lodge* trips are $695/adult, $395/children under 12. *Custom Guided Trips* are slightly higher and vary on the number of adults and children included. Straight outfitting costs $251/adult for three days, four nights, $126/child under 12; $499/adult for eight nights, $250/child.

ANTLER, BEAR, CANOE: *A Northwoods Alphabet Year,* by Betsy Bowen, depicts the lure and the lore of Minnesota life in 26 charming vignettes. The colored woodblock prints are exceptional. This book will delight young and old readers alike. (Little Brown)

CICLISMO CLASSICO (CC)
13 Marathon Street, Arlington, MA 02174
Phone: 800-866-7314/617-646-3377
Fax: 617-641-1512

IN THEIR OWN WORDS: Since 1988 we've been bringing you the best of Italy. Originally founded with the dream of creating culturally enriching, spectacular and fun cycling itineraries throughout Italy, we now offer 14 bicycling tours, six walking tours, a mountain bike escape plus a tour that utilizes a Renaissance castle as a base and combines cycling with Italian language lessons. Our customized family tours offer a variety of activities for all ages and several of our organized trips, such as *La Cucina Toscana* and *Tuscan Fantasy*, work particularly well for family groups.

THE TRIPS: Children ages 8 and older are welcome on many of CC's tours. The nine-day *Tuscan Fantasy* sounds simply terrific and cycles to many of the small towns we've explored with our own kids. Participants reside at the 12th century Castello di Montegufoni, a property boasting two swimming pools and recently renovated apartments, ideal for those of us traveling with kids. By not changing lodgings each night, your daytime options can be much greater than on other cycling trips. Another family recommendation from CC is its *Amalfi Coast Stroll & Roll* that begins in the charming seaside village of Positano and visits Capri, Amalfi, Ravello and other Mediterranean coastal jewels. Unfortunately, neither this trip nor the *Best of Southern Italy* (also recommended for families; it features biking through farmland and "passing these very funky stone huthouses with conical roofs, painted white buildings and roofs covered in painted abstract symbols; visiting a handmade pasta operation and an olive oil press; and boating through limestone grottoes with our own Italian Popeye, Giovanni") currently operate on dates when children are generally out of school. *Villas and Gardens of Veneto* cycles on flat ground with the backdrop of the Dolomites and visits a group of villages with fantastic trompe l'oeil frescoes and stops to see the giant chess board in the main square in the town of Maraostica, where a "live" performance is put on every two years with townspeople dressed in medieval garb serving as chess pieces. CC customizes these trips for families, complete with a support van, and also can arrange for villa rentals with "trustworthy" child care plus lots of other amenities.

RATES: Children between the ages of 8 and 12 receive a 30 percent discount when sharing accommodations with parents; ages 13 to 17, 10 percent. Rates for *Tuscan Fantasy* begin at $2,350/adult. Customized trips cost about 10 to 20 percent more than scheduled departures.

BOOKED FOR TRAVEL

Introduce children ages 6 to 9 to one of four foreign countries and its spoken language with the help of **Kingfisher's Little Library** series (various authors). Choose the GUIDE TO FRANCE, GERMANY, ITALY or SPAIN with its companion volume the FIRST 200 WORDS IN FRENCH, GERMAN, ITALIAN or SPANISH and your kids will be on their way to becoming citizens of the world. The language format is identical in the First 200 Words books (it helps if there is someone who understands rules of pronunciation), and all the Guides have maps and chapters on food and drink, games, celebrations, etc. The artwork is very good and the books are easily transportable. (Kingfisher)

CLASS VI RIVER RUNNERS, INC.
P.O. Box 78, Lansing, WV 25862-0078
Phone: 800-CLASSVI/304-574-0704
Fax: 304-574-4906

IN THEIR OWN WORDS: We believe that our greatest asset is that we listen to and react to what our guests want. Consequently, we're continuously adding to and upgrading every aspect of our operation. We're parents ourselves and are very attuned to the needs of families — offering half price for kids ages 6 to 16 on our one-day trips, providing a playground at our base and arranging child care for those too young to participate. Our trips are on the New and Gauley Rivers, part of the largest federally protected watershed in the eastern United States. The gentle upper sections of the New River are ideal for family adventures, while the lower section offers incredible whitewater challenges. The Gauley provides one of the most exhilarating experiences imaginable.

THE TRIPS: If you've read **Great Nature Vacations With Your Kids**, you know we're big fans of Class VI and have rafted with them many times. A highlight of Class VI is that guests can enjoy several days of rafting adventures without having to camp out (though that is an option). The advantage here is that different family members can pursue their own rafting preferences, from world-class whitewater to calmer (but still exciting) waters. We've done this ourselves, arranging a kids-only boat on the Upper Gorge, while the adults and teenagers took on the challenge of the Lower Gorge. There are specialty trips, including seven overnight ecology weekends designed for families, as well as a number of day trips on both the Upper and Lower New, dinner trips, and multi-day trips. Providing one-stop shopping, Class VI can arrange just about every aspect of your vacation, beginning with special air fares. They also operate a campground and can organize a wide range of lodgings — B&Bs, cabins in state parks, even luxury stays at The Greenbrier. Kayak clinics, fishing trips and customized packages which can include mountain biking, rock climbing and rappelling are all possible.

RATES: One-day *Lower New* and *Dinner on the River* trips are $83–$97/adult. *Upper New* trips (minimum age 12) are $78/adult. Children ages 6 to 16 pay half price. Multi-day trips begin at $194/adult for two days with $25 discounts for rafters age 16 and younger. Gauley River (minimum age 15) trips begin at $108/day to $314/three days. Combination rates are also offered.

CUTTING EDGE ADVENTURES (CEA)

P.O. Box 1334, Mt. Shasta, CA 96067
Phone: 800-594-8435/916-926-4647
Fax: 916-926-0846

IN THEIR OWN WORDS: We (Leif Hansen and Stefanie Abrishmian) were both born and raised in California and for the past 14 years have worked as river guides and managers. We were both certified Swiftwater Rescue Technicians and trained EMTs before we decided to open Cutting Edge Adventures. We've chosen our favorite California rivers — the California Salmon, the Scott and the Klamath — for their magnificent scenery, rugged terrain and spectacular whitewater. In the off season we offer destination ski trips in the U.S. and Europe, scuba diving and sailing in the Caribbean and other tropical locations, sea kayaking in Baja, Mexico, rafting and safaris in Africa, rafting and exploring Mayan ruins in Honduras and paragliding in California. Our kayak school teaches the skills and techniques of running a hard-shell kayak. We love having kids on all of our trips and carefully guide families toward adventures most suitable for their family make-up. One stretch of the Klamath River is unique in that we can comfortably and safely take kids as young as 3 years old and still satisfy the quest for adventure of the parents. Other trips are more suitable for parents traveling with teenagers. The kayak clinics have successfully taught children as young as 7 the intricate Eskimo roll.

THE TRIPS: One- to three-day trips are offered on the Scott, various sections of the Klamath, the California Salmon and Sacramento Rivers. The Middle/Lower Klamath is one of Stephanie's favorite choices for families because of its incredible wildlife viewing from the river, beautiful campsites, great side hikes and fun rapids. The dam-controlled river is runnable between April and October with Class II and III rapids. The 'Sac' is also "fantastic for kids!" Three- and five-day Kayak Schools operate during July and August. On CEA's kayak trips in the Sea of Cortez paddling instruction is provided in what it calls "the perfect place to learn sea kayaking." Brochure dates of these trips, unfortunately, do not match standard school vacations; but with the opportunity to paddle next to sea lions or whales and time to hike and snorkel or talk with the guides who are "well-versed in the natural and human history of the area," your teens might learn almost as much as a week of school can offer. CEA notes that they can offer these trips during the spring/Easter break.

Our friend Christine Loomis, author of Fodor's **Family Adventures** (see page 8) has taken several trips with CEA and sings its praises, in particular regaling us with stories of Stephanie's remarkable relationship with children and her seemingly never-ending good humor. We've spoken with Stephanie ourselves and were suitably impressed by her enthusiasm

— something you rarely find in an operation such as this, where none of the principals are parents themselves.

RATES: River trips range in price from $90/one day/adult to $340/three days. Youth prices for those 16 and under are only offered on the Middle/Lower Klamath trips and are in the 40 to 50 percent range. *Kayak School* costs $750/adult for five days, $560/three days. A new *Inflatable Kayak School* is $340/three days. Kids 16 and under pay 50 percent. Private kayak clinics are recommended for families and prices are determined by the number of family participants and the ages involved. The *Baja* trip is $1,100/person and currently does not offer a youth discount.

ECHO: THE WILDERNESS COMPANY
6529 Telegraph Avenue, Oakland, CA 94609-1113
Phone: 800-652-3246/510-652-1600
Fax: 510-652-3987

IN THEIR OWN WORDS: We remain faithful to our original goal: To run the highest quality river trips possible: safe, well organized, exciting adventures that promote a greater appreciation of wilderness and wild rivers, and that offer special meaningful experiences for all. We've hand-picked five rivers that best meet this criteria: the Middle Fork and Main Salmon in Idaho, the Rogue in Oregon and the Tuolumne and South Fork of the American in California. Families are a mainstay of our business, with kids, parents and grandparents welcomed and catered to.

THE TRIPS: River Trips for Kids (and their parents) are scheduled on the Main Salmon, Rogue and South Fork of the American Rivers, during which a *Fun Director* plans exciting activities, from finding crawdads and hunting for animal tracks to stargazing and congregating around the campfire. Two trips to Alaska are also featured. These trips are described in greater detail in **Great Nature Vacations With Your Kids.**

RATES: Youth rates are valid for ages 7–17. The two- to five-day *River Trips for Kids* range from $230 to $915/adult and $220 to $790/youth.

ENGLISH LAKELAND RAMBLERS (ELR)
18 Stuyvesant Oval #1a, New York, NY 10009
Phone: 800-724-8801/212-505-1020
Fax: 212-979-5342

IN THEIR OWN WORDS: Since the mid-1980s we've led walkers and hikers of all ages on Lakeland rambles through the most beautiful corner of England. Over hills and dales, past peaceful pastures, rambling stone walls and rose-clad stone circles, we pass through the scenery that inspired such writers as Wordsworth, Coleridge and Potter. A number of families join our trips each year, including groups that are comprised of three generations. We like to see families come together in the type of situation we provide and feel that grandparents particularly enjoy sharing our trips with their grandchildren. Our only requirement is that children be physically able to walk from four to 10 miles each day and we have found that when youngsters are about 7 or 8 years old, this is not a problem. Though we specialize in the Lake District, our tours in the Cotswolds and in Scotland are of comparable quality and value. No previous experience is necessary but if you're first-time hikers we particularly suggest one of our *One-Hotel Base* trips where the daily walks are easy. We've designed them to include a nice balance of walking and sightseeing, while staying at a hotel in an idyllic setting offering old-fashioned hospitality with modern comforts. Wonderful food is yet another highlight of our trips.

THE TRIPS: The six-night *One-Hotel Base* trips recommended by ELR Director Seth Steiner can be taken in the Lake District, the Cotswolds or in Scotland and do sound appealing — both relaxing and fun. In the Lake District you'll not only walk, you'll cross Derwentwater by launch, motor up the steeper sections of the area by minivan and board a narrow-gauge steam railway. Visits include a Roman Fort, Wordsworth's last home, a medieval castle and spectacular waterfalls. The steeped-in-history villages of the Cotswolds and the wooded valleys and lochs of the Southern Highlands of Scotland also feature interesting itineraries.

Additionally ELR offers similar programs with more challenging hikes, inn-to-inn and customized trips.

RATES: One-Hotel Base trips range in price from $1,530 to $1,640/adult and include everything except airfare and transfers to/from the hotel which ELR will be happy to assist with. Children traveling with either one or two adults receive a 10 percent discount. Most properties cannot accommodate four persons per room.

EURO-BIKE TOURS
P.O. Box 990, DeKalb, IL 60115
Phone: 800-321-6060
Fax: 815-758-8851

IN THEIR OWN WORDS: I started Euro-Bike 20 years ago to offer Americans a more relaxed way to experience Europe. Born and raised in Holland, bicycling was a way of life to me and I knew that a gently paced bike trip offered folks a unique opportunity to discover the continent I knew so well. On all of our trips we meet participants at the airport, knowing they may be jet-lagged and anxious to avoid the hassles produced by airports. Our trips are not tests of endurance, but rather active vacations designed for their ease of cycling along country lanes and locally traveled bike paths. Side trips and extra mileage options cater to those who prefer a hardier pace. Our European guides delight in sharing the joys of cycling through their homelands.

THE TRIPS: It's only recently that Euro-Bike (which also operates walking tours) has started permitting youngsters under the age of 18 on their trips, so we were both pleased and surprised to find them sounding so family-friendly when we spoke with them. For parents with young children, they recommend their eight-day trips in France or Holland as being the easiest.

La Loire: Valley of the Kings explores the romantic, fairy tale chateaux of the Loire Valley — Blois, Amboise, Chambord, Chenonceau, Azay, et al. Medieval towns, feudal fortresses and vineyards and are among the delights that await cyclists.

The Dutch Touch travels from the historic art center of Haarlem and continues on through the Lake District of Friesland, along the coastline of the old Zuyder Zee. Visit a wildlife sanctuary in Workum, see the famous earthenware pottery in Makkum, learn why Geithoorn is called the "Venice of the North," and watch peat cutting, butter churning and clog-making at Berkenrode. Holland is more than a land of windmills, cheese and tulips! Another trip we think might interest families is Euro-Bike's particularly kid-appealing itinerary in Scandinavia.

RATES: Loire Valley is $1,895. *Dutch Touch* is $1,835. There are no standard discounts for youngsters. Each trip is determined separately.

BOOKED FOR TRAVEL

We've been wishing that someday we'd find a really good book on biking in Europe with children, and now we've discovered two: **EUROPE BY BIKE: 18 Tours Geared for Discovery**, and **FRANCE BY BIKE: 14 Tours Geared for Discovery**. Authors Karen and Terry Whitehall traveled over 6,000 miles while towing their two-year-old daughter Sierra Jo along in a bicycle trailer. What this means in practical terms is that all routes are chosen with an eye to safety. The itineraries sound very appealing and there are lots of tips on which local foods to sample and where to find budget lodgings. We hope that as soon as Sierra Jo has learned to ride competently by herself the Whitehalls will update these volumes and share the benefit of their experiences with us. (Mountaineers)

EQUITOUR, LTD.
P.O. Box 807, Dubois, WY 82513
Phone: 800-545-0019/307-455-3363
Fax: 307-455-2354

IN THEIR OWN WORDS: We offer horseback riding holidays across the country and around the globe — from Argentina to Turkey, touching on the continents of North America, South America, Europe, Asia, Africa and Australia/New Zealand. For most of our trips, you must have a good knowledge of the basics of riding and some experience in riding cross-country at a gallop. On many of our overseas trips, only English-style saddles are provided and riders must be solid intermediate riders to participate. The best place to learn if any of our many trips are suitable is at our home base, the Bitterroot Ranch, the last ranch in a remote valley in Wyoming, bordering the Shoshone National Forest and the Wind River Indian Reservation. Up to 30 guests, including youngsters, stay in our 12 cabins and gather in the main lodge for meals and relaxed evenings. Our ranch programs are extremely flexible heading out on rides which take you through sagebush plains and along rocky gorges to high alpine meadows and forested mountains.

Cattle Drives in Wyoming, Utah and Arizona are another specialty of ours. Depending upon the selected trip, accommodations vary from luxury hotels to rustic inns and tents — all with a warm friendly atmosphere. There's no set minimum age for youngsters but the majority of the trips are more suitable for families with teenagers, though children as young as 4 have enjoyed staying at the ranch (a babysitter is available every afternoon so that parents can go off on a ride by themselves). There are ponies for the younger children to ride and kids 7 and older are invited to join our supervised rides. Several children have been raised at the ranch and visiting youngsters are drawn into life here.

THE TRIPS: There are simply too many to list here but suffice it to say that if there's a destination either in the United States or abroad that can be explored by horseback, Equitour has a trip going there. We're totally unable to come to a consensus about which sounds most compelling. We're certainly tantalized by the eight-day/seven-night *Star Beach Ride* in Portugal with six half-days of riding from a base in the seaside village of Milfontes, but we're equally tempted by the eight-day/seven-night *Relaxed Tuscany Ride* featuring six days on horseback from the woodlands of the Arno Valley to the mountains of Chianti. Even more exotic is an expedition to Botswana, "Africa's last frontier." There are numerous domestic trips as well, from California to Virginia, with many spots in between. There are not many children who join these rides though we're assured that children who have the stamina to spend five or six hours a day in a saddle are most welcome. The trips with half-day rides only are a good starting point for families. It is important to speak directly with Mel or Bayard Fox or their office folks before signing on as they prefer to discuss your child's capabilities directly with you in order to be certain the trip will be successful for all.

RATES: Stays at Bitterroot Ranch are $1,100/adult/week plus a 15 percent service charge. Children under 16 receive a 25 percent discount and those under 4 pay $25/day. The *Star Beach Ride* is $685, *Relaxed Tuscany Ride* about $1,095, *Botswana* (10 days/nine nights) is about $235/night. Some examples of domestic trip prices are *Pony Express Ride*: $1,195/eight days, seven nights; *Wyoming Cattle Drive*: $1,245/eight days, seven nights; *Old Virginia Ride*, $1,490/seven days, eight nights. Though other children's rates are not published, they may be possible so please don't forget to ask.

BOOKED FOR TRAVEL

For those in search of the inside scoop on cattle drives, pack trips, endurance rides, et al., Frommer's HORSEBACK ADVENTURES, by Dan Aadland, is a first-person, in-depth account of the many ways to enjoy life from the saddle. Aadland is an entertaining raconteur and more than willing to share the benefit of his equestrian expertise with readers. Not all of these adventures are suitable for kids, but we still recommend the book — it's full of history and savvy observations about the nature of man and beast that should appeal to riders and non-riders alike. (Macmillan)

EUROPEDS
761 Lighthouse Avenue, Monterey, CA 93940
Phone: 800-321-9552/408-372-1173
Fax: 408-655-4501

IN THEIR OWN WORDS: With 15 successful years behind us, we have fine-tuned our selection of walking and bicycling itineraries in France, Italy and Switzerland. When you join one of our trips, you see Europe in a memorable, exhilarating, rousing fun fashion. Uncluttered by enclosure, our trips expose you to the indigenous scents of the environment, bring you close to local folks and provide a uniquely clear view of the wonders of the world. The core of our philosophy is that the path sets the pace. We pride ourselves on taking care of all your needs so that you can relax, enjoy and have fun. Our enthusiastic and friendly guides look forward to serving as your window to local culture and providing the support and encouragement you may need. Those of us who own and operate

Europeds lead most of our trips. Our sag wagon not only shuttles luggage from one hotel to the next, it follows you along the route with refreshments, the opportunity to store local purchases and give tired riders a lift. We've taken lots of families on our trips, on a recent trip we had both a 13-year-old and his 76-year-old grandparent.

THE TRIPS: Europeds is "quite willing" to take children as young as 10 years old. However, for youngsters who may be less than five feet tall, Europeds might not be able to offer a bicycle small enough to fit (all Europed bikes feature 27" diameter wheels, not the 24" wheels required for smaller-sized children). Younger children who wish to participate should bring their own bicycle with them, a solution that has worked in the past. We have great enthusiasm for Europeds' excursions, so many of which sound appealing. Founder Peter Boynton specifically recommends the *Loop Trips* for families "because we stay multiple nights at each of two hotels." These six-night trips are offered in both the Dordogne and Provence regions of France.

In the Dordogne, the first three nights are spent in Les Eyzies, where local attractions include the Font de Gaum cave, the 12th Century Abbey of Cadouin, the incredible Roc St. Christophe and, of course, the spectacular Cave Lascaux II. Then it's off to Carennac for three nights where the sights on the daily rides include the underground chasm Gouffre de Padriac and the stunning castles of Quercy.

The *Provence Loops* trip is similarly inviting, as are many of the other cycling and walking tours. Combinations are also on the calendar. The hiking tours are for hikers of intermediate and above ability. *Pedal & Pole*, a seven-day trip featuring mountain biking and skiing sounds very exciting (but not easy) and spends five of its six nights in a hotel in Verbier, the sixth in a mountain hut not far below the ice fields. We think our well-skied teens would love this trip. Parents with younger children can participate in this trip so long as they make arrangements with Verbier's ski school and/or child care facilities to watch their children during the day.

RATES: Dordogne Loops costs $1,545/adult, *Provence Loops* $1,575. *Pedal & Pole* is $1,695. There are no discounts or reductions for children.

GREAT VACATIONS TIP: When it comes to outfitting yourselves for a family bike trip, you'll be happy to know that Cannondale, the manufacturer of biking gear, has added a children's clothing line with garmets constructed of the same materials used for its adult clothing. Kids will definitely think that the colorful clothes are cool. They'll love all the pockets on the jersey. You may find them donning these duds whether or not they're heading out on their bikes. To find the retailer nearest you, call 800-726-2453.

GERHARD'S BICYCLE ODYSSEYS
P.O. Box 757, Portland, Oregon 97207
Phone: 503-223-2402
Fax: 503-223-5901

IN THEIR OWN WORDS: On a bicycling vacation you become part of a world that is impossible to witness from behind a car's window glass. On our tours, you set your own pace and forget the hurried, worried world as you meander through villages and valleys alive with century-old traditions. We plan every detail of your Odyssey, offering you a hassle-free vacation. Our support vehicle is always available for you and will carry your luggage and assist with any mechanical problems. We've had young cyclists and seniors (our oldest thus far was 80!) join our groups of 20 cyclists. We meet you at the airport and arrange for English-speaking guides on the various sightseeing tours. On our trips you'll discover the Europe of Europeans.

THE TRIPS: This company has been in operation for more than 22 years. Each year, owner Gerhard Meng designs new and exciting bicycling options in Europe. Though the trips are not conceived with kids in mind, children are always invited to join a group with their parents. Of the organized trips, *Bike, Balloon & Barge* offers a combination that should enchant kids of all ages. The first three nights are spent in Fountainbleau, not far from Paris, before boarding a barge for six nights along the canals of Burgundy. The unhurried pace and varied cycling selections are particularly attractive.

An even better bet for families, in our opinion, is the new *Independent Cycling* series. Trips include accommodations, meals, luggage transfer when applicable, bicycle rental and much more. Choose from *A Week in Provence*, *A Week in Denmark* or, for experienced cyclists, *Roof of Norway*, all of which offer an enchanting basic itinerary. The Provence trip visits the historic cities of Avignon and Arles and the coastal plains of the Carmague and features a day at leisure near the shores of the Mediterranean. In Denmark, take in a number of castles and ride along the ancient paths of the Vikings stopping at the Iron Age village of Roskilde. In Norway, travel from Oslo to Bergen by mountain bike along gravel roads, in the company of a local guide, as well as by train and fjord steamer.

RATES: *Bike, Balloon & Barge* is $2,950/person, *A Week in Provence* is $1,065, Denmark, $1,095 and Norway, $1,685. There are no reductions for children.

BOOKED FOR TRAVEL

In BIKE ABROAD: *439 Organized Trips with 79 Companies in 49 Countries* author Gerri Alpert strongly advocates group, or at least pre-planned, touring as the most carefree and enjoyable way to take a cycling vacation. "Someone else has found the best routes and handles the logistics of booking hotels There's a sag wagon or van to carry luggage, you have a ready-made social group," etc., etc. Each trip is described in depth and all of them sound interesting. Company backgrounds are given and there's all sorts of practical advice on the best clothing, how to transport your bike, and more. There's plenty of color photography and a list of *Trips for Families* early on in the book. A fine work. (New Voyager)

GUNFLINT LODGE & OUTFITTERS
750 Gunflint Trail, Grand Marais, MN 55604
Phone: 888-GUNFLINT/218-388-2294
Fax: 218-388-9429

IN THEIR OWN WORDS: We actually run two separate businesses, Gunflint Northwoods Outfitters and Gunflint Lodge. The former provides food and equipment for people who wish to take a multi-day canoe trip in the Boundary Waters Canoe Area Wilderness. Guests can go out on their own, join one of our group guided trips or have a trip customized for them. Children are natural explorers, forever curious, and excited with the discoveries of the natural world. We paddle through beaver ponds, look for critter tracks and plants along a lake bog and call out to loons at night.

The Lodge is a traditional resort where guests stay in cabins, dine in the lodge and take day trips for canoeing or fishing. Our strong programs of nature-related activities are designed both for families to participate in together and for children on their own. The newest activity, *Pathway to Fishing*, is a weekly 12-step program teaching kids fishing basics: habitat, knot-tying, casting, lure, etc., followed by a guided half-day fishing trip. Our staff is trained to offer friendly service in its true meaning. Every guest's request must get a "yes" answer.

THE TRIPS: Owners Sue and Bruce Kerfoot, who are parents and grandparents themselves, invite families to enjoy their wilderness from a variety of perspectives, always suggesting routes with modest portages and allowing time to observe local wildlife, both on- and off-shore. Guided trips include *Family Discoveries by Canoe*, a week-long adventure where kids 6 and older learn the basics of camping, hands-on, and refine their canoeing technique as they paddle through the land of the moose and the beaver. For those who wish, lodge-to-lodge trips are also offered.

Fishing is a specialty of the Kerfoots and they offer fly-fishing schools, lodge fishing for serious fishermen and fishing packages and trips.

In winter, the adventures continue with one-hour, half- or full-day dog sled rides, a *Mushing Week*, on which you and your children 6 years and older learn how to harness dogs, and escorted cross-country excursions from the home base cabin complete with fireplace, whirlpool tub and sauna. During the summer months all age children are welcome at the Lodge; in winter when mushing is the primary activity, it's recommended that children be at least 6 years old.

RATES: Self-guided wilderness trips run from $352–$377/person for a six-night package. Guided seven-night trips are $695/adult and $395/child under 12. A one-week *Family Package* in the summer at the Lodge averages $2,200–$3,100 for a family of four. *Winter Mushing Weeks* are $1,040/person. Dog sled rides range from $53–$150/person.

BOOKED FOR TRAVEL

David and Judy Harrison, the authors of CANOE TRIPPING WITH CHILDREN: *Unique Advice To Keeping Kids Comfortable,* have been canoeing with their kids for twenty years. The book covers both canoeing and camping out and every page is filled with practical material focusing on the needs of families, whether novices or pros. There are chapters on equipment, clothing, cooking, wildlife, safety, diversions, etc. Their advice is to begin camping with your children when they're young (before time with their friends becomes more important than family time) and recommend starting out with a weekend trip, with state and national parks as good bets for first-timers. A really excellent resource. (ICS)

HEADWATERS RIVER COMPANY
P.O. Box 1, Banks, ID 83602
Phone: 800-800-7238/208-793-2348
Fax: 208-793-2348

IN THEIR OWN WORDS: The Payette Rivers are exceptional in their variety and accessibility, offering trips that range from easy float trips for the entire family to the most challenging whitewater to be found. I've (owner Conrad Fourney) run rivers in North and South America, Africa and New Zealand and feel that the experiences available on the Payette Rivers are among the most special in the world. I invite you and your family to experience the beauty of these rivers with us.

THE TRIPS: It was only by luck (actually by misdialing the phone) that I caught up with Conrad Fourney of Headwaters, who was not only our guide on our first-ever river trip with ROW (see page 77), but whose first guiding experience was with Class VI (see page 43), another of our favorite outfitters. Conrad's company offers trips on the Payette Rivers in Idaho. Children 5 years and older are welcome on the half-day *Main Payette* excursion, where there's a good balance of fun rapids and relaxation, as well as on full-day trips on the river's Cabarton section, a veritable "symphony of nature," teeming with wildlife. Teens 14 and older may opt for the "wildest half-day" on the *Staircase* trip (combinable with the *Main Payette*), the full day in *The Canyon*, which includes a portage around an awe-inspiring 40 foot waterfall, or the two- and three-day trips through the rugged granite canyons and world class whitewater of the *South Fork Payette,* with stops to soak in natural hot springs. Fourney is pretty strict about the age limitation, as he has found that parents have not always been honest with him about their youngsters' capabilities.

Headwaters also offers kayaking instruction for both beginners and intermediates, starting at about age 8, with a minimum of two participants.

On the trip we took with Conrad as our guide, he was like the Pied Piper — all the kids flocked to him. His partner, Betsy Bader, also has had her fair share of experience with kids, first through an outdoor education program for at-risk youth, which she implemented as a VISTA volunteer. Her commitment to troubled youth continues to this day, through Headwaters' ongoing involvement with a local children's home, which offers a "rafting and kayak program for young people with the aim of helping them develop personal strength, self control and the responsibility necessary for making good decisions — a rewarding experience for both staff and kids!"

RATES: Youth prices are for ages 12 and under. Half-day trips are $30–37/adult, $20/youth. Full day: $71–90/adult, $45/youth. Two-day trips: $248, three-days: $348. Full-day kayak lesson: $75/person.

HIKING HOLIDAYS
P.O. Box 711, Bristol, VT 05443-0711
Phone: 800-537-3850/802-453-4816
Fax: 802-453-4806

IN THEIR OWN WORDS: From Arizona to Vermont, Massachusetts to Ireland, Maine to Switzerland, the world is filled with great places to hike and walk. In these places, walking/hiking explorations offer something more precious than photographs — priceless memories that will last forever. We design trips for people of every age and level of experience and our groups are a mix of singles, couples and families. Whether you've trekked in the Himalayas or are a first-timer, one of our journeys will take you to some of the world's most beautiful locations in the most relaxed way possible.

THE TRIPS: An offshoot of Vermont Bicycle Tours (see page 89), Hiking Holidays offers a number of hiking and walking trips both in North America (Vermont, Maine, Massachusetts, North Carolina, Arizona, Quebec, New Brunswick) and Europe (Ireland, England, France, Switzerland). As with VBT's bike trips, children 10 and older are welcome on North American trips, 13 and older on European trips. North American trips are between five and seven days in length, in Europe from seven to eight days. The *Vermont Lake Country* trip offers a respite from the summer heat in the cool forests of the state's Northeast Kingdom and, with its daily swimming opportunities, should appeal to youngsters. Lodgings include an historic farm and an inn in the town of Stowe. Walking options are from two to eight miles per day. A trip in the Swiss Alps visits the Jungfrau, the Sunnbuel and the Matterhorn. The variety of transport — trams, cable cars, gondolas, and cog railways — is exciting for all. Each day there's a choice of an easy, moderate or challenging hike, with the car-free villages of Murren and Zermatt among the stops.

RATES: Children ages 10 to 17 receive a 10 percent discount only on trips in North America. When a child is sharing accommodations with two full paying adults the discount is 25 percent. Unfortunately, not all of the properties used can accommodate four people. On the five-day *Vermont Lake Country* trip, for example, there is a maximum of three people in a room. There are no youth discounts offered on overseas itineraries. *Vermont Lake Country:* $995/adult. *The Alps:* $1,795/adult.

HUGHES RIVER EXPEDITIONS, INC.
P.O. Box 217, Cambridge, ID 83610
Phone: 208-257-3477
Fax: 208-257-3476

IN THEIR OWN WORDS: We have a young family ourselves and especially enjoy outfitting family rafting trips. A whitewater river trip in the wilderness is an ideal and unique vacation opportunity for families. During the summer over half our clients are families with children 5 years and over. We truly value family trips and can fit a particular family into a style of trip that fits its own interests and needs. We've taken children as young as 3 but find that 5 is a better minimum age. We invite you to join us on the river where we promise spectacular rivers, expert professional guides, delicious meals, excellent equipment and first-class service on Idaho and eastern Oregon rivers.

THE TRIPS: Jerry Hughes and Carole Finley, whose children are 12, 10 and 5, have been welcoming families for twenty years. Like many operators in Idaho, they recommend the four- or five-day *Salmon River Canyon* trips for first-time families. These trips take advantage of the long summer days, the warm swimming water and the white sand beaches that make ideal camping sites. The gentle flow of the river is perfect for learning how to enjoy paddle rafts and inflatable kayaks. Catch-and-release trout and bass fishing is a popular diversion, as are the stops to inspect Chinese rock houses, abandoned mines and natural springs.

Other family favorites are: the five- and six-day *Middle Fork of the Salmon*, with a McKenzie Drift Boat option for fishermen, *Snake River/Hells Canyon, Seven Devils/Hells Canyon* (a backpack/float combo), *Wallowa-Grande Ronde, Bruneau Canyonlands*, and *Owyhee Canyonlands*. Minimum ages vary from 5 to 12 on these rivers and depend on the river selected and the time of year. For example, early spring and summer trips are best suited for families with older children. The *Seven Devils/Hells Canyon* excursion is best suited to families with teens who are in good physical shape.

RATES: Youths (college age and under) receive a 10 percent discount. *Salmon River Canyon* trips are $885/four days, $1,080/five days. *Snake River/Hells Canyon* range from $675/three days to $1,265/six days. *Middle Fork* five- and six-day trips are $1,140 and $1,360 respectively. Drift boat rates are additional. The *Seven Devils/Hells Canyon* with three days on the trail, three on the river is $1,245/person.

HURRICANE CREEK LLAMA TREKS, INC. (HCLT)
63366 Pine Tree Road, Enterprise, OR 97828
Phone: 800-528-9609/541-432-4455
Fax: 541-432-4455

IN THEIR OWN WORDS: Llama trekking is a novel and comfortable means of wilderness travel. Our friendly and companionable llamas handle the heavy loads (but not your children), leaving you free to carry only a day pack with your lunch, your camera and rain gear. Children are welcome on many of our treks and our leisurely-paced base camp trips are best suited to youngsters 6 years and older, when they are generally able to hike several miles each day, are willing to try a variety of food and can follow the guide's instructions. We've found that enthusiastic young hikers enjoy our more strenuous progressive trips as well. No special skills are needed — just good health and a positive attitude. We've been leading llama treks since 1985 and know that a really memorable vacation experience awaits you in Oregon backcountry.

THE TRIPS: Of the half dozen or more trips operated each summer in the Hells Canyon National Recreation Area or the Eagle Cap Wilderness in Oregon, by Stanlynn Daugherty of HCLT, the *Brownie Basin Base Camp Llama Trek* is the one most recommended for families. The four-night trip utilizes a base camp with easily accessible fishing and hiking and plenty of quiet space to relax. Favorite family excursions include a hike to an historic mine and visits to the string of alpine lakes nearby where the animal and plant life are abundant. Participants overnight at a B&B and hike to their base camp the next morning, where they spend the next three nights, before hiking back to the B&B for a final night's sleep before departing. Guests pack their own llama bags and set up their tents (instruction and assistance happily supplied) though the choice of leading one's own llama is a personal one. "People stick pretty close to the llamas since their alert behavior often helps us spot wildlife we might otherwise miss." Food is described as hearty and wholesome, an assortment of fresh and prepared meals with whole grain breads and fresh fruits and vegetables provided.

Another HCLT program of interest to families is its *Llama Rental Program* for more experienced hikers. We're particularly enchanted by HCLT's *French Alps Llama Trek*, operated in partnership with Les Lamas de Buech in France, traveling in the high mountain valleys in the Nevache region, just west of the Italian border. During the weeklong trip that welcomes children 10 and older, guests stay in gites and mountain cabins that provide dormitory style accommodations, modern plumbing and home-cooked country style French meals. These are currently only offered on a custom basis and while knowledge of French will certainly enhance your trip, it is not necessary as all of the guides are fluent in English.

Stanlynn Daugherty has written a comprehensive guide, **Packing With Llamas**, that is published by Juniper Ridge Press and available at many bookstores.

RATES: Brownie Basin Base Camp is $660/adult, 20 percent less/ages 6 to 18. *Llama Pack Clinics* are $160/person and *Rentals* (training session required) are $35/llama/day with a two llama minimum. The customized trips to France cost about $2,000/person and do not offer any discounts to youngsters.

BOOKED FOR TRAVEL

A LLAMA IN THE FAMILY, by Johanna Hurwitz (illustrated by Mark Graham), is an entertaining book about a Vermont family who starts a llama trekking business. Though Adam, the family's older child and the story's narrator, initially isn't sure what he thinks of the new llama, Ethan Allen, by the book's end their bonding is complete, with plenty of chuckles, several dramatic moments and some happy surprises along the way — plus lots of interesting facts about llamas. (Morrow)

JAMES HENRY RIVER JOURNEYS (JHRJ)
P.O. Box 807, Bolinas, CA 94924
Phone: 800-786-1830/415-868-1836
Fax: 415-868-9033

IN THEIR OWN WORDS: Since 1973 we've been introducing adventurous souls to the delights of river tours. Our focus is on adventure, learning and camaraderie. Rivers, like people, each have a unique character and personality. We invite you to explore the beauty of the Rogue, the grandeur of the Salmon, the magnificence of the Tatshenshini, the sublimity of the Noatak or the wildness of the Kongakut — or any other of our North American rafting adventures. We will challenge you and provide an entree into a world you might not believe exists. We are pioneers of hands-on outdoor learning and during our journeys the possibilities for participation and enrichment are endless. We use a combination of paddleboats, oarboats and inflatable kayaks and are known for our exquisite wilderness cuisine — which satisfies both vegetarians and picky kids. We are vigilant when it comes to safety and often take our own kids along. Our trips are designed for singles, couples and families — anyone who possesses an adventurous spirit and a desire to immerse himself or herself into incomparable wilderness experiences.

THE TRIPS: A great number of river trips are offered each season between April and October. There are four- to five-day trips on the Rogue River (Oregon) with optional hiking, two- to three-day trips on the Klamath River (California) and six-day trips on the Main Salmon (Idaho). However, it's JHRJ's special interest trips that truly do "provide an enriching dimension" to the journeys.

In Alaska, JHRJ has found what it calls "the ultimate wilderness journey" down the Tatshenshini-Alsek River, the pristine jewel of British Columbia and Southeast Alaska. The 13-day trip begins in Haines, Alaska, travels into Canada's Yukon Territory, then rafts through British Columbia past the world's "largest non-polar glacial system." Raft around floating ice sculptures and discover a land of mammoth icebergs, iridescent glaciers and snow-laden mountain ranges reminiscent of the Ice Age. During the four layover days, guests explore the valleys and tundra near camp, with a variety of hikes and rambles that visit both glaciers and meadows of wildflowers. Some of the trips feature world-class naturalists/ anthropologists and interpretive programs focusing on the natural history of the area or the mythology of the Alaskan wilderness. All sound quite intriguing.

Other themed trips that will interest families include the *Rogue River Natural History, Salmon River Gourmet Wilderness Cuisine* or *Salmon Natural History Trip.*

RATES: Youth prices are for children 17 and under. Trips in California, Oregon and Idaho have a minimum age of 7; in Arizona and Alaska, the minimum age is 12, 14 or 16. Some sample prices are: Three days on the Klamath, $335/adult, $285/youth; four days on the Rogue, $585/adult, $498/youth; six days on the Main Salmon, $865/adult, $735/youth; 11 days on the Tatshenshini-Alsek begins at $2,295 with no youth prices. The *Gourmet Wilderness Cuisine* trip on the Salmon is $950/adult, $840/youth.

LAREDO ENTERPRISES
P.O. Box 2226, Havre, MT 59501
Phone: 800-535-3802/406-357-3748
Fax: 406-357-3748

IN THEIR OWN WORDS: Ride with us and after six days on the trail you'll feel like a true cowhand. We'll teach you to ride, assist you in camp or on the trail and give you your own horse to ride and care for. Take advantage of the opportunity to get away from the rigors of everyday life and become a real cowboy when you join us on a cattle drive for an experience you'll never forget. In business since the late 1980s, we don't operate a dude ranch. Rather, we host guests on working ranches while they help move and work the cattle across the Montana frontier.

THE TRIPS: Drives take place from the middle of May to the end of June and resume again at the end of August to the beginning of October. Guests are welcome to join the drives for the entire time (six nights) or simply participate on a per day basis while staying at one of two ranches — the X Hanging H Ranch or the Rumney Ranch. Depending upon the time of year, the drives are slightly different: cattle are moved to summer pasture in the spring and the process is reversed in the early fall. The first and last nights are generally taken at the ranch while the nights in between are spent in camps with porta-potties and shower facilities available. If you're wondering about children, covered wagons accompany many of the drives, which means that even a 4-year-old can join in, opting for a wagon seat in lieu of a horse. Kids as young as 6 can ride if they've had some experience. On some trips, camp is moved every night; on others you return to a base for several nights. A bunkhouse may be used for overnights when the weather doesn't cooperate! Evenings are spent in true western camaraderie around the campfire, a nice contrast to days on the prairie.

RATES: Prices range from $999–$1,329/adult and $777–$999/children ages 4 to 12 depending upon the package you select. You can include transfers to/from the airport, bring along your own horse and tack or choose to pay only for a wagon seat. The daily rides cost $259/adult, $159/child.

BOOKED FOR TRAVEL

Activity cum coloring books are a great way to get kids interested and involved in new places. **CECIL'S MONTANA ADVENTURE,** by Sheri Amsel, teaches about animals and nature with mazes, word games, etc., and its relevance extends well beyond the boundaries of the Treasure State; take it along on any trip out west. (Falcon)

LAUREL HIGHLANDS RIVER TOURS (LHRT)
P.O. Box 107, Ohiopyle, PA 15470
Phone: 800-4-RAFTIN/412-329-8531
Fax: 412-329-8532

IN THEIR OWN WORDS: Our family-owned and operated company together with our staff have more than 350 years of experience in paddling rivers — by raft, canoe or kayak. We are located in the heart of Ohiopyle State Park, very near a licensed day care center for children too young to participate in our adventures. The entire area is rich with history and is one of Pennsylvania's premier outdoor recreational areas. We welcome children as young as 4 on several of our family float trips and recommend that families combine our one-day trips for a more enriching experience.

THE TRIPS: LHRT Vice President Terry Palmo highly recommends the gentle, calm, scenic guided float trip on the Middle Youghiogheny for families with young children. 12 years is the recommended minimum age for trips on the Lower Yough with challenging Class III and IV rapids. A two-day combination is offered, as is an overnight package. Youngsters 16 and older are welcomed on the Upper Yough, which is considered expert, and 14 and older can join trips on West Virginia's mighty Cheat River.

In addition to rafting adventures, guided fishing tours (minimum age 12), kayak and canoe instruction (minimum age 7) and individual raft rentals are offered. Ask about their special *Pedal/Paddle* that combines rafting and bicycle rentals. LHRT can also arrange for accommodations in local guest houses.

RATES: Middle Yough prices range from $15.50–$24.50/child under 12, $20.50–$29.50/adult. *Lower Yough* prices are about $8–$25 higher. Combinations offer a 10 percent discount. Overnight packages are $225/person. *Upper Yough* trips begin at $109.50. *Cheat River* trips start at $49.50. For an additional fee you can rent duckies or thrillseekers.

LE VIEUX MOULIN (LVM)
Patinges 18320, Jouet sur-L'Aubois, France
Phone: 800-368-4234/011-33-2-48-76-07-21
Fax: 011-33-2-48-76-07-43

IN THEIR OWN WORDS: From the Old Mill in the beautiful Loire Valley near Burgundy sits Le Vieux Moulin, a well-appointed country inn with an award-winning chef. From here unique biking and walking tours are personally guided through forests, vineyards and farmlands. Each day our guests head to a special destination, a centuries-old chateau, church or abbey and stop for a relaxed lunch in a scenic village followed by a visit to a site offering historic interest. Our charming country estate is situated on seven acres on a bank of the river L'Aubois, and features the comforts of home with its 12 guest bedrooms, all with private bath, in two charming petite maisons. Both the two living rooms and one dining room have wood-burning fireplaces. We offer 20 different tours to suit your abilities — and we do the guiding. We believe that Le Vieux Moulin is ideal for families because we are flexible and because the countryside surrounding Le Vieux Moulin is mostly level, with gently rolling hills. Our goal is to please. Though the majority of families who stay with us come with teenagers, we are happy to have kids of younger ages when they are capable of riding with the group. Our support vehicle is always close at hand to support young riders and to assist with any mechanical breakdowns. Our guides, fluent in both English and French, can answer any questions you may have, in addition to providing you with the historic backgrounds of the sights.

THE TRIPS: Using the estate as a base, cycling tours depart daily. Several weeks during the year, LVM offers walking instead of biking, although with the great demand for cycling excursions, the walking trips have been severely cut back of late. On the first day, guests begin with a short trip to local villages, a famous abbey under restoration and some local chateaux. During your stay, trips might include Apremont-sur-Allier, a famous flower village, the city of Vezelay or the famous wine village of Sancerre. Visits to wine cellars and goat cheese farms are included on many of the tour routes. For those who prefer to forego walking or biking for part (or all) of their stay, there's plenty to do: canoeing; fishing; golf; badminton; boules; horseback riding; or shopping. Up to 24 guests are accommodated at one time.

When LVM proprietor Frank Pettee came to tell us about his facility and its tours, he couldn't have made a better impression. He and his French wife (often described in the inn's guest book at LVM's "best asset") regaled us with stories of their experiences with families, including one that brought along a baby (and babysitter) and needed the requisite crib and high chair, which LVM was able to provide. Recently, LVM welcomed a family of ten, grandparents, parents and grandchildren. In reevaluating LVM's policy toward families, Pettee feels that families with children over the age of 9 will best enjoy their stay here. It has become very difficult to arrange for babysitting and consequently is no longer a provided service. Children dine with other guests and, when notified in advance, LVM will adapt the menu to accommodate young palates. No early dining situation for younger kids is possible. In the works are plans for a Jacuzzi and a suite of rooms at the Inn that would be ideal for a family stay.

LVM is a well-kept secret from families — too secret from our point of view for those of you who meet its new age recommendations. Several of the bicycles at LVM can accommodate youngsters but it's best to check in advance.

RATES: A six-night/seven-day package includes lodging, five dinners, lunch and six breakfasts plus a dinner in a local restaurant, daily escorted excursions, use of bicycles and helmets and transfers to/from the train station. Adults pay from $1,395-$1,595 per person depending upon accommodation. A three-night/four-day package is also offered for $795 as is another package that includes air from eight U.S. cities, three nights in Paris and six nights at LVM. Prices begin at about $2,300/adult. Discounts for families are determined at the time of booking.

BOOKED FOR TRAVEL

For those whose mode of travel is two-wheeled **Bicycle Books** *has a number of appealing titles, two of which are* CYCLING FRANCE: *The Best Bike Tours in All of Gaul by Jerry H. Simpson, Jr. and* CYCLING EUROPE: *Budget Bike Touring in the Old World by Nadine Slavinski. Both give numerous itineraries of interest to cyclists. The suggestions on planning are particularly thorough and the advice very sound (except on the subject of helmets; Simpson doesn't like them). The authors were not thinking about families when they wrote, nor did they travel with kids, so you'll need to look further to find attractions of interest to children on the suggested routes, and the like. August, when all of Europe hits the road, is not recommended for a cycling tour.*

MAHOOSUC GUIDE SERVICE (MGS)
Box 245, Bear River Road, Newry, ME 04261
Phone: 207-824-2073
Fax: 207-824-3784

IN THEIR OWN WORDS: We are Maine's most versatile guide service offering year-round activities for all seasons and adventures for guests with all levels of experience. One of our unique features is that we make much of the equipment we use on our guided trips, such as cedar canvas canoes, ash dog sleds and maple paddles — traditional equipment that is durable and functional, in many ways preferable to today's high tech, outdoor gear. We put the same quality of craftsmanship into the creation of our trips, which are not designed as tests of endurance but rather as an opportunity to enjoy the wilderness. Our base in the Bear River Valley, just north of Bethel, Maine, affords us easy access to some of the wildest areas of Maine, New Hampshire and Canada. From canoeing in summer to dog sledding in winter, we invite you and your family to explore our world. Just bring the right clothing and a sense of adventure — we provide the rest!

THE TRIPS: MGS's canoe program teaches traditional Cree paddling techniques as well as offering workshops for beginning to advanced-level whitewater. Its wilderness canoe trips use handmade ash, cedar and spruce canoes that are "a joy to paddle." Best for families are three- to five-night trips which might include paddling down the Penobscot (the "most popular introduction to Maine canoe camping"), St. John, Moose Bow (MGS's favorite for families) or Allagash Rivers. A nine-night trip, *Canoeing with the Cree,* heads for the Temiscamie River in Quebec and combines adventure with a unique learning experience.

In winter, dog sledding takes center stage. Owners Polly Mahoney and Kevin Slater have been raising and working with sled dogs for more than 15 years, and offer day trips, weekend overnights and Northwoods four- to 10-day trips. The day trips visit Umbagog Lake, home to an unusual number of moose and otter. You'll learn the ins and outs of training, handling and driving your own sled dogs while eating lunch cooked over an open fire. The two- or three-day overnights add a "gentle introduction to winter camping (though the first night is spent at a B&B) and no experience is necessary." The gear is loaded on a toboggan and guests can ski or snowshoe at their own pace in between riding on the dog sled. The longer trips all travel by dog teams with two persons per sled, with a layover spent learning to ski and/or snowshoe. One trip, *Chisasbi To Great Whale - Dogsledding With The Cree Of James Bay,* with travel by snowmobiles and dog sled, is scheduled in mid-March to coincide with the migration of local caribou. Accompanied by a Cree guide, you'll pass several species of seal and its predator, the polar bear. The 11-day trip covers 175 miles of trail, with several nights at a traditional Cree winter camp called a mithogan. Days "often end with a spectacular display of Northern Lights over the bay." *Dogsledding with the Inuit on Baffin Island* is another opportunity to meet and learn from Native Americans. Custom trips are offered in Maine, the James and Hudson Bays and Baffin Island.

Owner Polly Mahoney tells us that though the youngest age of participants to date has been 6, for both the canoe and dog sled trips, there are no steadfast rules. It depends on the parents, the capabilities of the child and, of course, the weather. She often will "join together a couple of families" and plan a special trip just for them.

RATES: Children under the age of 13 receive a 25 percent discount on all trips. Canoe trips cost from $395–$700/adult. The popular trip we mention above is a five-night trip on the West Branch of the Penobscot River and costs $595/adult. *Canoeing With The Cree* is $1,550/adult.

For dog sledding, day trips cost $115; weekend overnights $325 or $400; four-night trips are $800; 10-night trips $1,950. The 10-night trip to Baffin Island is $2,500. Prices include specialized winter clothing.

MARIAH WILDERNESS EXPEDITIONS

P.O. Box 248, Point Richmond, CA 94807
Phone: 800-4-MARIAH/510-223-2303
Fax: 510-233-0956

IN THEIR OWN WORDS: We pride ourselves on being the only raft company to offer a special series of raft trips for the whole family, designed to bring education, growth, fun and adventure to our guests. We rate the South Fork American River as the best in California for the beginner and intermediate rafter with its wide variety of almost continuous whitewater rapids and beautiful scenery in the heart of Gold Rush Country. Our special family trips offer you time together in the outdoors sharing the thrills of the river and sleeping out under the stars. Our professional storytellers will delight you as they weave their stories and spin their tales during lunches and around the campfire at night.

THE TRIPS: Two-day trips featuring two full days of rafting, two nights of camping and five meals are designed for different family configurations with children over the age of 8. There are a *Father & Kids* trip, a *Mother & Kids* trip, a *Single Parents & Children* trip plus several *Entire Family* trips. A shower, volleyball court and pingpong table are among the base camp amenities. Because the same campsite is used on both nights, Mariah allows parents with younger children to bring along a babysitter to take care of them while older children and parents are out on the river. There is a very modest charge of $25/day for the babysitter (or other adult) and no charge at all for kids 7 and younger. You need to ask directly about this as it is not listed in Mariah's brochure.

Mariah runs a number of other rivers as well, including the Middle Fork American, Merced, Tuolumne, Kings and Rogue. On all of these, except for the Kings River and the Rogue, the minimum age is 14. On the Kings and the Rogue, the minimum age is 8. Additionally, Mariah offers a selection of trips in Costa Rica (minimum age varies from 8 to 14 depending upon the river selected) and *Sea Kayaking in the Sea of Cortez* (minimum age 5).

RATES: Children 16 and younger accompanied by at least one adult receive a 10 percent discount on most trips. Rates on the family rafting trips are $204/adult, $102/ages 8 to 12, $154/ages 13 to 16. Youth discounts are for one child per each adult.

MICHIGAN BICYCLE TOURING (MBT)
3512 Red School, Kingsley, MI 49649
Phone: 616-263-5885
Fax: 616-263-7885

IN THEIR OWN WORDS: We're celebrating almost 20 years of offering hiking and biking vacation tours for all. Our vast, water wonderland state is a showcase of low-traffic backroads, dazzling waterfalls, sugar sand beaches and dense evergreen woodlands. We welcome young bikers ages 9 and older but have found that biking with little people is individual and varies from child to child. There's no rule set in stone. Children who are familiar with riding a 12-speed bike and have done rides of 15 or more miles (not necessarily hilly) will cruise on the shorter routes of most of our tours. Lots of kids often out ride the parents! In addition to our bicycle tours, we offer trips that include off-road cycling, easy kayaking, canoeing, day hiking and backpacking. You can bike with younger, non-biking children if you're willing to use a cart, rather than a child seat. If you don't have one, we can rent one to you.

THE TRIPS: In operation since 1978, MBT operates a number of varied two- to five-day outdoor adventure tours which range from biking and canoeing to kayaking and hiking. According to director Libby Robold, several are especially good for children. One suggestion for a weekend trip is the combination *Platte River Pedal & Paddle*, which offers easy canoeing, short bike rides and accommodations at Crystal Mountain Resort, where there is a kids' play area, heated indoor pool and washer and dryers for parents! In past years this trip has featured a family-only departure. *Crystal Lake Natural* is another good choice, says Robold, and adds that when alerted in advance that kids are along on the trip, the lodge, which specializes in vegetarian cuisine, is happy to prepare "more ordinary" food for young palates. The more challenging *Herring Lake Amble* is Robold's choice for teens (though kids 10 and older have been successful on this hilly terrain). It also works well for families with younger and older kids, as long as one parent is willing to stay put at the Inn and take the little ones to the nearby private beach on Lake Michigan, while the others in the family cycle off.

The five-day *Interlochen Sightseer* is a "nice beginner and family outing" for families with energetic, athletic kids. The majority of MBT's other five-day tours are for intermediate and above cyclers.

RATES: Platte River Pedal & Paddle costs from $330 to $360/person depending upon date selected; *Crystal Lake Natural* is $275/person and *Herring Lake Amble* is $290. *Interlochen Sightseer* begins at $699/adult. Children sharing accommodations with two adults receive the following discounts: 25 percent/ages 9 to 12; 15 percent/ages 13 to 17. When sharing with one adult, children receive a 10 percent discount. Burley Trailers are $35/weekend, $75/week. A nominal fee is charged for non-biking children, even infants. Non-biking adults receive a 20 percent discount.

MOUNT ROBSON ADVENTURE HOLIDAYS LTD.
Box 687, Valemount, B.C., Canada V0E 2Z0
Phone: 604-566-4386
Fax: 604-566-4351

IN THEIR OWN WORDS: At Mount Robson, we feature gentle adventures for all ages — even if you have little or no wilderness experience. Come with us and canoe through marshlands, view spawning salmon on a gentle rafting float trip or hike along scenic trails to alpine meadows — all with an eye toward nature observation. We offer you a variety of choices, from multi-day trips to half- and full-day excursions from our lodge base. The majority of our trips welcome school-age children and a number of them even encourage you to bring along infants! All of the excursions are ideal venues for grandparents to share with their children and grandchildren. These adventures are based in Mount Robson Provincial Park, home of the highest mountain in the Canadian Rockies — a nature lover's paradise that is home to moose, elk, bears, deer, mountain goats and more than 170 species of birds.

THE TRIPS: As with most adventure travel companies, Mount Robson recommends minimum ages but will work directly with you to determine just what will be best for your family. Ages 6 and older will enjoy its *Mount Robson Experience,* a three-day/four-night adventure that's "active but not strenuous" and includes a full-day guided trek, half-day guided canoe trip, a gentle rafting float trip, and a half-day nature tour. Guests stay in cabins with private baths at the Mount Robson Lodge. There are two *Berg Lake Backpacking* trips, one a fly-in, hike-out trip best for children 8 and older that begins with a spectacular helicopter flight, and a second for ages 10 and up. Both are designed for those who "enjoy backpacking but not all the work that goes with it." The Berg Lake Trail has been called the most spectacular hike in all of North America, passing Kinney Lake through the Valley of a Thousand Falls and Emperor Falls with its sheer drop of 60 meters. On the three-day/two-night trips participants camp in beautiful alpine surroundings. The weekly four-day/five-night *Lodge-to-Lodge Canoeing* trips with easy paddling by day and cozy comfort at night sound extremely appealing. Recommended for ages 10 and older, the trip begins with canoeing instruction.

Owner/Manager Wendy Dyson also recommends that families consider staying in the area and taking a day trip. The *Gentle Rafting Float* is open to all ages, even infants, and so is its three-hour *Nature Tour.* Guided hikes and canoe trips are also offered. Among the accommodations in the Mount Robson/Valemount area are the Mount Robson Lodge (604-566-4821) that is located three miles from the park and the Cariboo Lodge (800-661-0252), located two miles south of Valemount. There are several campgrounds, motels and B&Bs in the surrounding area. For more information, contact the Mount Robson Visitor Info Centre at 604-566-9174.

RATES: All prices are in Canadian dollars and are subject to a Federal tax of seven percent. *Mount Robson Experience* is $499/adult, $245/child 12 and under; *Berg Lake Backpacking,* with *Fly-In, Hike-Out* is $730/adult,

$664/child, all hiking costs $480/adult, $414/child. *Lodge-to-Lodge Canoeing* is $794/adult, $573/child. Day trips begin at $35/adult, $15/child. Lodging at the Mount Robson Lodge cabins begin at $60/two persons, the Cariboo Lodge at about $200.

NANTAHALA OUTDOOR CENTER (NOC)
13077 Highway 19 West Bryson City, NC 28713-9114
Phone: 800-232-7238 - Rafting and lodging only
        704-488-2175 - Travel and custom programs
        704-488-6737 - Instruction programs
Fax: 704-488-2498

IN THEIR OWN WORDS: We are an employee-owned organization comprised of a diverse bunch — from teenagers to retirees — coming from various parts of the U.S. and the world, with both rural and urban backgrounds. What we have in common is a love of our mountain and river environment and its adventurous activities. We have created a community of committed, fun-loving people whose mission is to help our guests experience the joys of the outdoors.

THE TRIPS: What sets NOC apart from other organizations is the outstanding quality of its instructional programs in kayaking, canoeing, mountain biking and rock climbing. As a basic rule of thumb, all of the organized workshops (whether one-day or longer) are open to anyone 16 years or older. *Samplers*, which usually include a half-day instruction combined with a half-day of exploring, allow youngsters 13 and older to participate. Private instruction for family groups is offered in all of the disciplines. In these sessions, minimum ages are determined on a one-by-one basis. A number of workshops are offered just for kids between the ages of 10 and 15. Moreover, NOC operates a fully-licensed day care facility for youngsters 6 weeks to 10- or 11-years-old at its Nantahala Outpost. It includes indoor and outdoor play areas and is open daily from 8 a.m. until 6 p.m. For children 5 and older the program is similar to a day camp with activities such as hiking and river swimming. Though it appears that the center is there for guests' children, we were surprised to read the following advice to adults signing on for standard courses: "Since your day will begin early and end well into the evening, we recommend that if you plan to bring small children, you arrange to bring someone along to care for them." While we understand the point here, we're a bit dismayed since we feel that it penalizes parents of younger children who may prefer the camaraderie of a group program for their kids as opposed to private arrangements.

The second area of NOC expertise is its outing and adventure travel trips, most of which can be customized for as few as six participants.

Families are welcome on these trips and though there is typically a minimum age of 14, some trips accept younger kids who have the adequate skills deemed necessary.

Whitewater rafting is offered on the Nantahala, French Broad, Chattanooga, Nolichucky and Ocoee Rivers with both guided trips and complete outfitting for experienced rafters. Age minimums range from 8- to 13-years old, except on selected guide-assisted trips on the Nantahala River, for which the Forest Service insists that participants weigh at least 60 lbs.

Domestic trips featuring sea kayaking float along the Georgian Coast and North Carolina's Outer Banks; canoeing, rafting or kayaking are found in Florida, Texas and Alaska. Overseas destinations include sea kayaking in Costa Rica and the Fiji Islands, plus whitewater adventures in Costa Rica, Chile, Corsica, Greece, Honduras, Ireland, Mexico, Nepal and Turkey.

RATES: Generally speaking, there are no special youth prices except for the youth-only clinics. *Samplers* are $35/half day, $70/full day. Lodging at NOC costs about $50/night.

BOOKED FOR TRAVEL

We've examined **Human Kinetics' Outdoor Pursuits Series:** CANOEING, by Laurie Gullion, HIKING AND BACKPACKING, by Eric Seabord and Ellen Dudley, WHITEWATER AND SEA KAYAKING, by Kent Ford, MOUNTAIN BIKING, by Don Davis and Dave Carter, SNOWBOARDING, by Rob Reichenfeld and Anna Bruechert, and WINDSURFING, by Ken Winner, and while we very much admire their format (especially the color photos and illustrations) and think they do a great job of presenting individual adventure skills, only the books on canoeing and hiking and backpacking make any mention of where children fit in and how to involve them. While we think you'd find any of these volumes valuable, you'll need to do additional research to find the family component. (Human Kinetics)

NEW ENGLAND HIKING HOLIDAYS (NEHH)
P.O. Box 1648, North Conway, NH 03860
Phone: 800-869-0949/603-356-9696
Fax: 603-356-7292, May-October/407-778-3806-November-April

IN THEIR OWN WORDS: There's no better way to experience the outdoors than on a guided country inn hiking tour. Participating in an active holiday doesn't mean giving up appealing luxuries. Our array of excellent inns feature comfort, hospitality and fine food. Your daily hiking/walking forays can be long or short, gentle or challenging, and you will always be accompanied by guides who are eager to share their love and knowledge of the natural world. Our small personalized groups are generally a mix of couples, singles and families. Regardless of your age or hiking ability, as long as you're in reasonably good physical condition, we think you'll love a New England Hiking Holiday.

THE TRIPS: Trips, which range from two to eight days, are offered near NEHH's home base of the White Mountains of New Hampshire, in the Northeast Kingdom of Vermont, Maine's Acadia National Park, the Berkshires of Massachusetts, the Colorado Rockies, California's Lake Tahoe, Hawaii, the Blue Ridge Mountains of North Carolina, the Shenandoahs of Virginia, as well as in Canada and Europe. Though owners Clare and Kurt Grabher recommend the White Mountain trips for families, we also liked the sound of the five-day Vermont trip because it includes inns we know like kids, such as the Wildflower Inn in Lyndonville. Both the New Hampshire and Vermont itineraries include lots of opportunities for swimming in the many local lakes along the hiking routes. The Lake Tahoe itinerary would also be a good family choice, since it combines a two-night stay at the very family-friendly Resort at Squaw Creek with three nights right on the lake. We're also tempted by the Devon Coast and Moors in England, an itinerary rich in historic sites and natural phenomena that should enchant kids as well as parents.

BOOKED FOR TRAVEL

BEST HIKES WITH CHILDREN IN CONNECTICUT, MASSACHUETTS & RHODE ISLAND by Cynthia C. Lewis and Thomas J. Lewis features 75 hikes and nature walks for toddlers to teens, both day trips and overnights, through forests, mountains and beaches. The authors, who are parents, have provided practical information on distance, difficulty and elevation as well as "turnaround points" for tired hikers who want to head back early. An example of the tempting choices: a hike to the "storybook" Gillette Castle and its riverside grounds. "Encourage the grandparents to take the children on this hike. It's perfect for the oldest and youngest members of the family." The book is part of a series that includes other areas: Vermont, New Hampshire and Maine; the Catskills and Hudson River Valley; New Jersey; Colorado, Utah; San Francisco's North and South Bay (2 vols.); Western and Central Oregon; Western Washington and the Cascades (Vols. 1 and 2). With one of these books in your backpack as your guide, you can head for the hills on excursions specifically geared to your child(ren)'s age(s).(The Mountaineers)

RATES: In spite of stating "regardless of age," NEHH welcomes children only 10 years and older and offers them a 10 percent discount when sharing with parents. It should be noted that the majority of the lodgings can only accommodate three persons per room. The Vermont trip costs $895–$995/adult, White Mountains $875–$895, Lake Tahoe $995 and England $1,795. Prices may be slightly lower in spring and fall.

NORTHERN OUTDOORS
P.O. Box 100, Route 201, The Forks, ME 04985
Phone: 800-765-7328/207-663-4466
Fax: 207-663-2244

IN THEIR OWN WORDS: We are Maine's oldest and largest adventure company, having pioneered whitewater rafting in New England in the mid-70s. Over the years we have earned the reputation of offering the most popular and exciting rafting trips in the Northeast and have continuously added to our roster of adventures. Northern Outdoors now offers a host of activities including rafting, kayaking, hiking, fishing, camping and rock climbing. We are unique in several areas. First, we maintain a year-round staff who have the time to turn their experience and attention to those details that can often turn a good trip into a great one. Moreover, we operate two Resort Centers for adventurers to return to after an active day, each of which features a restaurant, licensed bar, hot tub, sauna, entertainment center and overnight lodging. Our all-inclusive two-day packages allow guests to combine whitewater rafting with hiking, biking or fishing.

THE TRIPS: We'll start with the action-packed *Family Overnight Wilderness Adventures*, which run weekly during the height of the summer season (minimum age 8). This trip gives you a terrific smorgasbord of adventures: easy whitewater, swimming, tubing, traveling by motor boat, overnight camping lakeside with a lobster cookout, and an exciting finale on day two where you tackle the 12-mile descent of the Kennebec Gorge. One-day *Kennebec River Whitewater Adventures* have a minimum age requirement of 12 on the Upper Gorge and 8 on the Lower Gorge. Here, too, you get a chance to swim and frolic on the river in inflatable kayaks. The one-day *Penobscot River Whitewater Adventure* is more challenging, with a minimum age of 15 on the Upper Gorge section, 12 on the lower. For relaxation and a touch of adventure, *Kennebec River Float Trips* depart each afternoon, June to September (minimum age 8). *Rock Climbing* instruction is offered on a day-long expedition for ages 12 and older.

RATES: The *Family Overnight Adventures* are $209/adult and $109/child under 16. *Kennebec River* and *Penobscot River* day trips are $79/adult weekdays; $99/adult weekends. On the Kennebec, one child per adult rafts for half price, weekdays only. Children are welcome on weekends but do not receive any discount. *Kennebec Float Trips* are $25/person in a single inflatable; $20/person in a double. *Rock Climbing* costs $75/person. Neither of these two offers a youth discount.

OUTDOOR ADVENTURES (OA)
P.O. Box 1149, Point Reyes Station, CA 94956
Phone: 800-323-4234/415-663-8300
Fax: 415-663-8617

IN THEIR OWN WORDS: It takes a lot more than simply substituting peanut butter for brie to make a river trip special for kids. We were the first California-based company to offer specially-structured trips with kids in mind — with organized activities such as bug collecting, fishing, sand castle contests, music making with natural objects, nature hikes, story telling, gold panning, stick carving, weaving and sing-alongs, to name a few. We want your trip with us to be the best part of your summer and we work hard to structure family trips that are relaxing, safe and memorable. Our life vests are fitted specifically for kids. Our guides review safety frequently, not just the first day. We carry extra snacks for kids and plan other activities for the entire family to enjoy.

THE TRIPS: OA offers specific recommendations for families. First is to go when the weather is warm, on a date when other families will be going. We couldn't agree more. Among the trips they suggest for families are the Salmon River in Idaho, the Rogue River in Oregon, the American River in California (all with a minimum age of 7) and the Lower Kern in California (minimum age 9). In addition to the regular four- and six-day Salmon River trips, two six-day departures feature *Kids Float Free* for youngsters 16 or younger. On lively whitewater Kern River trips, where nights are spent on sleeping platforms with comfortable mattresses, special family rates are offered twice weekly on two-night trips. Attractive rates combined with great weather and just the right number of fun rapids make one- or two- day trips on the South Fork of the America particularly appealing. Three- and four-day trips on the Rogue raft one of the river's wildest sections.

RATES: Salmon River trips cost $1,095/adult, $895/youth for six days; $895/adult, $695/youth for four days. Families taking advantage of the *Kids Float Free* program need to pay $195/child for off-river costs. Kern River trips cost $238–268/adult. Family rates, depending on the number of people in your party, are offered on Monday and Wednesdays. American River one- or two-day trips range in price from $99–$259. On these trips ages 7 to 17 pay about 20 percent less. Rogue River trips cost

$498 or $568/adult and $498–$518/youth for three- or four-day trips.

OUTDOOR ADVENTURE RIVER SPECIALISTS (OARS)
P.O. Box 67, Angels Camp, CA 95222
Phone: 800-346-6277/209-736-4677
Fax: 209-736-2902

IN THEIR OWN WORDS: Vacations are a special time that should bring a family together, providing fun as well as family bonding — a chance to rediscover the people closest to you in the sharing of a memorable experience. There are few experiences more memorable than river rafting. The giddy sense of anticipation as the raft moves into the current to slide downstream, the exhilaration and thrill of challenging and conquering a rapid, the excitement of camping under the stars combined with the scenery of the American West are some of the reasons why river running is rapidly becoming the vacation of choice for today's active family. Our family trips offer a strong emphasis on safety, experienced guides who understand families, kid-friendly food, a "Fun Director" to entertain the kids plus a "Fun Bag" stocked with games and toys for all ages.

THE TRIPS: While OARS was not among the first companies to recognize that river rafting is an appealing family vacation, its special *Family Trips* are thoughtfully designed and very tuned into the needs and desires of both parents and kids. Several of us have taken trips with OARS and we're particularly impressed with the way they describe their age guidelines: "Age limits are decided upon by a combination of factors including how well most kids can handle the duration of the trip, their ability to feel comfortable in the water and so on. Don't think of these limits as barriers to adventure, but as thresholds!" Trips are offered on the San Juan River (three, four or six days, minimum age 5) and on the Green River (four days, minimum age 8) in Utah; the Lower Salmon (four or five days, minimum age 7), Main Salmon (six or seven days, minimum age 7) and Middle Fork of the Salmon (six days, minimum age 9) in Idaho; the Lower Klamath (two or three days, minimum age 4), the South Fork American Stanislaus Combination (one or two days, minimum age 7) and Tuolumne (one, two or three days, minimum age 12) in California; and the Rogue (four or five days, minimum age 7) in Oregon. There are also two options in the Grand Tetons of Wyoming, a raft/float trip (two days, minimum age 4) and a sea kayaking trip on Jackson Lake (one, two or five days, minimum age 4). There's also a raft/kayak combination (four days, minimum age 4).

Believe it or not, that's just the beginning. In business for more than 26 years, OARS can also arrange for lodge trips on the Main Salmon, dory (in hard-hulled boats) and raft trips through the Grand Canyon, sea kayaking in Mexico, *Inside Passage Adventures* in British Columbia and more. For Grand Canyon trips, OARS recommends its trips that begin at Lees Ferry or terminate at Phantom Ranch. A *Grand Canyon Sampler* which begins and ends in Las Vegas is a recommendation that will probably appeal to many families since it offers an interesting combination of a stay on a cattle ranch, whitewater rafting and hiking through some spectacular scenic areas. We're also turned on by a sea kayaking trip to *Espirtu Santo Island* in Baja, Mexico on which kids ages 8 and older are welcome. The seven-day trip is filled with discovery from snorkeling with sea lions to exploring sea caves.

RATES: On all OARS' *Families Only* trips, the first two family members pay the full rate with each additional family member receiving a 15 percent discount. These rates apply only to designated family departures on the Rogue, Salmon, Klamath, Snake and San Juan Rivers. On other trips, children ages 17 and younger usually receive a 10% discount. Here's a sampling of prices for some of the trips we've described: *Lower Klamath* is $219/adult, $199/child for two days, $319/adult, $289/child for three days; *Rogue* is 595/adult, $540/child/four day or $690/adult $630/child/ five days; *Grand Tetons Raft/Kayak* trip is $535/adult, $426/child; *Grand Tetons Sea Kayaking on Jackson Lake* is $190/adult, $99/child/one day, $290/adult, $199/child/two days and $680/adult, $585/child/five days; *Grand Canyon Sampler* is $1,091/person with no youth discount; *Espirtu Santo Island* is $1,030.

OUTDOOR BOUND INC. (OBI)
18 Stuyvesant Oval #1a, New York, NY 10009
Phone: 800-724-8801/212-505-1020
Fax: 212-979-5342

IN THEIR OWN WORDS: For more than 20 years we've organized thousands of trips for thousands of folks just like you. We've taken kids as young as 5 on our canoe and raft trips, as young as 8 out hiking and cross-country skiing or snowshoeing. Kayak trips are also a specialty of ours and we have recently added new challenges to our roster of offerings. All of our trips are rated by difficulty and can accommodate all levels of expertise. Our guides are experienced — each with an area of specialty: canoeing, kayaking, skiing, backpacking, etc. — and are skilled and personable. Trips include lessons and equipment. Meet us in New York or at our destination, the choice is yours. We'd love to have you join us.

THE TRIPS: The sister company of English Lakeland Ramblers (see page 45) OBI features day trips from New York City plus a number of weekend jaunts that venture as far afield as Quebec. There is also an eight-night trip to the Pacific Northwest. On the overnight trips accommodations may be at a country inn, a rustic cabin or a campground in the woods. Unlike many other adventure companies, OBI offers hiking trips year-round.

RATES: Day trips begin at $42/adult with a $10 discount if you meet up with the group rather than taking OBI's transportation option. Weekend trips start at $179 if you provide your own transportation, $249 if not. The Pacific Northwest trip is $1,300 plus airfare. Children receive a 10 percent discount on all rates.

POCONO WHITEWATER ADVENTURES (PWA)
Route 903, HC-2, Box 2245, Jim Thorpe, PA 18229
Phone: 800-WHITEWATER/717-325-8430
Fax: 717-325-4097

IN THEIR OWN WORDS: For 20 years our family has been running trips on Pennsylvania's Lehigh River. We specialize in one-day adventures for both the novice and accomplished rafter and have grown to now offer biking trips as well. We thank everyone who has shared an adventure with us and look forward to welcoming new adventurers to join us and learn about Pennsylvania's natural heritage, the Lehigh's million-year-old gorge and experience a lot of fun.

THE TRIPS: Three- to four-hour long *Family Floatrips* that feature a free riverside barbecue and lots of swimming along the Class I and II whitewater are offered daily July through August. *Upper Lehigh Gorge* trips with Class II and III rapids run from mid-March through June and again from mid-September through October with a minimum age of 10. *Sit-A-Top* float trips offered between mid-May and early October are ideal for learning how to kayak. During the summer PWA also schedules one and two day kayak clinics on weekends. Class IV and V whitewater trips through the Cheat River Canyon are designed for those 14 years and older with rafting experience.
  Easy self-guided or professionally-led mountain bike day trips, lasting from three to six hours, follow the route of the river and welcome all ages. Youth bikes, child seats, trail-a-bikes and tandems are all available for rent. A combination *Pedals & Paddles* trip operates every weekend.

RATES: Family Floatrips cost $33/adult, $19.95/ages 5 to 16, with the first child accompanied by two adults free. *Lehigh Whitewater:* $48/adult, $39/youth 10 to 16; *Cheat River Canyon*: $70/adult, $59/youth ages 14 to 17. Guided bike trips cost $37. Kayak clinics: $65 each, $120 for both.

REI ADVENTURES
6750 South 228th Street, Kent, WA 98390-0800
Phone: 800-622-2236/206-395-8111
Fax: 206-395-4744

IN THEIR OWN WORDS: In the same spirit in which REI provides quality outdoor gear, our adventure vacations offer high-quality trips for active travel enthusiasts. Our family departures are specially designed to handle the comfort needs of young adventurers. On all of our trips your perspective of the world will be changed by the natural splendor you witness. Our numerous trips give you the choice of camping, hiking, biking, trekking, kayaking and rafting (or combinations of these) as alternative means of travel. Our staff and leaders help make your trip a breeze and we work hard to find the best quality at the lowest prices.

THE TRIPS: REI Adventures recently introduced a few specific departures which welcome families with children 8 and older. Among them is *Day Hiking California's High Sierra*, which takes place in the Ansel Adams Wilderness, spending two nights at a lakeside resort and four nights at a base camp on Saniford Lake, six miles uptrail. Each day there's time for hiking, fishing and relaxing. All gear is included and is carried to the camp via mules. Passengers need only to carry a day pack. *Olympics Day Hike* explores the rugged coastline, temperate rain forests and mountain meadows of Washington State's Olympic Peninsula, staying at historic lodges and hotels along the way. *Cataract Canyon Raft Trip* takes you down the Colorado and Green Rivers through this spectacular Utah canyon buried in the heart of Canyonlands National Park, floating past brilliantly colored cliffs. There's plenty of time to hike and explore the grottoes and relics of the ancient Anasazi ruins.

When your children reach age 12, your choice of trips with REI is greatly expanded. You can pedal through Massachusetts, New Hampshire and Vermont on a New England biking holiday. A car-camping adventure awaits you on its *Alaskan Hidden Treasures* trip. In the Hawaiian Islands, you can hike, kayak, swim and snorkel on the Garden Island of Kauai on *Hiking Hidden Hawaii*. And, on the *Australia Tropical Discovery* trip you can kayak, hike/bike, explore the rain forest and even scuba dive or snorkel at the Great Barrier Reef. Several combo trips allow you to do it all — hike, camp, bike, kayak and raft — including one in Canada's parklands and another in Hawaii.

Though solo travelers and couples between the ages of 30 and 60 comprise the majority of REI participants, families are definitely beginning to have their presence felt. Remember, if having other kids along is important to you, ask for a trip on which another family is already signed on.

RATES: Folks who are members of REI (a one-time $15 lifetime membership) receive reduced land rates plus dividends on purchases at REI stores. Sample prices are: *High Sierra*, $895/person; *Olympic Peninsula*, $1,050/person; *Cataract Canyon*, $875/person; *Hiking Hidden Hawaii*, $895/person. REI does not yet offer youth prices nor does it work with travel agents.

RIVER ODYSSEYS WEST, INC. (ROW)
P.O. Box 579, Coeur d'Alene, ID 83816
Phone: 800-451-6034/208-765-0841
Fax: 208-667-6506

IN THEIR OWN WORDS: Few vacations offer families the opportunities for sharing as does a river trip. We've taken kids as young as 4 and folks as old as 83, some who have never camped, other with extensive wilderness experience, including the physically disabled. To travel by river is to go at nature's pace. The mix of river, rapids and wilderness create dynamic, magical times, most rewarding when sharing it with others. You'll be hard pressed to find a more fun-loving, safety conscious organization. We hope you'll join us to share our lives and the places we love.

THE TRIPS: ROW offers trips on nine rivers in Idaho, Oregon and Montana. The relatively new raft-supported hiking trips have been very well-received by participants. Proprietors Peter Grubb and his wife Betsy Bowen took their own two young children out to explore the river before they were able to talk. Among the first outfitters to offer family river trips, and the company that hosted our first of many rafting trips, ROW currently operates four or five *Family Focus* trips each summer for children as young as 5, as well as several *ParenTeen Fun* departures. Two to three trips each season span both age groups for those who have children in both chronological brackets. ROW only allows family "units" to go on its *Family Focus* trips — no singles or couples unaccompanied by a child or other family member with kids.

We know first-hand how much fun and how rewarding ROW's *Family Focus* trips are. Our group consisted of a real mix: another two-parent/two-child family, three single mothers and their sons and five sundry adults. We spent five days of unending excitement on the Salmon River, passing through Hell's Canyon into the Snake River. We understand completely why these three- to five-night *Salmon River Canyons* trips are Peter's top choice for families with young children, since they offer a perfect rafting and camping experience for first-timers. We especially liked the wide sandy beaches where we pitched camp each night and were continuously surprised by the quality and quantity of food that was served each and every mealtime — fresh fruit, freshly baked cakes at dinner and other treats. River time took over our spirits quickly, our ears always perked for the next rapid.

ROW's brochure lists many other domestic options and gives age guidelines for each of its trips. Trips on U.S. rivers generally run from May to September when the hiking/rafting-supported trips are also scheduled. About 20 percent of the *Salmon River Canyons* trips host multigenerational family groups. The hiking/walking trips take advantage of the trails that roughly follow the shoreline paths along the Snake and Middle Fork of the Salmon Rivers. Trips average six to eight miles of walking/hiking and are raft-supported. The raft transports all luggage and travels ahead to set up camp. You need only carry a day-pack with water, camera and binoculars. Children 12 and older are welcomed. If the hiking is too tiring, you can make arrangements to ride in the boat for parts of each day. Your kids can even go in the boat while you hike. Ask about *Raft & Ranch* and *Raft & Horseback* combinations.

Internationally, ROW offers yachting tours along the coast of Turkey, nature-oriented rafting trips in Ecuador and barging along the canals of France. Their newest program features trekking in Nepal. ROW has already taken along kids on these trips and recommends them for youngsters 10 and older. We won't be surprised to discover a family trek being offered soon. As experienced rafters with kids over age 14, we're looking forward to joining a *Raft Ecuador* trip this winter. We've yet to decide whether to opt for the *River of the Sacred Waterfalls* or *Wings & Whitewater*, both are appealing.

ROW's yacht trips along the Turkish Coast and *Barging In Europe* will be covered in detail in **Great Cruise Vacations With Your Kids.**

RATES: Youth prices are for kids 16 and younger are valid on all of ROW's trips. Five-day *Salmon River Canyons* trips are $920/adult, $795/youth. Rio Upano/*River of the Sacred Waterfalls* is $1,750 with a $100 discount for youths; *Wings & Whitewater* is $850/adult, $650/youth sharing with parents. A five-day/five-night *Market Towns and Inca Ruins* extension is $800/adult, $650/youth.

ROADS LESS TRAVELED (RLT)
P.O. Box 8187, Longmont, CO 80501
Phone: 800-488-8483/303-678-8750
Fax: 303-678-5568

IN THEIR OWN WORDS: At Roads Less Traveled our wish is to share with you the magic of the special lands we call home — the Rockies and the Southwest. We believe that to truly experience this majestic region one must leave the main roads and venture only those that are visited by few.

Only on the forgotten backroads and trails can you discover an unspoiled wilderness of emerald lakes and hot springs, isolated ghost towns and herds of elk and deer. Every year we have seen an increasing number of people join our programs that cater to families. Popular for families with children over 8 are our *Pedaling 'n Paddling* and *Hiking 'n Biking Samplers* and our *Backwoods Getaway*, which combines traveling by foot and mountain bike between a series of remote high mountain log cabins. Adults and children alike love the opportunity to stay deep in the mountains with hiking trails and wildlife right out the door.

THE TRIPS: Offering a variety of biking and hiking adventures, RLT trips are designed for children over age 8 though young participants are generally between the ages of 10 and 14. Because experience and skills vary greatly among children RLT prefers to talk to parents on a "case-by-case basis to ensure that the child will enjoy the program." Most popular with families are the *Sampler Vacations*, which encompass mountain biking, hiking, rafting and/or horseback riding with inn stays; the company's customized trips are also popular. On the latter, RLT recommends putting together a small group of two or three families. Younger children can more easily be accommodated on these trips. Recommended *Family Samplers* head for Arizona, New Mexico, Colorado, Grand Teton and Glacier Parklands. The reason these trips are so highly recommended (over RLT's "beginner" level for example) is because of the variety of activities. Almost all of the *Sampler* programs include dirt-road biking, a sure-fire child pleaser. Warm-weather winter trips to Dominica in the Caribbean, Costa Rica and Belize in Central America, and Hawaii are operated by other outfitters in cooperation with RLT.

RATES: Samplers, which are generally six days and five nights in length, cost anywhere from $1,025 to 1,295. All of the trips have supplements for singles.

BOOKED FOR TRAVEL

"My mother and I are going backpacking in the desert canyonlands. As we drive the road to the beginning of the trail, I can see that this is a magical place. All around us are huge rocks that look like castles against the desert sky." DESERT TRIP, by Barbara A. Steiner (illustrations by Ronald Himler), conjures up the imaginary journey of a mother and child, following them step by step as they hike the back country trails of Utah's Canyonlands National Park. The mother is the seasoned instructor, the child the wide-eyed novice, marveling equally at the great — mammoth canyons, starry firmament — and small — the soapweed yucca, cliff rose and cottontail rabbit. (Sierra Club)

ROCKY MOUNTAIN RIVER TRIPS (RMRT)
Winter: P.O. Box 2552, Boise, ID 83701;
Summer: P.O. Box 207, Salmon, ID 83467
Phone: Winter: 208-345-2400/Summer: 208-756-4808
Fax: 208-345-2688

IN THEIR OWN WORDS: It's clear that people are seeking quality time with their families and rafting trips are still under-rated by the conventional wisdom. We are doing our best to educate the public. All of our trips are along the legendary and awesome Salmon River in Idaho. The Middle Fork rips through 105 miles of the most primitive country in the world, a land with the remains of mining successes and failures, tattered remote homesteads, lonely grave markers — all signs of the people from the past who tried, in one way or another, to temper an area too rugged. Part of our experience is wrapped in the simplicity of an outdoor adventure in an environment in rapport with nature. There's lots of time for hiking, bird-watching or fishing, plus observing the enormous diversity of wildlife that thrives in the area. Since we make all of the camp and food preparations, there's plenty of time to relax. Speaking of food, we take a special approach to food preparation. It's Sheila's Dutch-oven cooking and our attentive, experienced crew of Middle Fork guides who get credit for so many folks returning again and again.

THE TRIPS: In business for almost 20 years, RMRT offers nine six-day trips on the Middle Fork each summer, departing from the Mountain Village Lodge in Stanley, ID. Children 6 years and older are welcome to participate and the Mills recommend that younger children visit during July and August when the water in the river is at its warmest. Oar-powered boats carry only four passengers (meaning there is a guide for every four guests) but those who wish can opt to crew a six-person paddle boat or an individual inflatable kayak. Camping is on sandy white beaches located near natural hot springs and sleeping bags, pads, pillows, and rain suits are provided by RMRT. A complimentary t-shirt is given to each rafter. A handful of four- and five-day trips are also possible each season.

Owners Sheila and Dave Mills are among the most highly respected river outfitters in the country and have been awarded the *Outstanding Achievement in Recreation* award from the Idaho's Governor's Conference for their "efforts to provide a quality whitewater rafting experience while preserving Idaho's environment." Sheila is the author of **The Rocky Mountain Dutch Oven Cookbook** (McGraw Hill) and these trips serve as her test kitchen! It has been said the RMRT's crew is the most experienced in Idaho with the guides averaging 40 years of age.

RATES: Six-night trips cost $1,475/adult, five days/$1,060 and four days/$850. Kids age 15 and under receive a 10 percent discount except on trips in July. Idaho sales tax and a Forest Service user fee are additional.

SEA TREK
P.O. Box 561, Woodacre, CA 94973
Phone: 415-488-1000
Fax: 415-488-1707

IN THEIR OWN WORDS: In operation since 1982, we are considered California's premier sea kayaking outfitter, offering a wide selection of classes, trips and adventure vacations for outdoor enthusiasts — with or without paddling experience. Experience the thrill of gliding past a curious sea lion, observe a pelican dive as the sun sets over Mt. Tamalpais or watch the river churning with spawning salmon in Alaska — this is the magic of sea kayaking. Our friendly, experienced instructors will initiate you to the pleasures of exploring the world by sea kayak. Our kayak fleet includes single, double and triple craft as well as junior-sized and sit-on-top models.

THE TRIPS: Take The Kids Sea Kayaking is a gentle three-hour adventure featuring "a sea lion's perspective of Richardson Bay." This terrific introduction to the sport with games and activities designed to interest youngsters of all ages is offered once or twice a month from February through October. There are a number of day excursions and clinics for novice and more experienced paddlers in the San Francisco Bay Area. Week-long trips head to Baja, Mexico where two nights in a hotel in Loreto are combined with five nights of "catered" camping along the Sea of Cortez. In Alaska, two types of trips are offered, one includes seven days of kayaking from camp to camp and a *Base Camp* program with relaxed paddling jaunts from two different areas, a better choice when traveling with kids. For both of these programs it's best if kids are comfortable around adults who comprise the majority of the guests. 12 is generally the youngest age. For youngsters between the ages of 9 and 14, a *Sea Kayak Summer Day Camp* is offered.

RATES: Take the Kids costs $50/adult, $40/child under 12. *Baja* trips, which run during March and April, cost $990/person. *Alaska* journeys, which operate during July and August, range from $1,190 to $1,420/adult with discounts available for youngsters up to age 16. Sea Trek blocks air seats for participants on all of these trips.

SHERI GRIFFITH EXPEDITIONS, INC.
P.O. Box 1324, Moab, UT 84532
Phone: 800-332-2439/801-259-8229
Fax: 801-259-2226

IN THEIR OWN WORDS: We call our trips soft adventures because they are soft on risk and high on adventures that provide a glowing sense of pleasure hard to find in today's high pressure world. Our "touch of class" adds just the right sense of pampering and comfort. Each season we offer special departures such as *The Family Goes to Camp — Expedition Style*, where we take the kids on structured outings where they'll interact with nature, other children and our wonderful guides. These trips are designed to give you the luxury of a guided expedition while the kids "go to camp." We camp on sandy beaches, bring along water toys and prepare meals for both adult and child appetites.

THE TRIPS: The family trips offered on the *Majestic Canyons of the Green River* begin with a scenic flight to the put-in point. The 50+ rapids are interspersed with relaxing stretches, making the river ideal for those as young as 5 and seniors. They are welcome on all the Green River departures, though only the family camp trips feature special kids' activities.

Coyote Run: An Introduction to Family Camping is considered a float trip (utilizing both rafts and inflatable kayaks) with teepee camping in "authentic Sioux Indian teepees" on an "Old West homestead" and is "for every kind of family" and children 4 and older. Participants will not only enjoy the scenic float on a mild stretch of the Colorado River, they'll get a glimpse of how life was at the turn of the century. For those averse to sleeping on the ground, cots are set up in the heavy canvas teepees and there's even a cabin available for the less intrepid. As the rafts pull into camp, staff is already on-site, ready to "attend to the kids, from snacks through interpretive walks, water activities, games and crafts."

Ages 10 and older are welcome on the company's Colorado River trips through Cataract Canyon and Westwater Canyon. A combination mountain bike and raft trip is also offered.

RATES: Youth rates are offered to those up to age 16. *Family Camp* and Majestic Canyon trips are $783/adult, $499/youth on five-day/four-night trips. A four-day/three-night option is $712/adult, $418/youth. The two-day/one-night *Coyote Run* trip is $195/adult, $165/youth. Two-to-five-night trips in Cataract Canyon cost $638 to $837/adult while one-or two-night trips in Westwater Canyon cost $314 and $472 respectively. Some trips include the camping equipment; others offer ground pads and tents for rent. Personal inflatable kayaks can be rented on some trips.

SLICKROCK ADVENTURES, INC.

P.O. Box 1400, Moab, UT 84532
Phone: 800-390-5715/801-259-6996
Fax: 801-259-6996

IN THEIR OWN WORDS: We began as a kayak school in 1977 seeking to create an instructional program in a wilderness setting. Twenty years later we've expanded to offering trips in both North and Central America and have become on of America's top kayak outfitters. All of our trips feature instruction for all levels. From Canyon County of the Colorado Plateau, famous for its spectacular scenery, to a pristine island reef in Belize, all our trips are designed to be hassle-free, led by guides who are top professionals in their field. We're dedicated to fun and safety and carefully select itineraries guaranteed to provide experiences you'll long remember.

THE TRIPS: We learned about Slickrock from a reader whose family took a trip with them to Belize. In her enthusiasm describing what was their "best family trip ever" with "superb guides" and "unforgettable experiences," our reader neglected to include her name. A call to Slickrock explaining that the trip included a 4-year-old helped trace her since, at that point, Slickrock only accommodated children this young on custom tours. We're pleased to note that they now include a *Kid's Price & Policy List* for their *Glovers Reef* expedition in Belize that begins at age 3! However, Slickrock's other international trips and all of its domestic trips continue to have a minimum age of 16.

    Sea Kayak Glovers Reef is described as the "premier sea kayak trip in Belize, offering the best of everything from comfortable chartered transport and a gourmet seafood feast to top equipment and guides." During the six- or 10-day trips, guests stay in thatched cabanas or tents on the beach. Days are spent paddling among the patch reefs where dolphins, sea turtles, rare coral and myriad tropical fish are encountered. Certified divers have the opportunity to dive the outer wall. Trips are offered from December through April. There are a number of other enticing trips to Belize and Honduras also (minimum age 16).

    Back in the States, trips through the Canyonlands region include kayaking along the Green River and can be combined with a mountain bike trip. A similar trip is offered to the Maze and Lake Powell.

RATES: Sea Kayak Glovers Reef costs $950/adult for six days, $1,495/10 days. Children ages 3 to 6 receive a 65 percent discount, ages 7 to 12, 30 percent. Discounts are lower when you book through a travel agent. The three-day Canyonlands kayak trip is $430 and the four-day mountain bike trip is $545. A combination trip is $975.

BOOKED FOR TRAVEL

SNORKELING FOR KIDS OF ALL AGES, by Judith Jennet, published by the National Association of Underwater Instructors (NAUI), covers all the proper techniques, skills and equipment a snorkeler (child or not) needs to derive the most out of the snorkeling experience. Very little is said about surface snorkeling; the focus is on snorkel diving. There are chapters on Pressure, Hypothermia, Hyperventilation and Overexertion and safety issues are given the highest priority throughout the book. In fact, the only features that make this a children's book are the instructional drawings and the simple language employed. Although children who have mastered the art of snorkeling can, in theory, go diving in safety (of course, with a buddy and after having asked permission), we believe that an adult companion should be part of the diving party, something that this book does not advise.

SUNRISE COUNTY CANOE EXPEDITIONS, INC. (SCCE)
Cathance Lake, Grove, ME 04657
Phone: 800-RIVER-30/207-454-7708
Fax: 207-454-3315

IN THEIR OWN WORDS: We've been in the business of guiding and outfitting river-based canoe trips for nearly 25 years and are respected throughout the country for the integrity of experience that we offer our clientele. Our staff includes some of the finest veteran river and expedition professionals in North America, and our technical instruction, which is integral to all our trips, is very highly regarded. We consider canoe voyaging an art and, although we offer the most extensive selection of itineraries of any outfitter, our heritage remains that of the professional Maine Guide, stressing instruction, comfort in the outdoors and safety of participants. Our trips are all-inclusive with a staff to guest ratio of 1:4.

THE TRIPS: Directors Martin Brown and Kendra Flint say that many of their trips are good bets for families. In particular, the *Saint Croix River* — one of Maine's "real gems," and recently nominated as a Canadian Heritage River — features miles of easy to moderate rapids, making it suitable for all levels of expertise and ideal for learning technique. SCCE operates special family trips along the river almost every week.

SCCE also recommends trips on the legendary Rio Grande River on the Texas/Mexico border. Journeys into the isolated Lower Canyons are seven days in length and operate during March and April when it is springtime in the desert and the scenery is at its most spectacular with no rain or bugs — just abundant sunshine and premier wilderness.

SCCE wasn't joking when it said it offers more trips than other outfitters. Other choices include the San Juan River in Utah, the Verde River in Arizona, the Machias and Saint John Rivers in Maine, the Bonaventure, Chamachuane, Moisie, and Cascapedia Rivers in Quebec, plus trips in the Arctic, Newfoundland, Baffin Island, Iceland and numerous customized itineraries in Maine and Canada. For those looking for an unguided experience, SCCE offers complete outfitting services throughout the Eastern Maine Waters region.

RATES: Six-day, Tuesday to Sunday *Saint Croix* trips cost $689/adult; four-day trips are $495/adult. There is a 50 to 66 percent discount for both youngsters and young adults under 20 years old. The Rio Grande trips cost about $895/adult, with discounts offered for groups of two or more, including children's discounts the same as on the Saint Croix trip. Working with a travel agency, they can assist in securing economical airfares. All beverages except for soda, beer and liquor are supplied. Wine is served to adults with evening meals and, on special occasions, such as the *Mexican Night* on the Rio Grande trip, when margaritas are served.

TOWPATH TREKS
15 Penrith Way, Aylesbury, Bucks HP21 7JZ England
Phone: 011-44-1296-39556

IN THEIR OWN WORDS: We are the only U.K. organisation specialising in canal-side walking holidays — activity with tranquillity, where you can escape the madding crowd and discover the hidden world of nature. The inland waterways system of England and Wales comprises some 2,000 miles of interconnected canals and navigable rivers. One of the principal attractions of this kind of holiday is that you can walk without strain where the environment complements rather than competes. By the very nature of the route, you are always beside water. A wealth of wildlife and hundreds of species of wild flowers and plants are there to be discovered. Also, many of the original bridges and lock cottages still exist, as do many of the pubs and inns!

THE TRIPS: We found this company through a reader of ours who took her then three- and five-year-old boys on a walking tour which Towpath Treks arranged. Having spent an idyllic honeymoon hiking and driving through the English countryside, she and her husband had long dreamed of returning to hike along small country lanes, with only a small knapsack on their backs, nestling in at night at cozy farmhouses where their luggage awaited them. Once she became a mother, she put her vision on hold, until, that is, she found Keith Pyott at Towpath Treks, who was able to make her dreams a reality, then and there, children and all. By customizing a trip with special pickups, shorter routes, etc., their holiday turned out to be even better than they had anticipated. Walking from Oxford to Leamington Spa at a rate of three to six miles a day, the boys were never bored — they played tag on the canal paths, stroked ponies that they met and picnicked along the way. When the kids tired, the family cleverly hitched rides with local boaters on the canals in exchange for cranking the lock gates. They spent one night at a farmhouse in Kings Sutton where the farmer's wife took the boys to collect eggs for a delicious home-cooked breakfast. By day's end, with all the fresh air and exercise, one and all slept tight.

Curiously, when we asked Pyott if he wanted to add any comments on families, he declined, though he definitely seemed quite pleased to be included in our family guide. Moreover, several of the brochures he sent that describe the canal walks highlight the fact that these expeditions are "perfect for family explorations." Pyott researches the routes for the walks himself, designing various possibilities for each trip which is offered year-round so long as the accommodation is available. Customization of the routes is always possible for those signing on for a minimum of three nights and guests can often select their own starting point within the planned itineraries. Among the routes which range in length from three to 12 nights are: Stratford to Birmingham; Worcester to Birmingham; Newport to Brecon; Aylesbury to Northampton; Northampton to Coventry; Stratford to Worcester; London to Aylesbury; Oxford to Northampton; and Reading to Bath. Lodging (many with family rooms) may be in a hostel, motel, farmhouse, inn, guest house or family home.

RATES: The cost of the family trip described above was $120/day for two adults and two children and included lodging with breakfast, luggage transfers and detailed route notes.

TREK & TRAIL (T&T)
P.O. Box 906, Bayfield, WI 54814
Phone: 800-354-8735/715-779-3595
Fax: 715-779-3597

IN THEIR OWN WORDS: We offer a number of outdoor learning adventures. For more than 17 years we have been providing knowledge and enthusiasm for the land, expert technical sport instruction and safe, rewarding experiences. Our home base offers immediate access to the 21 islands that comprise the Apostle Islands National Lakeshore, a reserve with miles of white sand beaches, sandstone cliffs, shipwrecks and a rich history. If you're looking for a family trip that is adventurous, educational, safe and fun, we've designed a number a trips for families of all ages.

THE TRIPS: We asked owner Mary Sweval to highlight which of T&Ts kayak trips she considered best for families and were pleased to discover so many possibilities. The majority of these water-based adventures explore the Apostle Islands National Lakeshore of Lake Superior, near the company's headquarters. *Sea Caves* is their most popular excursion, a full-day, six-and-a-half mile kayak trip with a picnic lunch on the beach that begins with instruction on basic skills and safety. Double kayaks are used for greater stability and paddle boats are substituted when waters get rough. *Shipwrecked I* is a half-day trip that's ideal if your kids are young. All it requires is "an attitude for fun and adventure."

Shipwrecked II is a more challenging, full-day adventure that also includes the basic safety course and lunch. On both you'll visit shipwrecks which date back to the 1860s. Another good choice for families is *Sea Kayaking Introduction*, a two-hour trip which includes both instruction and an excursion to an abandoned shipwreck. Overnight trips include a weekend trip to Sand Island and a five-day adventure on Madeline Island staying at a base camp in Big Bay State Park. Each day the group makes short forays to local beaches, lagoons, hiking trails and sea caves. Instruction, fishing, naturalist led-hikes combined with fun and relaxation all make for a terrific family experience.

Come winter, when the snows cover northern Wisconsin, families can join up with a professional musher and a team of experienced dogs for a weekend of hands-on mushing instruction on T&Ts *Dog Sledding & Cabin* overnight. At night, they'll repair to a cozy, rustic cabin and listen to the Newago family retell the lore and legends of the Ojibwas.

For those looking for a springtime warm weather adventure, T&T heads to Mexico and the remote reaches of the Sian Ka'an Biosphere, where there's kayaking, snorkeling and bone fishing, while staying in a large Spanish-style hacienda along the coast. Seven-day trips run during March and April. T&T's *Paddling School* welcomes children 12 and over.

RATES: On all T&T trips, children 12 and under receive a 50 percent discount. *Sea Caves* is $79/adult, *Shipwrecked* from $48 to $79, *Sea Kayaking Introduction*, $30. The *Sand Island* overnight is $199 and the *Madeline Island Base Camp* is $439. Adults pay $300 for the *Dog Sledding & Cabin* overnight while the Mexico trip is $1,695.

TURTLE RIVER RAFTING COMPANY

P.O. Box 313, Mt. Shasta, CA 96067
Phone: 800-726-3223/916-926-3223
Fax: 916-926-3443

IN THEIR OWN WORDS: Our love of running rivers is the heart of our business. To share our world of river adventures, we have created trips for families with children as young as 4 years old. One of our greatest rewards each season is seeing children learn and grow on the river.

THE TRIPS: Kids' Klamath & Trinity river trips are designed for children 4 years and older. The small, yet exciting, rapids are ideal for youngsters. Along the way, there are side creeks to explore, warm water to swim in and deer and turtles to discover along the riverbanks. Children ages 7 and older are invited to join trips on the Klamath, Trinity and Rogue Rivers, while excursions on the Upper Sacramento and Owyhee are reserved for those 10 and older. For the more intrepid, with teens 14 and older, there is the Class IV Upper Klamath River and the Class V California Salmon and Scott rivers. Trips range in length from one to seven days and most offer a discount for those 17 and younger. While the majority of these are camping trips, there is also a lodge trip on the Rogue River in Oregon.

RATES: Some examples of pricing are: One-day trips: $78 to $116/adult, $62 to $72/youth; three days: $284 to $366/adult, $236 to $66/youth. The seven-day Owyhee trip is $752/adult, $636/youth.

UNICORN RAFTING EXPEDITIONS, INC.
P.O. Box T, Brunswick, ME 04011
Phone: 800-UNICORN/207-725-2255
Fax: 207-725-2573

IN THEIR OWN WORDS: Families looking for a fun, affordable vacation will find that Unicorn Rafting Expeditions offers one of the best values for whitewater rafting anywhere in the East. Our *Family One-Day Adventures* on the Lower Kennebec River and summer Dead River trips are geared toward the young family and novice rafter. Moreover, we believe that the popularity of our three-day and night *Family Vacation Adventure* package is due to its flexibility and affordability. For over 17 years we have been offering trips where your safety and enjoyment are as important to us as our own children's welfare. We have so much confidence in our programs that we are the only river outfitter in Maine to guarantee our outdoor adventures. We provide the best-trained and friendliest guides and offer the best lodging. Our guests are treated as family. All of the rivers we raft are dam-controlled, assuring plenty of water all season. An escape with Unicorn is an outdoor adventure you'll cherish forever.

THE TRIPS: On most of Unicorn's trips the minimum age is 8. The family trips on the Lower Kennebec River (offered twice weekly) and on the Dead River (offered once a week) feature mild yet exciting whitewater experiences. After a day on the river, guests are invited to use the facilities of Unicorn's Lake Parlin Resort, including its heated pool, hot tub, game room and lounge. On several Dead River departures inflatable funyaks are available for youngsters 12 and older and adults. Kids 14 and older are invited to join five other paddlers (at least two of whom must be adults) for a guide-your-own-raft adventure.

Family Adventure begins on Sunday afternoon with lodging in a cabin at Lake Parlin and is followed by a full-day Kennebec River trip and a full-day guided bike trip. There's time to canoe, hike, sail and relax and there are numerous children's only activities. Two breakfasts, two lunches and one dinner are included and families can either cook the other meals in their cabin or take them at the restaurant at Lake Parlin Resort.

Families with kids over 12 might consider the three-day *Moose River Canoe Trip* into a remote wilderness area. Ideal even for beginners and exciting enough for intermediates, this weekend trip includes both river and lake canoeing, hiking and camping. Big Moose Inn and Campground is Unicorn's base for its *Penobscot River Adventures* where the minimum age is 14. Guided fishing expeditions for smallmouth bass are offered June through August and welcome children 12 and older.

RATES: Family Kennebec trips are $59/adult, $39/child 16 and under; Dead River trips are $65/adult, $55/child. The *Family Adventure Package* is $642/family of four staying at fully furnished lakeside cabins with modern bathrooms and kitchenettes. The *Moose River Canoe* trip is $249/adult, $169/child under 18. On multi-day trips participants bring their own sleeping bags.

VERMONT BICYCLE TOURING (VBT)
P.O. Box 711, Bristol, VT 05443-0711
Phone: 800-245-3868/802-453-4811
Fax: 802-453-4806

IN THEIR OWN WORDS: At Vermont Bicycle Touring, we don't think of what we do as bicycling, we think of it as sightseeing by bicycle. The world is filled with so many wonderful things that people in a rush never get to see — like the friendly smile of a farmer as he proudly offers you a taste of homemade cheese. Because you'll be seeing the world at your pace, you won't miss a thing. No matter which VBT vacation you choose, rest assured that we've painstakingly arranged everything . . . down to the last detail. We've selected and tested our routes to find the finest cycling, the most breathtaking views, and the best accommodations. Our groups are a happy mix of couples, singles and families who share your interest in exercise, fine food and accommodations, and a sense of adventure. We keep our groups small so you'll have plenty of opportunity to meet and make new friends along the way.

THE TRIPS: In business for 25 years, VBT has recently added *Family Tour* options welcoming children as young as 5 on three of its established itineraries: Plymouth, Vermont; Acadia National Park in Maine; and Colonial Williamsburg in Virginia. Though not limited to family participants, the destinations have been specially selected for the activities available, the degree of safety offered by the road conditions and the attitude of the accommodation used. Although "no extracurricular activities are planned for children or families," the trip leaders are knowledgeable about the given area and will be able to direct families to interesting and appealing stops. Minimum age for children on other domestic trips is 10; 13 on international excursions. Note that if a van shuttle is needed for any children up to 17 years old, parents must ride with them. VBT's rental bikes accommodate children 4'10" and taller, but peripherals, such as trail-a-bikes, trailers and bike seats, are not rented by VBT and cannot be attached to any of its equipment. Before booking any of VBT's other trips, ask if there are bookings from other families or if any of the lodgings where you'll be staying in often have young guests.

RATES: Family Tours cost from $269 to $695/adult for two to three nights. Like its sister company Hiking Holidays (see page 54) children ages 10 to 17 receive a 10 percent discount on North American trips; no discounts on international trips. When a child shares accommodations with two full paying adults the discount is 25 percent. Unfortunately, not all of the properties used can accommodate four people

VERMONT ICELANDIC HORSE FARM (VIHF)
P.O. Box 577, Waitsfield, VT 05673
Phone: 802-496-7141
Fax: 802-496-5390

IN THEIR OWN WORDS: We offer a most unusual vacation in the Mad River Valley of central Vermont. Come with us and explore the mountains, meadows and forests on one of the oldest and purest breed of horses in the world — the Icelandic horse. Since 1988 we've catered to experienced and novice equestrians trekking in exceptional riding comfort from one country inn to another. We may lead our horses at times, explore a tempting swimming hole or just relax and enjoy the spectacular scenery. You'll return home fit and rested with the memory of newly found friends and shared adventures.

THE TRIPS: Treks, on what are reputed to be personable, sure-footed and extremely comfortable steeds, can be as short as a half day or as long as six days and five nights. Owner Karen Winhold welcomes children 10 years and older who have riding experience. Most popular with families are the *Weekend Adventures* and the four-day/three-night *Vermont Fun Treks*. *Winter Treks* through the snowy countryside are also offered. On these trips participants get to try "skijoring" which is described as similar to water skiing behind a horse. All trips, with the exception of day rides that are always available, are inn-to-inn. We were pleased to see the family-friendly Mad River Inn among the stops along the way.

RATES: Weekend Adventures range in price from $335 to $385/adult for one or two nights. Two-night/three-day *Vermont Fun Trek* and *Winter Treks* cost $775/adult, $885 during fall foliage season. Children receive a 10 percent discount on most trips.

WESTERN RIVER EXPEDITIONS (WRE)
7258 Racquet Club Drive, Salt Lake City, UT 84121-4599
Phone: 800-453-7450/801-359-0246
Fax: 801-942-8514

IN THEIR OWN WORDS: A rafting vacation is a wonderful way to get in touch with both nature and yourself. Abandon cellular phones, fax machines, traffic and congestion for the solitude of the river, where city sounds are replaced by the roar of rapids, whispers of river birds and the haunting quiet of Anasazi Indians whose dwellings hang on canyon walls. Hike to picturesque waterfalls, sleep under brilliant stars and enjoy the excitement of huge rapids. To best experience this rugged beauty without roughing it, we provide sleeping cots for guests and set up potty tents at each camp, offering real adventure with a measure of pampering.

THE TRIPS: The nation's largest rafting company, in business since 1956, WRE operates trips in the Green River Wilderness, Cataract Canyon, Westwater Canyon, on the Main Fork and Middle Fork of the Salmon River and, of course, in the Grand Canyon. There are also trips which combine rafting with lodge or ranch stays. Green River trips are recommended for families with children as young as 7-years-old; Salmon River trips, 8 and older. The youngest age suggested for Cataract and Westwater Canyons is 12. Trips in the Grand Canyon offer several options, with the shorter trips accepting youngsters 9 and older. Though no specific family departures are planned, there are always family groups on WRE trips, many of which offer youth prices.

RATES: Green River three- or four-night trips are $795/adult, $397.50/youth 7 to 17. Three-day Grand Canyon trips begin at $755/person, no youth discount. The four-day trip, with an overnight at the Bar 10 Lodge is $910. Salmon River trips, six days/five nights, begin at $1,033/adult, $705/youth.

WOLF RIVER CANOES, INC. (WRC)
#21652 Tucker Road, Long Beach, MS 38560
Phone: 601-452-7666
Fax: 601-452-3784

IN THEIR OWN WORDS: With its white sand beaches, the cool waters of the Wolf River offer the perfect playground for family canoe or kayak trips. Though minutes from Mississippi's casinos and Gulf beaches, the river meanders past peaceful woodlands and ancient clay formations, creating a sense of serenity.

THE TRIPS: Proprietor Joe Feil often works with families and kids. His most popular trip is a 10.6 mile one-day outing, averaging five to seven hours, allowing for stops to swim, fish and explore. A shorter 4.5 mile trip is also operated daily (two times per day on weekends). Both of these can be accompanied by a guide. Other day trips include *Paddle Around*, *Shuttle* and *To Go*. Unguided camping trips are another possibility. On these outings, you choose your distance and provide your own camping equipment, while WRC supplies the canoe, paddles, life vests and lots of terrific advice and support. Kayaks and tubes can also be rented.

RATES: The *10.6 Mile* is $27/canoe; *4.5 Mile*, $25/canoe. *Paddle Around*, *Shuttle* and *To Go* are $15/canoe. Two-days/one-night of camping is $45/canoe, two nights, $60.

BOOKED FOR TRAVEL

BUCK WILDER'S SMALL FRY FISHING GUIDE is a delightful and whimsical how-to introductory handbook to fresh-water fishing in North American waters for kids. Buck Wilder is the creation of Tim Smith and Mark Herrick (the book's author and illustrator respectively), whose aim throughout is to let kids know that fishing is fun, and pretty easy once you know about basic equipment, techniques and the foibles of individual species. This is one book we feel will appeal to a wide range of ages, with no upward limit. Though it's available in bookstores, if you order through the publisher, the author will be more than happy to inscribe your copy personally. "Buck" has a new book coming out next year: **The Small Twig Hiking & Camping Guide.** (Alexander & Smith, 800-994-BUCK)

CHAPTER 3

STAY & PLAY

We have no doubt that while you've been reading the previous pages, many of you are thinking that although the adventures sound absolutely terrific, there's no way you would join a full-blown organized group excursion. Perhaps your children are too young. Perhaps not every member of your family is anxious to experience these types of adventures. Perhaps it all sounds too exhausting. In the pages that follow, you'll find options that address these very issues.

There are countless adventures that families can enjoy when they're staying in traditional vacation settings, from country inns and dude ranches to luxury resorts and family camps — and these are just some of the numerous possibilities that exist, both at home and abroad. There are several advantages to this type of adventure vacation. For many, coming back to the same room each night is reason enough. Younger kids will certainly find this more comforting than moving around each day. Moreover, not all parents want to take their children out on each and every outing — nor do kids want to spend their holidays hip-to-hip with their parents. Just about each and every spot included in this chapter offers an active program for children to participate in with their peers.

Also, those traveling in multigenerational groups may find this an easier vacation to plan. After all, while your kids may want to ride all day, it's likely that your parents will want less strenuous activity (at least part of the time). We've found that not all family members want to be active all the time. One day we might go out on a hike together, the next, perhaps one of us will take a canoe trip while the others relax or meet up with new friends.

Yet another advantage of choosing a single place to stay is that it allows you try out a number of activities and determine which ones appeal to you the most. You may discover that you enjoy a specific adventure more than another and decide to take a trip involving this activity on a subsequent vacation.

Following the section on Club Med, our *Stay and Play* selections contain a *DESCRIPTION* of the property, details about the specific *ADVENTURES* on tap, the *FAMILY FEATURES* that you'll need to know in order to make a good choice for your own family, and the *RATES*. We remind you once again that all prices are for 1996 unless otherwise stated.

CLUB MED

We're always a bit shocked to learn that many folks don't know that Club Med (800-CLUB-MED) villages are often wondrous choices for families, with an eclectic variety of outdoor adventure and sporting opportunities. Those of you who don't realize that Club Med has been offering family vacations for many years will be doubly surprised to learn that a number of Club Med villages offer some of the same adventure activities we highlight throughout this book. We've visited a number of the *family villages* with our kids and have loved each and every visit. If we have any complaint, it's that our kids are so anxious to join their groups that we don't spend as much time together as we might like. The Club realizes that part of every family vacation entails spending time together and has been adding more family-together activities each season. For those families who have been anxious to travel abroad and don't know where to go with children, the news gets even better, as a number of clubs across the globe offer special facilities for children as young as 4 months.

Since Club Med is so well known for its sports facilities, we traditionally recommend that parents first find the clubs which offer the specific activities they enjoy before choosing a destination. If it's adventure you're after, the following clubs will more than satisfy your craving — they all offer activities for kids. Many, many other clubs welcome kids (most specify a minimum age) but do not provide any special facilities for them. With the exception of Copper Mountain, we've saved details on Club Med's 19 ski villages for our sports guide. The chart below tells you the name of the club, its location and the adventures offered (those with an * carry an additional fee) and the ages accepted in organized programs (all are year-round unless otherwise stated). Clubs marked with ** are primarily French-speaking villages.

BOOKED FOR TRAVEL

IN THE OCEAN, a "pull-the-tab and lift-the-flap book," is a marine adventure on dry land that both toddlers and preschoolers can enjoy. The format is engaging, with a cheerful text by Dawn Apperley and amusing and vibrantly-colored drawings by Kate Burns. The book is part of a new Hide and Seek series; a second volume, IN THE SAND, is equally appealing. (Little Brown)

CLUB	LOCATION	ADVENTURES	KIDS' PROGRAMS
Bali	Indonesia	windsurfing, kayaking, circus	Mini and Kids' Clubs for ages 4 to 12
Caravelle	Guadeloupe, French West Indies	kayaking, deep sea fishing*, circus	Kids' Club for children 6 to 11 during school holidays
Chateau Royal**	New Caledonia	windsurfing, circus with climbing wall	Mini and Kids' Clubs for ages 4 to 11
Copper Mountain (winter season only)	Copper Mountain, Colorado	snowshoeing*, backcountry skiing*	Petit, Mini, Kids and Teen Clubs for ages 3 to 17.
Coral Beach	Israel	windsurfing	Mini and Kids Clubs for ages 3 to 12
Forges-les-Eaux**	France	mountain biking, BMX biking for kids, horseback riding*	Mini and Kids' Clubs for ages 3 to 11
Huatulco	Mexico	kayaking, deep sea fishing*, circus, mountain biking*	Teen Club for ages 12 to 17; clubs for ages 6 to 11 during school holidays.
Itaparica	Brazil	windsurfing, circus, horseback riding*	Mini and Kids' Clubs for ages 4 to 12
Ixtapa	Mexico	kayaking, deep sea fishing*, horseback riding*, circus	Baby, Petit, Mini and Kids Clubs for ages 1 to 11 years .
Jerba la Douce**	Tunisia	windsurfing, kayaking, horseback riding*	Kids' Club for ages 8 to 11
Opio	France	biking and mountain biking, circus (seasonal), horseback riding*	Mini and Kids' Clubs for ages 3 to 11
Pompadour**	France	horseback riding*, biking, guided hikes	Mini and Kids' Clubs for ages 3 to 11
Punta Cana	Dominican Republic	windsurfing, kayaking, deep-sea fishing*, horseback riding*, circus	Petit, Mini and Kids Club for ages 2 to 11.
Rio de Pedras	Brazil	kayaking, rain forest hikes	Mini and Kids' Clubs for ages 4 to 12
St. George's Cove (opening Spring 1997)	Bermuda	windsurfing, kayaking, deep-sea fishing*, scuba-diving*, circus	Mini and Kids' Clubs for ages 6 to 11

As a general rule of thumb, Club Med kids' programs are broken down into *Baby Club* (babies under 24 months old), *Petit Club* (children ages 2 to 3) *Mini Club* (children ages 4 to 7), *Kids' Club* (children ages 8 to 11) and *Teen Clubs* (children ages 12 to 14 and 15 to 17). In certain overseas clubs, ages vary for specific programs, but kids are never mixed with those either too young or too old to enjoy the same activities.

The newest addition to Club Med is *Club Aquarius*, described as a "European-style village for the budget-conscious family." A limited number of meals, sports and activities are included in the basic price, but many others have an extra fee. They will, however, include children's programs for kids up to age 16 (only *Petit Club* will have a supplement). Windsurfing (and boardsailing) are included while scuba diving, horseback riding and go-carting require an extra fee.

Although Club Med vacations are no longer the bargains they were twenty-five years ago, their overall comfort level has vastly improved since those early days. In order to make a visit to a club more affordable, the company offers frequent specials. For example, a number of family villages throughout the world offer *Kids Stay Free* weeks (for children under 5) and a *Family Wild Card* price based on the number of people in your family. These specials bring the all-inclusive price to about $800/person per week except in peak periods.

BEAVERKILL VALLEY INN (BVI)
Lew Beach, NY 12753
Phone: 914-439-4844
Fax: 914-439-3884

DESCRIPTION: Just steps away from the birthplace of American fly-fishing, within Catskill State Park, lies the Beaverkill Valley Inn, an elegantly understated country inn with the "recreational opportunities of a wilderness retreat." It is in its 100th year of operation and is listed on the National Register of Historic Places. BVI offers a warm welcome to families — immediately obvious upon checking out its facilities: an indoor swimming pool, ice-cream parlor and children's playroom among them. Owner Larry Rockefeller, father of two active boys, has added a number of safety features that parents of young children will appreciate, including child-sized handrails that have been installed to the inn's staircases. The Inn itself, just two-and-a-half hours from midtown Manhattan, has 21 guest rooms, each decorated with distinctive wallpaper, homemade quilts and antique furniture. Other public rooms include a large front parlor and a card room, each with fireplace. The Inn takes great pride in its food, using the freshest seasonal fare available, with most (but not all) of the meals served buffet style, offering several choices both at lunch and dinner. All breads, desserts and pastries are made on premises. There is a no tipping policy at the Inn.

THE ADVENTURES: BVI encourages its guests to be adventurous and explore the Valley. Knowledgeable local guides for fly-fishing, cross-country skiing or hiking can be arranged. Depending on the season, you can join a guided hike and nature walk up Balsam Lake Mountain, tour the saphouse and check out the maple sugar operation or take a horse-drawn sleigh ride. There are numerous hiking and skiing trails on the extensive, breathtaking property and the one mile of privately-owned stream allows guests to fish without a license. A backcountry cabin is available for overnight use by cross-country skiers. Cross-country skis are available at the Inn. Rafting or canoeing down the Delaware River is easily accessible. Bike riding (bring your own bikes) is also popular.

For additional recreation there are two tennis courts and a pond for summer fishing and winter ice-skating. The Inn also operates a General Store, gallery and pub that guests are welcome to use.

FAMILY FEATURES: Kids of all ages are warmly welcomed and love swimming in the indoor pool and enjoy the free ice-cream parlor. "Children love it here so much, they don't want to leave." On weekends a Saturday evening supervised kids' dinner followed by time in the stocked playroom provide a quiet interlude for parents. During the summer a day camp is operated from Monday through Friday for children ages 2 to 14. It is open to Inn guests as well as other guests of the Beaverkill area (so you'll never have to worry as to whether or not there will be children in attendance). Whenever you choose to visit you will find both kids-only and family-together events on the schedule. At the Inn you can expect a variety of games, from soccer in the summer to ice-hockey on the pond in winter. There's an outdoor basketball hoop and pingpong and pool tables in the Inn. Family barbecues are also featured (all meals are included at the Inn). The local area attractions are plentiful: nearby mountains, lakes, downhill skiing and golf all within a half hour of the Inn. Evening entertainment is even sometimes on tap.

RATES: American plan rates that include all meals, tennis, use of pool and trails and fly-fishing in season, are the same year-round. Charges are per room. Two adults pay $330/night in a double with private bath, $260/shared bath. Single rooms are $195 and $160 respectively. Charges for children ages 3 to 13 are based on whether they are sharing with an adult, another child or have a room of their own. When two children share a room, the room rate is $230/private bath, $160/shared bath. A child in a single room by his or herself pays $145/private bath, $110/shared bath. There is no charge for children under age 3. There are no service charges but there is a seven percent sales tax.

CASTLE ROCK RANCH
412 Country Road 6NS, Cody, WY 82414
Phone: 800-356-9965/307-587-2076
Fax: 307-527-7196

DESCRIPTION: Castle Rock Ranch is located along the pristine waters of the Shoshone River in the Absoroka range of the Rocky Mountains. Hosted by Derek and Gina McGovern, Castle Rock offers a wide variety of outdoor adventure activities for the whole family. The ranch consists of 10 homey, rustic cabins that can accommodate as many as six people. The cabins are furnished in western style and all have views of the surrounding mountains. Guests round up at the Saddle Saloon for complimentary cocktails and socialize around the river rock fireplace in the main lodge. In addition to the outdoor heated pool, guests enjoy volleyball and horseshoes at the outdoor barbecue area.

THE ADVENTURES: The ranch program features a full range of outdoor activities in addition to horseback riding. Rock climbing, kayaking, river rafting, mountain biking, fishing (spin and fly), cattle team penning and an overnight pack/camping trip are part of the weekly schedule, as are a trip to the Cody Nite Rodeo and Yellowstone National Park (approximately 50 miles).

FAMILY FEATURES: For children ages 3 to 9 Castle Rock offers a first-rate children's program. The agenda includes hiking, mountain biking, nature and bone hunts, arts and crafts and swimming. For younger children, the McGovern's own nanny is sometimes available to take on extra kids in addition to their own five. Guests are asked to compensate the nanny separately. Another unique and special feature at Castle Rock is its guest laundry service, part and parcel of the daily housekeeping. What a treat!

RATES: All-inclusive rates which include activities, equipment, instruction and meals, range from $1,200-$1,400/adult; children ages 5 to 9 pay half the adult rate, under 3/$250. Older children pay a third person rate starting at $900. Fishing licenses are additional and are required for children 14 and older. The ranch is open from June through September with off-season weeks available for groups.

COFFEE CREEK RANCH

HC2 Box 4940, Trinity Center, CA 96091
Phone: 800-624-4480/916-266-3343

DESCRIPTION: Calling itself "Northern California's finest guest ranch," Coffee Creek offers a wide range of adventures combined with services and amenities designed to provide "fun and relaxation, the beauty of the outdoors and a friendly western atmosphere" — quite a goal to fulfill. Located on 127 acres surrounded by National Forest and the Trinity Alps Wilderness Area, the ranch is perched along Coffee Creek, an excellent trout stream, eight miles above Trinity Lake. Up to 50 guests stay in individual cabins (most have two bedrooms) secluded in the woods or in orchards around the ranch house where meals are taken. Several cabins are open in winter as well, making Coffee Creek a year-round destination. The stables and corrals, swimming pool, pond, shuffleboard, basketball, volleyball/badminton and horseshoe courts, archery range, pingpong table, health spa, rec room and guest laundry are all located on-property; some facilities are accessible via a walk-bridge across the road. Guests are invited to come for the better part of a week (Saturday to Friday) or just for a few days. In summer, priority is given to guests who stay a full week.

Most meals are served in the dining room, with lunch generally served buffet style and dinner as a sit-down affair. There are a number of breakfast and picnic rides, poolside BBQ lunches and a weekly cowboy cookout at the lake. Weekly rates include all meals, horseback riding (extra charge in summer), plus a wide range of activities, from hiking and gold panning to tennis and canoeing plus evening entertainment. Weekly prices can also include an overnight pack trip.

THE ADVENTURES: In addition to the daily (except on Fridays) riding opportunities (these are in addition to the pack trip) from the end of March to November, each season brings adventuresome delights for the entire family. Participants in *Wilderness Pack Trips* (spring, summer and fall) head for the 517,000 plus acres of the Trinity Alps Wilderness area and can choose from "spot trips" where a packer takes you and your gear in by horseback to a designated campsite, "dunnage packing" when gear is brought to a designated spot that you hike to at your leisure or "all-inclusive" trips on which everything but your sleeping bag and personal items are seen to by a packer and trail cook. Hiking is a major draw, especially in spring with the area's explosion of wildflowers. Beginning in November, tubing, ice-fishing, cross-country skiing, snowshoeing and dog sledding are featured. A snowboard park is on the drawing board.

FAMILY FEATURES: With the exception of specifically designated *Romantic Weekends*, families are always welcomed at Coffee Creek.

Owner/managers Ruth and Mark Hartman have raised their two children on the ranch and are very attuned to the desires of parents and kids. Summer youth programs, supervised by counselors from overseas, operate from 9 a.m. to 5 p.m. Saturday through Thursday and are broken down into various age groups: *Cowboys & Cowgirls* (ages 3 to 7); *Jr. Wranglers* (8 to 12; note: this age group is given two complimentary riding lessons early in the week "for maximum riding results") and *Bronc Busters* (13 to 17). With the exception of private lessons, the riding is always included when children are in their groups. For children under 3, babysitting is provided at the *Kiddie Korral* during the scheduled horse rides. During the rest of the year, activities for children are offered on an as-needed basis. None of the programs are mandatory and families can spend as much time together as they wish, and are encouraged to do so!

RATES: Summer rates range from $675 to $695/adult, $555 to $575/child 3 to 12, and $655 to $675/teen. Children under 3 pay $250. In spring, winter and fall, expect to pay about 15 to 20 percent less. Nightly rates are also offered. Taxes and gratuities are additional. In summer, weekly riding which include all rides, an overnight pack trip and guest rodeo costs $250/adult. Two-hour rides are $27.50/ride; all-day rides are $55.

BOOKED FOR TRAVEL

Pat Dickerman first published **FARM, RANCH & COUNTRY VACATIONS** in 1949 (it's now in its 29th edition) so her opinions definitely carry weight, and one of her views is that a vacation in rural America is the best kind of family holiday possible. From Alaska to Florida, Dickerman introduces readers to farms, lodges, ranches, inns, B&B's and even B&B&Bs (bed, breakfast and barn) for people who want to travel with their own horse. The majority of her choices "are focused for families, with back-to-the-land activities and special events for children." Each entry clearly indicates where families are particularly welcome and whether there are discounts for kids and/or children's programs. Her fulsome descriptions and page-by-page four-color photos are so beguiling that they make you want to pack your bags and hit the trail. (Adventure Guides)

FIR MOUNTAIN RANCH
4051 Fir Mountain Road, Hood River, OR 97031
Phone/Fax: 541-354-2753

DESCRIPTION: Located at an altitude of 2,500 feet on the eastern ridge of the Hood River Valley, this 120-acre ranch is a B&B that boasts classic fireplaces and a wrap-around deck with sweeping views of Mt. Hood and the Cascades. Licensed outfitters Maria and Franz Brun describe their home, dating back to the 1890s, as "authentic arts and crafts," with old photos and written history readily at hand for guests to peruse. Its casual atmosphere and spacious living arrangements are "ideal for families with children and great for the outdoor enthusiast." It is this warm feeling that led us to put Fir Mountain Ranch in this chapter, as opposed to *Adventure Travel Companies.*

THE ADVENTURES: In addition to "adventurous" guided trail rides (kids must be 7 to ride their own horse; younger kids may be led on a lead rope and are not permitted to double up with parents), families may also indulge in river rafting, windsurfing, biking and hiking. Overnight trail rides, up to two weeks in length, are truly the Brun's specialty. Accommodation during these trips is in fully outfitted spacious tents with foam mattresses. A similar program is offered in Arizona from November through April. The minimum age for participating in these trips is 7.

FAMILY FEATURES: On the overnight rides, fresh gourmet-quality meals are brought into camp daily, so special food requests for a child with finicky tastes can easily be catered to. Small groups (six maximum) mean the pace can be adjusted as necessary. Washing facilities, warm showers and a toilet are available at the camps. There's always a passenger van in camp to take riders briefly back to civilization to catch a local rodeo or other festivity.

RATES: B&B rates are $80/night/room. Children under 3 are free; older children are charged $10 for an extra bed. If you stay seven nights, the last night is free. Trail rides begin at $165/adult/day. A one-week trip is $975, two weeks, $1,850 with no discounts offered to youngsters.

THE GROVE PARK INN RESORT
290 Macon Avenue, Asheville, NC 28804-3799
Phone: 800-438-5800/704-252-2711
Fax: 704-253-7053

DESCRIPTION: Built from boulders that were hewn from Sunset Mountain (upon which it perches) and hauled to the site by wagon trains, "The Inn" opened back in July of 1913 and has been listed on the National Register of Historic Places since 1973. The 510-room resort has successfully preserved its old-fashioned ambience and has remained open to guests year-round since 1984. Almost a third of the rooms are located in the historic Main Inn, the centerpiece of the 140-acre complex in the Blue Ridge Mountains located two miles from downtown Asheville. Guests have the option of dining at various restaurants, both formal and informal, most of which offer spectacular views of the surrounding mountains. When it's time to play, there's a choice of golf, indoor and outdoor tennis, indoor and outdoor swimming pools, aerobics, racquetball, squash and a fully-equipped sports center. Themed weekends are offered throughout the year from Halloween Weekend featuring *Wanda the Witch* to annual *Comedy Classic* and *Festival of Flowers* events. The Inn has two museums of historical interest on its grounds: the Homespun Museum and the Antique Car Museum. Christmas is a particularly enchanting time at the Grove Park Inn when the entire property is dressed up for the holiday with gingerbread houses and all.

THE ADVENTURES: There are two jogging trails on the property and bike rentals are offered at the Sports Center. The surrounding area abounds in adventure activities for the whole family. The Inn concierge can put you in touch with a number of operators or you can make your own arrangements in advance. Unless you are part of a group, you need to arrange for your own transportation to and from the hotel. and the off-property activity The Nantahala Outdoor Center (see page 68) is within easy driving distance. Southern Safari (800-454-7374) believes that "outdoor expeditions should be extraordinary" and can arrange for hiking, mountain biking, luxury camping excursions, llama trekking, whitewater rafting, nature hikes and more, just moments from the Inn. Whitewater enthusiasts with children over the age of 7 (for the French Broad River) or over 10 (for the Nolichucky River) should call Carolina Wilderness (800-872-7437) for half- or full-day trips while canoeists and rafters have a choice of quiet or white water with Southern Waterways (800-849-1970). Mark and Laura Moser of Avalon Llama Treks (704-299-7155) invite you to trek with them for a day or longer, or fly high in the sky on Mount Pisgah Balloons (704-667-9943) with David and Erma Woods. There are also a number of riding stables in the area.

FAMILY FEATURES: In addition to a Children's Playground (located between the Main Inn and the Sports Center) a fully-supervised day camp is offered for children ages 3 to 12. *Operation Kid-Nap* offers full- and half-day sessions daily May through Labor Day and Saturdays year-round. *Supper Club,* Monday to Thursday, is also seasonal and runs from 6 to 9 p.m. *Kids' Night Out* is offered every Friday and Saturday night throughout the year from 6 to 10 p.m. All are fee based. Activities run out of the children's playroom located at the indoor pool and pre-registration is recommended, though not required. A minimum of three children must enroll in order for the programs to operate. A number of activities are featured throughout the year for families to participate in together.

RATES: Children under age 16 are free when they're sharing with one or both parents. Rooms are rated *Value, Standard* and *Deluxe* with prices ranging from $75-$195/night depending upon season and selected accommodation. A Club Floor is open only to those 16 and older. A number of packages can include various meals and activities; surprisingly, the only family-oriented package is one for groups, requiring a minimum booking of five rooms.

HIGH HAMPTON INN & COUNTRY CLUB
P.O. Box 338, Cashiers, NC 28717-0338
Phone: 800-334-2551/704-743-2411
Fax: 704-743-5991

DESCRIPTION: Set amid 1,400 acres in the Blue Ridge Mountains of North Carolina, High Hampton Inn & Country Club has been owned by the McKee family for three generations. Families —who return here year after year singing its praises — can be assured they'll find the best of two worlds: a country inn with rustic accommodations, friendly, homespun ambience and regional cooking; and a carefree resort lifestyle with a full range of activities and facilities that "keep everyone happy from morning to night." The atmosphere at High Hampton is one of old-fashioned elegance, with jackets and ties de rigueur at dinner and rocking chairs gracing the Inn's three front porches. Most accommodations have no telephones or televisions and mixed drinks are only available between the hours of 6 and 10 p.m., and not in the dining room (though wine and beer are). As you might have guessed, afternoon tea is served daily.

"Not everyone will like High Hampton" says its brochure. Folks seeking luxury accommodations or casino/showtime evening entertainment will be disappointed. However, those who appreciate breathtaking scenery, enjoy meeting other people and value gracious hospitality will find High Hampton a special home away from home.

The main lodge of the Inn, with its four-sided lobby fireplace, is a hub of activity and home to the main dining room which serves three full meals a day. In addition to the Inn's 33 rooms, 19 cottages, all convenient to the Inn, have an additional 97 guest rooms with private baths. Many have porches and some feature living rooms. If you can't possibly live without phone or TV, ask about the privately-owned homes on the High Hampton estate. Guests who select these accommodations receive full Country Club privileges but meals at the Inn can be optional.

Listed on the National Register of Historic Places, High Hampton serves up abundant recreation. There's a children's play area, an exercise trail, a golf course with golf schools (more on these in **Great Sports Vacations With Your Kids**), six tennis courts, a private 35-acre lake, plus a gift shop and an art gallery. Various educational workshops from visiting artists are scheduled each year. High Hampton is open from April through November and has no service charge and a no-tipping policy.

THE ADVENTURES: There's no lack of outdoor adventure available. Many hiking trails for all abilities meander across the length and breadth of the estate and guided walks are scheduled weekly. The fitness trail is professionally designed. Lakeside sailing, canoeing and fishing are all convenient. There is a series of mountain bike trails throughout the property and guided bike treks are offered. Bring your own bike or rent one at the pro shop.

FAMILY FEATURES: High Hampton has been a family resort since its inception. Its highly regarded *Kid's Club* for ages 5 to 12 is offered daily from 9 a.m. to 2 p.m. and nightly from 6 to 9 p.m. and is run from the Noah's Ark playhouse, located across from the boathouse. *Play Group*, for the 2, 3, and 4-year-old age group operates from 9 a.m. to 2 p.m. Both programs, which cost $2/hour/child, include lunch. If your child does not take a nap, check the daily *Play Group* schedule as on some days there's a two-hour period devoted to lunch and nap time — much too long a "quiet" time for a child who would prefer more activity.

RATES: Inn and cottage rates are $72–93/adult/night, with children under 6 paying from $41–$51/night. Children 6 and older pay $52–58/night. Rates include room, private bath and all meals. On stays of seven nights or longer, there's a five percent discount. The privately owned two- to four-bedroom homes with daily maid service cost $196–$268/night and $1,128–$2,097/week. A three-meal-a-day plan costs an additional $33/person/day, $20/child under 6. Taxes are additional and there are modest charges for golfing and boating. Though pets are not permitted in the guest rooms, if you absolutely must bring yours along, there's a kennel on the premises. Parents of young children who want to give their children freedom of movement should request accommodations that do not require crossing a street to access the Inn.

THE HOMESTEAD
P.O. Box 2000, Hot Springs, VA 24445
Phone: 800-838-1766/540-839-1766
Fax: 540-839-7670

DESCRIPTION: Often called "America's Premier Mountain Resort," The Homestead is located in the Allegheny Mountains of Virginia and takes great pride in its combination of rich historic ambience and present-day elegance. Operated by Club Resorts, Inc. more than $17 million has recently been invested in property-wide renovations that include major restoration of its 103-year-old European-style spa. "Since 1766, The Homestead has offered its visitors an incomparable retreat and is a resort full of activity for your whole family — 15,000 acres of recreation and relaxation with as much to do — or as little — as you could possibly wish. We are your home in the mountains — on a grand scale." The list of activities is prodigious: swimming, tennis, canoeing, golf, horseback and carriage riding, skeet, trap and sporting clays, biking, fly-fishing, skiing, ice skating, bowling and, of course, The Homestead's renowned spa and hot springs.

The more than 520 guest rooms are large and spacious, easily accommodating a family of four. Suites are available for larger families. Dining possibilities rival its recreational fare with a dozen restaurants and bars available to guests. Room service dinners are even possible on the MAP packages. Several of the restaurants require jackets (and/or ties) in the evening. Afternoon tea is served daily in the Great Hall.

The active family will find themselves busy morning, noon and night with lots of time to enjoy activities together. Two outdoor pools are complemented by the newly refurbished spring-fed indoor pool and the indoor bowling lanes, movie theater and billiards room are favorite family spots.

THE ADVENTURES: Virginia Outdoor Adventures maintains an operation at The Homestead from May through October, offering guided or unguided mountain biking, hikes to the Warm Springs and canoe excursions. Biking and canoeing tours welcome kids from age 3 when accompanied by an adult. Teens may go without parents but need written permission to do so. The bike equipment rentals include child trailer/joggers and trail-a-bikes. There's also trout fishing in a three-mile long stream, an equestrian center, and more than 100 maintained miles of scenic walking/hiking trails on the property. The *KidsClub* features many active, outdoor events.

FAMILY FEATURES: As one would expect from a resort of this caliber, The Homestead has a number of family-friendly amenities, not the least of which being no charge for cots or cribs in the rooms. *KidsClub* is offered daily, year-round for children 3 (potty-trained) to 12 and runs from 9 a.m. to 4 p.m. except on Sunday when it ends at 1 p.m. Seasonally a dinner club is offered from 6 to 11 p.m. several times a week. All of the sessions are fee-based. The program is operated under the direction of the Curry School of Education from the University of Virginia and is designed to "appeal to kids' interest, understanding and sense of adventure based on their developmental level." The resort's *Ultimate Family Vacation* package includes registration for all kids in the Club.

RATES: All of this is not cheap, but for active families the *Ultimate Family Vacation* summer package (from mid-April to early November) can offer good value. Priced at $695/family-of-four/night (three night minimum) it includes accommodations (with suite upgrade if available), three meals/person/day, *KidsClub*, unlimited golf (with a cart) and tennis, a family horseback or carriage ride, unlimited use of the shooting club (ammunition extra), unlimited bowling, mountain biking, fly-fishing, canoeing, one spa therapy for each adult, guided nature and historic tours plus service charges and taxes.

A less expensive MAP package for a family of four, without many of the above features but including *KidsClub*, ranges in price from $153–206/weekday night, $178–$231/weekend night per person. Children under 18 are free (maximum four per room) and an adjoining room for children is $120/night. A 15 percent service charge and a four-and-a-half percent state tax is additional. Nightly MAP rates begin at $117/adult in a standard room and go as high as $909/adult in a two-bedroom suite. Children under 4/free, ages 5 to 12/$29, 13 to 18/$50. Service and tax is additional.

LEON HARREL'S OLD WEST ADVENTURE
1120 Spur 100, Kerrville, TX 78028
Phone: 210-896-8802
Fax: 210-792-4292

DESCRIPTION: A visit to the Harrel family ranch, just 60 miles from the city of San Antonio, is unique — definitely not one you're likely to have at a resort-style ranch. This is the place where professional horse cutter Leon Harrel promises you one of the most exciting times in your life — the opportunity to become a cowboy by participating in *Cowboy Camp.* Guests in this program bunk down over at the Y.O. Holiday Inn Hotel (a different property from the Y.O. Ranch described on page 124. This is a ranch-style hotel near the Harrel ranch) and take all meals out on the ranch range — hearty breakfasts, lunches and dinners served from a cookshack located next to a chuckwagon that was actually used in cattle drives in the 1800s. Two-, three- and five-day camps are offered.

THE ADVENTURES: Harrel's aims to get guests to understand who the cowboy is, what his skills are and how to implement these skills. Instruction of all sorts is given — from catching your horse to saddling, mounting, bathing and grooming — in addition to basic riding techniques needed for the program. You'll learn how to round up cattle, sort and pen them, even the master art of "cutting" or separating individuals from the herd. At the end of your visit, there's a *Ranch Rodeo Competition* day that's great fun for all. Days are a combination of work and play — becoming familiar with and practicing cowboy skills plus lots of recreational time in the saddle. We're ready to sign on anytime! Check out their video of the adventure (you have to promise to return it), and we think you'll be ready to do the same.

FAMILY FEATURES: The Harrels prefer that children be at least 9 years old but, if they have enough families at one time with younger children, they would be happy to arrange for a babysitter to offer non-riding activities just for them. It is always easy to secure babysitters. Kids are taken out on the range to meet up with parents at mealtimes and for evening entertainment.

RATES: Special, greatly reduced family rates (for those with children between the ages of 9 and 15) are as follows: five days/six nights: $3,600/ two adults, one child; $4,200/two adults, two children. Three days/three nights: $2,000/two adults, one child; $2,400/two adults, two children. Two days/three nights: $1,200/two adults, one child; $1350/two adults/two children. Single parents should ask about special prices.

BOOKED FOR TRAVEL

LET'S RODEO!, by Charles Coombs, goes behind the scenes of this quintessential Western American entertainment. Entries on bareback riding, calf roping, steer wrestling, cowgirls and more will fascinate and educate young readers. (Henry Holt)

LOCH LYME LODGE & COTTAGES
70 Orford Road, Lyme, NH 03768
Phone: 800-423-2141/603-795-2141

DESCRIPTION: The 50th anniversary of family ownership is being celebrated by Loch Lyme Lodge, where families have been the mainstay of its business for more than 70 years, enjoying casual, relaxing, inexpensive vacations. "We're a rustic vacation spot —no telephones, no televisions, simple furnishings, no wall-to-wall carpeting, no video arcade, no hot tubs, no microwaves and no bar with nightly entertainment." What Loch Lyme does have is 135 acres of fields and woodlands to explore, fresh air and clean water, a private lakeside location and "an emphasis on family fun."

There are four double rooms at the lodge and 24 one- to four-bedroom cottages to choose from. During the winter months, only the lodge rooms are open to guests. The summer cottages are located on a hillside overlooking Post Pond and each has a private bath, fireplace and living room; some have kitchen facilities and outdoor grills for those who prefer to prepare their own meals. For guests in these "housekeeping" cabins, meals may be purchased separately at the Lodge.

For guests on the B&B or MAP programs, meals are taken in an informal dining room, each family at its own table with the requisite high chairs or boosters readily available. Though there's no children's menu, entrees are chosen "with children in mind and can be tailored to a youngster's taste." Breakfast is served family-style on the sunporch.

Adirondack chairs are set along the lawn facing the lake and the recreational pleasures are plentiful. The swimming area at the beach has a sandy bottom and a raft. A separate cottage, Playwood, is where guests head for equipment for badminton, to play pingpong, read by the fireplace, watch a video or play with young kids on Little Tykes playground equipment. There are two clay tennis courts and guests are entitled to use the town facilities as well. A baseball field, soccer net, horseshoes and basketball court are all appreciated and well-used. Kids can often be found jumping off the float in the lake and particularly like the picnic tables where light lunches can be served. Rates can include breakfast, breakfast and dinner or no meals at all. Early risers are invited to come to the kitchen for a cup of coffee or cup of juice. Babysitting can be arranged starting at $5/hour. A particularly thoughtful insert in the guest information folder found in the rooms includes articles on summer safety in the playground, at the beach, near the water and in the house. Present owners, Judy and Paul Barker, are parents of two boys and they are very attuned to the needs of families and extremely knowledgeable about which local attractions kids most enjoy.

The staff is an eclectic mix of European students, and guests are encouraged to invite off-duty staff to join them on outings as a way of showing them both the area and the American way of life.

THE ADVENTURES: Adventure begins at the waterfront, where boats, kayaks, canoes, a paddleboat and a windsurfer (ages 16 and older only, instruction available) are available to guests at no additional charge. Life jackets, which are required, are supplied by Loch Lyme. There is a hiking trail on the property and several longer trails close by. The Barkers steer guests to the hiking trails at the Montshire Museum of Science in nearby Norwich, Vermont. Similarly, horseback enthusiasts are asked to contact Kedron Valley Stables in South Woodstock, Vermont. Fishing is popular so don't forget your fishing tackle. Bait and licenses (required for ages 12 and older) can be purchased in town. In winter, the focus is on cross-country skiing, snowshoeing and sledding.

FAMILY FEATURES: Though there are no special activities planned just for children, families thoroughly enjoy their visits here. Dartmouth College in Hanover with its rich cultural life is a short drive away. Cribs, junior-sized beds and refrigerators are available ($6/stay).

RATES: Summer B&B rates begin at $32/adult/night in the lodge, $43/adult/night in a one-bedroom cabin. A two-bedroom cabin for two adults and two children between the ages of 5 and 15 costs $156/night, $988.50/week. MAP rates which include breakfast and dinner for the same family in the same accommodation would be $1,126. State tax and the suggested staff gratuity is additional. Inquire about pre-season June discounts and winter rates.

MONTECITO-SEQUOIA LODGE
1485 Redwood Drive, Los Altos, CA 94024
Phone: 209-565-3388
Reservations: 800-227-9900/415-997-8612
Fax: 415-967-0540

DESCRIPTION: Located on 42 acres at a 7,500 foot elevation on Lake Homavalo between Sequoia and King's Canyon National Forests, Montecito-Sequoia Lodge promises "A Great Family Adventure" at its one-of-a-kind *High Sierra Vacation Camp*. During both summer and winter seasons, extensive family programs are in operation. In fall and spring, the Lodge offers a splendid country getaway.

With such an awesome roster of activities, guests feel as if they've gone back to summer camp — with their kids in tow. Accommodations are either in the 13 rustic cabins that sleep three to eight people, each of which are basically furnished with either a king or queen bed, with bedding supplied, and bunk beds, for which you provide sleeping bags. The cabins are not outfitted with private baths or running water, but a bathhouse is nearby. The lodge rooms, which do have private baths, have similar sleeping arrangements. There are no telephones, televisions, radios or air-conditioning in any of the rooms and guests staying in cabins must bring their own towels. Limited maid service is provided once during the week in the lodge rooms.

On the other hand, if you're sociable and physically active, with a yen to take part in any number of outdoor activities with like-minded folk — all of whom bring along their kids — you'll have a great time here. In addition to the "real" adventures listed below, you'll also find waterskiing, paddleboarding, tennis, swimming, volleyball, trampoline, fencing and arts and crafts, plus an interesting *Artist of the Week in Residence* program. There are a heated pool, a 10-jet spa, rifle and archery ranges and a stable.

Buffet meals feature lots of fresh fruits and vegetables, with trail lunches provided for those on day-long excursions. There's also a 24-hour hospitality bar with coffee, fruit, juice and snacks.

There is no longer a supervised activity program for infants to 23-month-olds but there is a separate area for this age group where parents and babies can play.

THE ADVENTURES: Canoeing, sailing, stream fishing, hiking and horseback riding are all possible. A natural rock slide at Stony Creek is a popular outing and an extensive array of guided nature walks and hikes are featured each week, as are overnights. There are two naturalists on staff. Each day, after breakfast, adults and children can participate in two peer-group activity periods; two more are offered each afternoon. Families can choose to spend as much or as little time together as they like.

The winter program, with its focus on cross-country skiing, snowshoeing and skating, is not quite as extensive as the summer one. During holiday periods supervised one-and-one-half-hour activity periods are offered each morning and afternoon for ages 4 and older and are included in the rate. Additional babysitting is possible for $8/child/one-and-one-half hours, $5/each additional child in the same family. During non-holiday times, youngsters in the same age group are charged $5/hour-long activity ($3/sibling). Younger children who do not cross-country ski enjoy a variety of fare from snowball tosses to an eclectic sampling of arts and crafts. Guests' autos are escorted to the Lodge with the lodge's 4x4 vehicle from the park gate. Lessons and equipment for all ages are included in the many of the winter packages.

FAMILY FEATURES: The programs are designed to strike a nice balance of kids-together/family-together time. Programs are divided as follows: *Minnows* (age 2), *Tadpoles* (3 to 4), *Chipmunks* (5 to 6) *Marmots* (7 to 9) *Cougars* (10 to 12), *Bears* (13 to 18), *KILTS, Kampers in Leadership Training* (14 to 18) and *Adults* (19 and older). *Guppies*, from 6 to 23 months, are welcome in what is called the *Primary Area* when accompanied by a parent, teenager or responsible adult. Be forewarned that while babysitters are available during mealtimes and in the evening, the Lodge cannot secure babysitting during the activity hours.

Before dinner it's *Family Time* in the Sports Arena, with volleyball, horseshoes, tennis, basketball and pingpong. Counselors help coordinate this activity period so they are not on hand to supervise kids. Evening programs are for the entire family to enjoy together. Laundry service is available each Wednesday for a nominal fee.

RATES: Prices include all meals and most activities. Gratuities (which are not added on to the bill) are encouraged upon departure and are shared by the staff members, many of whom depend on these tips as part of their salary. Week-long (Sunday to Saturday) and mini-week (four days, limited availability in high season) packages are offered. Riding and waterskiing cost extra. Weekly rates in cabins are about $595/adult, $565/ages 13–17, $535/2–12 and $95/infants. Rates in the lodge rooms are slightly higher and different configurations are possible, including a second room for kids. *Winter Holiday Rates* range from $267/adult/cabin to $342/adult/lodge room for three days. A five-night ski week costs $276/adult/cabin, $356/adult/lodge. Youth rates are offered for children from age 2.

PINEGROVE DUDE RANCH
Lower Cherrytown Road, Kerhonkson, NY 12446
Phone: 800-346-4626/914-626-7345
Fax: 800-367-3237/914-626-7365

DESCRIPTION: Nestled in the Catskill Mountains, just under a three hour drive from New York City, Pinegrove Dude Ranch offers a unique western ranch experience east of the Mississippi. We've been visiting with our kids for almost ten years, during which time this incredibly family-friendly property has continuously upgraded its facilities and programs. Owned and personally operated by Dick and Debbie Tarantino and their families, we know of nowhere more welcoming to parents traveling with children — and the kids sense this immediately. Pinegrove is not a quiet getaway spot, but rather, a bustling and active full-fledged vacation destination, attracting, for the most part, an eclectic group of families. Accommodations, while not luxurious, are more than adequate and prices are all-inclusive.

The roster of indoor and outdoor facilities is mind-boggling. In warm weather, horseshoe pitching, badminton, basketball, boating, fishing, nature hikes, golf, archery and skeet shooting are on tap, while winter snows bring a small downhill ski slope, cross-country skiing and night snow tubing. Lessons and equipment are available.

Need more? Check out the teepee village, the indoor and outdoor pools, miniature golf, bocce, pingpong, hayrides, the children's playground, the baby animal farm, campfire marshmallow roasts, etc., etc., etc. Even massage therapy is offered.

Of course, there's year-round horseback riding with several daily trail rides for adults and children age 7 and over plus pony rides for the younger kids. Riding instruction sessions are also scheduled for both adults and kids. The *Jr. Wrangler Instructional Rides* are designed specifically for kids ages 5 to 7. During our last visit, one of the teenagers with us who'd taken riding lessons as a child, swore he learned more in his one lesson here than in all of his years of instruction at home!

Three all-you-can-eat meals daily are supplemented by free hot dogs, burgers and fries from the lobby chuckwagon (10 a.m. to midnight), plus daily evening cocktail parties. A full activity schedule changes daily, and evening entertainment invites the participation of the entire family.

THE ADVENTURES: In addition to all of the above, Pinegrove features a *City Slicker Cattle Drive*, intended to give you a "taste of what it was like in the old West." We've participated in one of these and enjoyed it tremendously, learning that it's not the ability to lope (or gallop) that's important, but to have control over your horse (rather than vice versa), as the drive is primarily a slow-movement exercise. The almost two-hour adventure is one you're certain to remember for years to come. While not out on the range, indoor steer-roping lessons are offered in the lobby to both kids and adults and cattle-calling sessions are also on the weekly agenda. Young children will find the cow-milking just the right-sized adventure.

FAMILY FEATURES: L'il Maverick Day Camp and the *Belle Star Nursery* accommodate kids of all ages from 10 a.m. to 1 p.m. and again from 2 to 5 p.m. One-on-one care is offered for the youngest children (under age 3 or still in diapers) while older kids' (ages 3 to 11 and teens) activities range from a variety of indoor fare such as arts and crafts, story time and swimming in the indoor pool to playground time, hay rides, pony rides, feeding and petting the baby animals, outdoor games and swimming. Private babysitters and an evening night patrol are also offered. Kids are welcome to join with parents in almost all activities. Bingo games, family scavenger hunts, Native American legend-telling, square dancing, karaoke and riding demonstrations are among the offerings parents enjoy sharing with their children.

RATES: Daily summer rates begin at $125/adult/night in a room with two double beds and go as high as $675/adult/seven nights-eight days in a one- to three-bedroom country cottage. Children ages 4 to 16 pay 50 percent of the adult rate when sharing with two adults. Single parents pay the adult rate for themselves, 75 percent for the first child and 50 percent for additional children. Children under 4 are free. A *Family of Three* package is $999/six days and five nights and runs from mid-June through July and again at the end of August. Holiday weekends carry a $5/night surcharge. There is an additional $25/person charge for the *Cattle Drives*.

BOOKED FOR TRAVEL

In **RANCH VACATIONS**, Gene Kilgore writes not only of ranches where you can ride, but also about ranches with fly-fishing, cross-country skiing and other eclectic adventures. Kilgore gives readers plenty of background and data, including a full run-down of what's offered for kids. At the end of the book are handy listings of *Special Ranch Features*, a *Calendar of Annual Western Events* by state, and more. The format is especially nice, and lets you can see at a glance whether or not there are children's programs, how many guests are accepted, and the general price range. Another plus are the many pages of color photos. (John Muir Publications)

SCOTT VALLEY RESORT & GUEST RANCH
P.O. Box 1447-GWAK, Mountain Home, AR 72653
Phone: 501-425-5136
Fax: 501-424-5800

DESCRIPTION: Located in the midst of the Ozarks, Scott Valley Ranch is set among 275 acres of meadows, streams, rocky cliffs and woodlands and is open to guests from March through November. In business for over 40 years, the owners Tom and Kathleen Cooper live on the ranch ensuring "each and every guest a happy, memorable and comfortable visit." The Coopers have packages to meet everyone's needs, from single parents to non-horse enthusiasts and would-be ecotourists. Among the facilities are a heated swimming pool, a whirlpool spa, tennis court, playground, hiking trails and more. Two nearby 18-hole golf courses are available for ranch guests. Trail rides depart at least four to five times each day in three different categories. Nightly activities operate during the summer months and feature hayrides, cookouts and ferry tours with dinner on Lake Norfolk.

Guests are accommodated in simple, motel-like rooms with more than half of the 28 rooms able to fit up to six persons comfortably. Each has a private bath and a ground floor location.

THE ADVENTURES: In addition to the mountain trail rides (guaranteed to "take your breath away") horseback rides are offered daily. The Coopers raise their own horses and specialize in Missouri Foxtrotters. Hiking trails, canoe trips through scenic river gorges and local cave explorations are among the daily options. World-class trout fishing on the White or North Fork Rivers is moments away and the Coopers provide boats, pack lunches and, for an additional charge, arrange for guided fly- or float-fishing trips.

FAMILY FEATURES: Though no special children's programs other than its "outstanding riding program" are featured, Scott Valley describes itself as the "ideal family experience," one in which "parent and children spend time together learning how to interact." However, for time off from your toddler or teenager, the Coopers can arrange for child care or an energetic ranch activity while parents enjoy some free time. A full playground and a petting zoo are favorite spots for kids, who also delight in the evening hayrides and cookouts. Teens love the recreation room and the overnight trip or they can head for Lake Norfolk for adventurous jet-skiing or sailing experiences. There's no minimum age for riding and youngsters can ride double with their parents.

RATES: Weekly rates range from $560/adult/spring and fall to $650/summer. Children 7 to 12 pay $450 and $530 respectively, ages 2 to 6, $285 and $340. Under age 2 are free. Nightly rates are also offered. There is a 10 percent discount for four or more people sharing the same unit. Prices include lodging, three meals/day, all recreation on the ranch including riding, complimentary boats and canoes on the White and North Fork Rivers (both off-property). A five percent gratuity and seven and a half percent sales tax are additional.

SUNRIVER RESORT
P.O. Box 3609, Sunriver, OR 97707
Phone: 800-547-3922/503-593-1000
Fax: 503-593-5458

DESCRIPTION: Considered one of the Northwest's premier family destinations, Sunriver, though known for it extensive golfing facilities, offers families much, much more — horseback riding, rafting on the Deschutes River, and boating, to name just a few examples. Located at the foot of the Cascades, 15 miles from Bend in the center of the state, it is said that the area has more than 275 days of sunshine a year, making it an outdoor lover's paradise.

There's a wide choice of accommodations at the 3,300 acre year-round resort: 211 guest rooms and suites in the Lodge or more than 200 condominiums and hundreds of private homes, all of which feature stone fireplaces and full kitchens. Suites also have kitchenettes plus loft bedrooms. There are three restaurants located in the Lodge itself, one serving gourmet continental cuisine, the others lighter fare. Minutes away in the resort's commercial center are a dozen more eateries. The resort, with the Lodge as its focal point, was planned as a residential community where "man and nature can strike a deep and resonant chord of harmony." Today, it considers itself more a mountain retreat than a resort, where "the scenery is always spectacular, the hospitality unforgettable and the recreation opportunities endless." From tennis and basketball courts to a full-service marina and playground, plus a number of indoor and outdoor swimming pools and the aforementioned world-class golf, Sunriver appears to have surpassed its original goals.

THE ADVENTURES: Available on-site are horseback riding, more than 30 miles of paved bicycle trails (with rentals at the Bike Shop, including kids' bikes, child trailers and mountain bikes), whitewater rafting, fishing and canoeing. Sunriver High Adventures offers challenge ropes and orienteering courses (and family discounts). Pacific Crest Mountain Bike Tours and High Cascade Descent both offer a variety of guided cycling trips. Deschutes River Outfitters has fly-casting lessons plus a number of guided lake or river trips. Sunriver Nature Center has regular nature walks (some just for kids, some for the entire family) and stargazing evenings, plus raft trips on the Deschutes River in conjunction with Sun Country Tours which operates the half- and full-day "family oriented whitewater rafting" trips for the resort from the marina. Wanderlust Tours handles the hiking programs while the canoe and kayak trips are taken care of by the folks who run the marina.

Wanderlust Tours continues to offer exciting outings in winter, including snowshoe excursions and wilderness camping, a choice of nature tours and hiking trips, several of which explore large lava fields, remnants from volcanic eruptions. The resort stables are also open year-round. Nearby, *The High Desert Museum* schedules family outings.

FAMILY FEATURES: If you're dazzled by the choices of adult and family-together fare, wait until you see the far-ranging selection for kids. *Kids Klub* is now comfortably ensconced in its new home next to the Bike Shop and during the summer season offers organized fare for children between the ages of 3 and 10 in both the day and evening. The center is called a "frontier dream come true with authentic Native American teepees and nomadic yurt." The *Youth Adventure Academy, YAA*, is an active, outdoors-oriented programs for youngsters from 10 to 14. *Pedal, Paddle, & Fish, Hike & Bike* and *Excursions & Explorations* are among the themes of YAA. For little ones, babysitting can be arranged.

In winter, *Kids Klub* continues with up to three sessions offered each day. Over holiday periods, kids have the opportunity to be tucked into bed by one of Santa's elves, teens enjoy their own New Year's party, and the entire family is invited to head for the resort's ice-skating rink for day or evening family fun. YAA operates on an as needed basis during the winter months. Daycare for little ones is available at Mt. Bachelor, 18 miles from Sunriver. Transportation to and from the ski area is not provided by the resort.

RATES: All prices are based per unit, not per person. Lodge Village guest rooms accommodating a maximum of three persons range in price per night from $89 to $130/May to October, from $79 to $89/November to April. A Lodge Village suite, accommodating up to six persons, costs $145 to $185/May to October, $119 to $145/November to April. A two-bedroom condominium, with maximum occupancy of six persons, costs $184 to $190/May to October, $130 to $162/November to April. Holiday rates are higher.

THE TYLER PLACE
Box 1, Old Dock Road, Highgate Springs, VT 05640
Telephone: 802-868-4000
Fax: 802-868-7602

DESCRIPTION: We never seem to find enough kind words for The Tyler Place where we, along with other lucky families who have by now become good friends, return the same week year after year to this 165-acre haven for active families on Lake Champlain. Mrs. Tyler, who developed and managed the property for more than 40 years, passed away in 1996 and leaves behind a legacy that more than fulfills her original goal: to create a family resort that not only caters to the needs of children but where the atmosphere allows the romance of marriage to be rekindled. In her words, "The magic of The Tyler Place is having opportunities to recharge as a couple, with the peace of mind and pleasure that comes from sharing a vacation with your children. For children, the Tyler Place *is* magic."

We couldn't agree more, nor could our kids, to whom a vacation at The Tyler Place is synonymous with "the best family vacation ever." In fact, they love Tyler Place so much that one year when they were bickering during the six-hour drive and we pulled off the road for a 15-minute time out, they were so distressed at being "late" they managed to refrain from sibling strife for the remainder of the trip!

Guests stay in a choice of fireplace cottages (of which there are 27), at the Inn or in several lodges with family-sized suites. All of the attractively decorated simple accommodations feature king or queen beds in the air-conditioned master bedroom and separate bedroom(s) for children. Those lodgings which have kitchens are also equipped with microwave ovens. Each family has its own preference. We particularly like the cottages located between the pools and the boat dock; friends of ours wouldn't consider staying any place other than the Inn since they can let their kids go to their groups on their own. There are no TVs, telephones or radios in any of the rooms. Guests' messages are posted on the Inn's information board as they come in and there are two TV rooms at the

Inn. There are indoor and outdoor pool complexes and dozens of activities with separate programs for kids (divided into eight categories).

As for the food, suffice it to say that we all gain weight, in spite of our high level of activity. With one adult vegetarian, one youngster with a delicate digestion, one picky eater (and another adult who eats everything), we all love the served buffet-style meals, with its wide range of selections. There are always lots of fresh fruit and veggies and, of course, Ben & Jerry's ice cream for dessert.

One of the resort's finest qualities, however, is its staff, beginning with the Tyler family. Each year we meet more members of this interesting, eclectic clan, the newest being Mrs. T's grandson and his wife from Australia, who spent the summer in Vermont before heading to make their mark in Hollywood (they were both accomplished performers Down Under). Even non-family staff members return year after year. There is a unique sense of camaraderie that evolves during one's visit to the Tyler Place. Our sons can't wait to be juniors at college so they can apply for a position here, and they don't care what they do (with the exception of housekeeping). Guests regularly come from as far as California and as close as Burlington, and you're just as likely to meet salesmen or women physicians as teachers or lawyers. While not all families are comprised of two working parents, a fair number are. There are relatively few single-parent families and a limited number of multigenerational groups, though both are warmly welcomed.

Before going on to the resort's specific offerings, it's important to understand the basic structure that has been at the core of TP's success. Each morning (with the exception of those who opt for "family breakfast") kids meet in their groups and stay together until after lunch. While the kids enjoy a wide range of camp-type activities, a full roster of adult activities is offered, from guided canoe trips and mountain bike tours to tennis round robins and water aerobics. After lunch (family lunch is also a possibility), at 1:30, it's family time and each afternoon features at least one activity that families can participate in together. Kids meet up with their groups again at 5:30 for dinner and an evening activity. The older the child, the later the evening activity ends. An unbelievable choice of rainy day fare is offered at those times when the weather doesn't cooperate. Our visits have all been different weather-wise. The first year we had a mix, the next it was sunny and gorgeous every day, another it rained every day. Yet, weather has never been a factor when it comes to planning our return visit.

THE ADVENTURES: With its location on Lake Champlain, it's no wonder that sailing, windsurfing, kayaking and canoeing are all popular. With the exception of water skiing, free instruction and unlimited use of watercraft are included in the weekly price. Guided canoe and kayak trips are offered several times a week and self-guided trips are always possible. If you're a water rat, you can't go wrong. Some weeks, fly-fishing clinics are offered by a local guide and instructor, as are hikes with noted local naturalist Doug Flack. Family hikes that search out local caves and cemeteries are great fun. A fleet of one-speed bikes is maintained at the Bike Shed. Guests can select one and use it for the entire week at no additional charge. Kids' bikes (including tricycles), baby seats and helmets are also provided. Mountain bikes are included during the guided excursions (several are featured each week) and are available for a modest charge if you want to take one out on your own. Lest the weekly schedule not offer enough activity, *The Tyler Place and Beyond* . . . booklet that guests receive upon check-in describes a number of do-it-yourself bike routes and hiking trails, farms to visit (including several working dairy farms), eleven listings for Parks & Outdoor Entertainment plus a number of interesting side trips into neighboring Canada, just three miles north.

FAMILY FEATURES: The extensive kids' programs begin officially at age 2 1/2 and are broken up into groups that span anywhere from a six-month to two year age difference. Additionally, parents are encouraged to bring babies and young toddlers. One-on-one parents' helps are organized for little ones, and during the resort's early and late season a morning *Toddler Program* operates. A nice touch if your child isn't feeling well is that the front desk will arrange for a sitter for little kids or "game-playing companion for older children" for which they pick up the cost during the time children would have been with his or her group.

Our kids are in heaven here. When they're not on bikes, at the basketball court, swimming in the pool or schmoozing with friends, they manage to find some time to spend with us. The weekly softball game is always fun and we never miss the opportunity to join *Ted's Treasure Hunt*. David plans as many tennis hours as he can and I sign up for as many massages as reasonable. The first day of our stay the boys head for Martins Store at the end of the road and stock up on snacks for the week. Martins is also well known for its fishing trips and is the place that anyone over 14 needs to go for a fishing license. Every year we say we'll spend a day in Montreal. We haven't made it yet. Maybe next year.

RATES: Prices range from $110 to $174/night/adult, $45 to $64/ages 2-1/2 to 5, $48 to $68/ages 6 to 10, $52 to $74/ages 11 to 16 and include all meals and most activities.

BOOKED FOR TRAVEL

THE VERMONT OUTDOOR ADVENTURE GUIDE by Flip Brown is one of the best-organized books we've come across. Chapters appear alphabetically by adventure, and each adventure is rated by icons on a scale of one to five in the following categories: Cost Factor, Potential Thrills, Immersion in Nature, Fitness Level, Crowd Factor, and Family Friendly. Mixed in with the anticipated chapters on canoeing, downhill skiing, and hiking and backpacking, etc., are a few surprises. Did you realize there is good scuba diving in Vermont? Lake Champlain has numerous historic wrecks and Lake Willoughby is known for its underwater rock cliffs. Other out-of-the-ordinary adventures include ice sailing, speed skating and sculling. Names, addresses and phone numbers of sources and resources appear at the end of each chapter — it's a breeze to use. (Northern Cartographic)

VISTA VERDE RANCH

P.O. Box 465, Steamboat Springs, CO 80477
Phone: 800-526-7433/970-879-3858
Fax: 970-879-1413

DESCRIPTION: Suzanne and John Munn invite families to experience personalized attention and a warm friendly atmosphere at their "high mountain hideaway, an upscale ranch — not a resort." This working cattle ranch, located at 7,800 feet 25 miles from Steamboat Springs, is home to more than 60 horses, 80 cattle, and lots of farm animals for children to visit, pet and tend.

Up to 30 guests, including children, stay either in spacious lodge rooms with balconies or in cabins with rustic-looking exteriors. The interiors have recently been enlarged to create a master suite for parents and a separate bath for the kids. The cabins also have wood stoves and some even have private hot tubs. Meals, with a gourmet menu that features healthy choices for nutrition-conscious adults and special dishes for children, are taken in a new lodge, and another building boasts an espresso machine and coffee bar, plus a game room for the kids. A spa facility with a sauna, outdoor hot tubs and exercise room is popular with young and old alike. The ranch's vans transport guests into Steamboat Springs for the rodeo, raft trips, hot springs visits and swims, shopping, kayaking and more.

THE ADVENTURES: John Munn believes that Vista Verde's program is "the most varied in the industry with cattle drives, rock climbing, river rafting, hot-air ballooning, as well as customary horseback riding" on the weekly agenda. Kayaking, hiking in the adjoining Zirkel Wilderness area, fly-fishing, and mountain biking are also possible. *Cattle Drive* weeks take place at the end of May and again during the middle of September. Overnight guided *Pack Trips* head for local wilderness areas where guests rough it "Vista Verde style" — with just the amount of comfort guests expect.

Kid-sized adventures include gold panning, campouts and hiking, though families are encouraged to participate together in many of the featured adventures.

During the autumn months five-day/six-night elk-hunting packages are offered as are five- or seven-night fly-fishing adventures. When the winter snows fall at Vista Verde, the ranch offers guided backcountry tours for novices and the experienced alike on the ranch's groomed cross-country trails, hills and adjoining wilderness. Snowshoeing, luging and winter horseback riding round out the cold weather fun. For an additional fee, Vista Verde can arrange half-day dog sled trips, ice-climbing instruction, snowmobiling and snowcat skiing.

FAMILY FEATURES: The Munns are extremely proud of the ranch's strong children's program, which is "structured to allow youngsters time together as well as sufficient time to spend with their parents when they can ride, rock climb, raft, etc. as a family." Readers of our newsletter, **Family Travel Times®**, have been singing the praises of Vista Verde for the past several years. The seclusion of the ranch setting allows parents to give children unique freedom of movement, something all of us are pleased to be able to do in this day and age.

RATES: The ranch is open from June to October and mid-December to mid-March and is best suited for children 5 years and older (though younger children are accepted). Sunday to Sunday summer rates are either $1,595 or $1,395/adult and $1,095 or $995/child under 12 depending on date. Transfers to/from Yampa Valley Regional Airport in Hayden are included. Winter rates are nightly and begin at about $200/night/adult, $100/child with rates higher over the Christmas/New Year's period. Of the activities above, only ballooning costs extra.

WHITNEYS' INN
P.O. Box 822, Jackson, NH 03846-0822
Phone: 800-677-5737/603-383-8916

DESCRIPTION: Located in the White Mountains of New Hampshire, at the base of Black Mountain and less than two miles from Jackson Village, Whitneys' Inn has been operating since 1936. Best known as a cross-country ski destination, the town of Jackson boasts an unusual number of legendary Nordic skiers. Guests at the Inn can start skiing the moment they walk out the back door, where 150 kilometers of trails that comprise the Jackson Ski Touring Foundation await. However, Bill and Betty Whitney originally purchased the Inn specifically because of the "hill" (Black Mountain) behind the farmhouse. Named the "Best Eastern Slope Family Resort" by the *New England Travel Guide*, there are 29 guest rooms in the Main Inn, two cottages and a chalet building with a number of family suites, all of which have private baths. The restaurant serves American cuisine with an emphasis on classic New England fare; a summer highlight is its weekly pondside lobster bake and hayrides.

THE ADVENTURES: In addition to the cross-country and Alpine skiing options which abound (the Inn is within easy striking distance of Attitash Bear Creek, Cranmore and Wildcat Mountains), the Inn has a backyard skating rink and a tube run on Black Mountain's Whitney Hill. In summer, there's paddleboating plus a number of hiking trails on Black Mountain, where a petting zoo is a perennial family favorite.

Nearby, guests can hike with the Appalachian Mountain Club at its Pinkham Notch Center (ask about its family hikes, 603-466-2721), canoe or kayak along the Saco River with Saco Bound in Center Conway (603-447-2177), learn rock climbing at the Cranmore Sports Center (603-356-6301) or fish in the many surrounding ponds, rivers and streams. A number of easy biking and mountain biking trails are moments away in the town of Jackson where, at Nestlenook Farms Recreation Center, kids can feed reindeer in the woods during the winter months. Kids 11 and older with their parents can join an Off Road Cycling Adventure in North Conway (603-356-2080) and Echo Lake State Park (603-356-2672) has a number of hiking trails that are ideal for families with young children. Tuckerman's Ravine and Mount Washington are extremely popular year-round. For more adventures in the area, see the section on Attitash Bear Peak on page 128.

FAMILY FEATURES: In addition to a warm welcome for kids, the Inn activity director organizes a number of children's activities each Monday, Wednesday and Friday morning (9:30 a.m. to 12:30 p.m., $5/child) during the summer for kids 5 and older. Tennis, badminton, swimming, whiffleball, arts and crafts and nature hikes are among the fair weather activities, some of which the kids choose themselves. Babysitting is possible for younger children; though it is not mandatory to make arrangements in advance, it is recommended. Also during the summer and on holiday weeks and weekends throughout the year (or whenever there are a sufficient number of children), the Inn hosts a children's dinner table (kids eat at 5:30 and can be supervised until approximately 8:15), though they are always welcome to dine with their parents. If they do, "the waitstaff is trained to ask if they would like the children's entrees served as soon as they are cooked or if they would like to all eat together."

Kids who decide to wait can play a game, watch a movie or even go outdoors and ice skate. A game room is located in a separate building, the Shovel Handle, where there's also pingpong, a TV and VCR with free movies, games and puzzles. Open until 10 p.m., the building also has an après-ski pub that serves light lunches, and has a pool table, video games and a juke box. From April through Labor Day, children 12 and under staying in the *Family Suites* in the Chalet building stay and eat free off of the Inn's children's menu.

In winter the Inn continues its children's dinner table but, because so many ski school and nursery programs for children operate so close by, there are no in-house daytime activities for children. Whitneys' tells us that they're finding that "parents who learned to ski at Black Mountain are now bringing their children to learn here." Celebrating its 60th anniversary in 1996/97, the mountain sells a value-priced *Family Passport* lift pass for two adults and two children.

RATES: Rates are per person per night and do not include an eight percent tax or service charges (10 percent for B&B guests, 15 percent for MAP). Children's rates are for kids 12 and under and assume they are eating from the children's menu and sharing accommodations with two adults. Single parents who indicate that they have read about the Inn in this guide can have the two-adult minimum waived (in all categories except in the cottages and on the children stay and eat free program). The main difference between the standard and deluxe rooms is that the latter have larger sitting areas and are the same price as the Chalet suites that feature a bedroom, living room, TV and small refrigerators. There are two two-bedroom cottages and one two-bedroom suite in the main inn. Daily adult MAP rates, which vary by season, are as follows: Standard/$52–$73; Deluxe/Chalet: $62–$83. B&B in the cottages are $124–$165. Children's rates, when applicable, range from $12–$25/night. B&B prices are $20 less/adult, $5–$10/child.

BOOKED FOR TRAVEL

ME & YOU & THE KIDS CAME TOO: A Comprehensive Guide to New England's Finest Accommodations for Families by Dawn and Robert Habgood is a pleasure to read. The Habgoods compiled this well-researched resource after discovering that many of the B&Bs, inns and resorts they visited before they had children simply weren't appropriate for families. As a result, they sought out family-friendly establishments, from farms to luxury resorts, that also convey the charm and character of New England. Their delightful descriptions of more than 200 appealing places include information on cribs, babysitting, organized activities and age restrictions (if any), rates, nearby attractions and other details. (Dawbert Press)

WILD HORSE/DERRINGER RANCH
P.O. Box 157, Quemado, NM 87829
Phone/Fax: 505-773-4860

DESCRIPTION: We had a hard time deciding whether to put the Derringers in this chapter or under *Adventure Travel Companies*, since guiding and outfitting trips are the crux of its business activity. However, since its *Family Package* encompasses a stay at Susan and David Derringer's 40-acre ranch, and includes a choice each day of one activity, we believe that this option offers families the best opportunity for adventures.

Located about 200 miles from Albuquerque, 20 miles south of Quemado, and surrounded by national forest, the ranch is located at an elevation of 8,000 feet, which means that, in spite of warm daytime temperatures, evenings can be quite cool. The ranch takes up to 10 guests per week "and can give each guest much personal attention." Lodging is in a 35 foot RV with a separate bath, bedroom and living room or in a cabin furnished with antiques. On request, guests can stay in tents and teepees both of which have access to a large outside bathroom with shower facilities. Wholesome, homecooked meals are "tasty and authentic hearty ranch (e.g., chuckwagon style barbecues are done in an outside pit) or New Mexican, depending upon your taste." The majority of the food is organically grown on the ranch with fresh eggs and milk gathered twice a day. Corn-fed beef and chickens are raised on the ranch.

The Derringers' minimum age limit used to be 10-years-old but they now report, "We have become much more flexible and have recently hosted many children between the ages of 5 and 9 on the ranch." Don't let the low prices lead you to believe that you'll be shortchanged in regard to experienced, quality excursions. The Derringers do most of the guiding and cooking themselves and they are certified in CPR, Lifesaving, First Aid, New Mexico Boating Safety, Advanced PADI (Professional Association of Dive Instructors), Advanced National Swift Water Rescue and Advanced Scuba Schools International, plus they're proficient in a great number of other outdoor skills. High quality equipment is kept in excellent condition, with safety a prime concern. Susan Derringer says, "We love the outdoors, people and animals and we are lucky enough to be able to share experiences with others."

THE ADVENTURES: Goat packing, whitewater rafting, canoeing, kayaking, horseback riding, horsepack trips, hiking, fishing and cliff dwelling tours are among the adventures you can select from, during which time you'll be introduced to many wilderness skills. Overnight trips (minimum two days/two nights) are also scheduled year-round. *Training Seminars* (not included in the *Family Package*) are offered in many wilderness activities, from rope climbing and backpacking to advanced river boating and horse care/horsepack skills. There is an outdoor museum of old horse-drawn equipment, remains of an old sawmill and ancient Apache ruins on the property. The elk come in in droves to drink in the stream and graze in the fields. "So enter the wilderness and have an adventure or 'cowboy up' for a day of horseback riding."

FAMILY FEATURES: Though nothing is listed as especially for families with kids in the Derringer brochure, Susan and David customize all of their guided trips and adventures to meet your family's needs and do their "utmost to accommodate the families that visit, discussing interests and food choices before arrival." Not surprisingly, kids particularly enjoy having the company of "environmentally nice companions that help carry your load" on the goat pack trips. Kids also love being able to fraternize with all the other farm animals. It is also possible to get a babysitter (at no additional charge) for a young child for whom a particular activity might be too strenuous while other family members go off for a morning or afternoon.

RATES: The five-day/six-night *Family Package* is $600/adult, $400/child under 16 and includes lodging, all meals plus daily activities. Training seminars and overnight trips are not part of the package but can be included for additional costs.

BOOKED FOR TRAVEL

Among the books Usborne publishes for children are **THE CHILDREN'S BOOK OF WILD PLACES: *Mountains, Jungles & Deserts*,** by Angela Wilkes (illustrated by Peter Dennis). It uses a format of heavily illustrated text to present the subject matter in a highly enjoyable way. There's a ton of information here, including lots of fun facts.

Y. O. RANCH
Mountain Home, TX 78058
Phone: 800-YO-RANCH/210-640-3222
Fax: 210-640-3227

DESCRIPTION: This 40,000-acre working ranch in Texas Hill Country, just an hour and a half from San Antonio, is home to the largest collection of natural-roaming exotic animals in the United States (including zebras, giraffe, wildebeest, scimitar-horned oryx and more), as well as to the largest privately-held herd of Texas Longhorns in the world. Overnight lodging, for up to about 35 people, is in old-west 1880-era cabins that have been lovingly restored and converted. One was a former stagecoach stop, another a schoolhouse. Accommodations include meals (the ranch chef has been featured on *Great Chefs of the Southwest*). Calling itself "an adventure camp for youth and an out-of-your-rut getaway for adults," Y.O. Ranch offers a number of unique opportunities in addition to horseback riding and swimming in the ranch pool.

THE ADVENTURES: For more than 100 years the Schreiner family has been "Living the Texas Legend" and inviting guests to share in this experience. Full-day and overnight trail rides, cattle drives, round-ups, branding and other opportunities to work with Texas Longhorn are all possible. Other options include afternoon trail rides culminating in a bonfire/campfire cookout, evening hayrides, roping lessons and "showdeos." Budding and experienced photographers should ask about the *Sunrise to Sunset Photo Safaris.* The youngest age for the riding programs is about 7 or 8, "an age at which some youngsters are comfortable being on horseback most of the day." It's recommended that all activities be pre-booked. In July and August the property features kids'-only *Adventure Camps.*

FAMILY FEATURES: Children's prices, babysitting with advance prior arrangements and tours of the historic property are all possible.

RATES: Nightly lodging with three meals/day begins at $75/adult, $50/ages 12 and under, free/infants under age 2. A *Weekend Package* that includes room, meals, a one-hour horseback ride and a property tour is $185.50/adult, $105.50/ages 15 and under. Round-ups begin at $150/person/one day, $250/overnight.

BOOKED FOR TRAVEL

BEST PLACES TO STAY IN THE MIDWEST: *Unique and Distinctive Accommodations for All Budgets* by John Monaghan is a welcome addition to this ongoing series. Whether you're seeking a grand resort or cozy B&B, a city stay or a place in the country, you'll find numerous choices throughout the six states covered. There's a chapter called *Family Finds,* and all listings indicate if children are welcome or if there are restrictions on families. (Houghton Mifflin)

CHAPTER 4

MOUNTAIN ADVENTURES

We admit it — we love mountain vacations. Regardless of the time of year we've discovered that just being in the mountains rejuvenates us. Best of all, from the time our kids were infants we've been able to spend our family mountain vacations enjoying the great outdoors without ever having to worry about what to do (either together as a family or without our kids) or finding socialization for our children. Over the past 15 years or so many ski resorts have become year-round vacation destinations, though as far as families are concerned, the key seasons are winter for the skiing, and summer when our kids are out of school. In spite of the many summer offerings, in most cases, these months are often considered the "off-season" which translates into bargains for lodging options.

The ski industry has long been a leader in offering an incredible variety of family fun — both for family activities and also for those moments when kids and parents wish to go their own separate ways. Skiing, both downhill and cross-country, and snowboarding will be covered in greater depth in **Great Sports Vacations With Your Kids**. In this chapter, we tell you where at ski areas to easily sample all the other popular winter adventures such as dog sledding, snowcat skiing, snowshoeing, backcountry touring and even hot air ballooning.

In summer, when the snows have melted and the earth has come to life, mountains are natural areas for adventurous exploration, be it on foot (hiking), bicycle (mountain biking) or boat (canoeing or kayaking). In fact, when you speak to people who have relocated to ski resort areas, you'll discover that though they initially came for the winter ski experience, they stayed because the glory of summer won their hearts: majestic mountains framed by clear blue skies, warm days and cool nights, wide open spaces, and easy and quick access to a variety of outdoor activities and sports. We once owned a house in Vermont, and seriously contemplated taking up the country life full time.

As someone who grew up thinking summer meant beach, I'm still surprised these days that when warm weather comes, my inclination is to head for the hills rather than the shore. I've yet to try mountain biking, the current rage, but I've had no end of other rewarding experiences. On a mountain vacation, I can choose to do something different every day — hike uphill one day and head down the river the next, get a massage or play some tennis, skipper a sailboat or take a trail ride, try my luck at fishing or take in an outdoor music or dance festival performance. On lazy days, we've been known to leave our hiking shoes at home and simply take a chair lift to the top of the mountain and walk down.

Also, when we go to the mountains, we get to spend lots of time with our kids when they're not off taking advantage of the many children's programs offered for babies to teens. Be sure to check in advance whether you will need reservations (especially for the child care) and what, if any, cancellation policies may prevail. Complete details on nursery and children's facilities at ski areas are also covered in our sports volume in this series though these listings give you the bare bone facts.

Another plus to this type of vacation is that often you won't need the family car — many times the area has local transportation free of charge!

Following we have highlighted nine ski resorts/ski destinations around the continent which we feel epitomize the best of mountain adventures — winter and summer. We hope that you'll be as turned on by the getaways as we are. Each write-up is broken down into a brief *DESCRIPTION* of the area, a round-up of winter and summer *ADVENTURES* for you to explore with or without your children, details of child care options and other *FAMILY FEATURES* and some suggestions on where to stay, *BEST BEDS*. Before you book anywhere, check out the variety of package vacation options (they often include a selection of adventurous outings), many of which offer incredible value and often (especially in the winter ski season) even special air fares.

When you sit down as a family and list everything that each family member would like to do on your next vacation, with the exception of the obvious choices that don't head for the hills (such as a cruise vacation), we think that ski resorts offer more than meets the eye. Check it out. The mountains may never have looked so good!

> **GREAT VACATIONS TIP:** Everyone who travels with small kids knows how difficult it is to schlep along all of the mandatory equipment, which can turn family vacation experiences into the *Battle of the Bulge!* Don't despair. Help is at hand with **Baby's Away**, a Colorado-based company which rents baby supplies across the continent.
>
> Currently, Baby's Away offers rentals in California (Monterey, North Lake Tahoe, South Lake Tahoe), Colorado (Aspen/Snowmass, Breckenridge/Copper/Keystone Mountains, Durango, Steamboat Springs, Telluride, Vail/Beaver Creek), Florida (Clearwater/St. Petersburg, Ft. Myers, Sanibel/Captiva, Naples, Marco Island), Hawaii (all major islands), Idaho (Sun Valley), South Carolina (Charleston, Hilton Head, Myrtle Beach), Utah (Park City area), Wyoming (Jackson Hole), Canada (Banff, Lake Louise, Edmonton, Calgary, Blackcomb/Whistler, Toronto, Ottawa and Montreal).
>
> Whether you need a crib, stroller or playpen, a box of toys, breast pump, VCR or car seat and much much more, Baby's Away can set up all your needs in advance and deliver them to your destination. Call them at 800-571-0077 or 800-984-9030 for the phone number of the facility best for you.

EAST

ATTITASH BEAR PEAK, Bartlett, New Hampshire

Information/Reservations: 800-223-7669/603-374-2368
Attitash Mountain Village Reservations: 800-786-6754/374-6500
Mt. Washington Valley Visitors Bureau: 800-367-3364/
    603-356-3171
Unless otherwise stated, the local area code is 603.

DESCRIPTION: Located in the heart of New Hampshire's Mount Washington Valley, Attitash Bear Peak is both a paradise for intermediate skiers and a haven for warm weather recreationers. The two mountains are a short five-minute drive from each other and facilities (but, alas not a children's ski school) are available at both. There are also no novice trails on Bear Peak.

Every December, the Conway Scenic Railroad in North Conway delights kids with its Polar Express trip, inspired by Chris Van Allsburg's Caldecott Medal-winning book of the same name. It's said that "believers" actually terminate their journey at the North Pole. Cross-country ski enthusiasts will find they're within easy striking distance of the Jackson Ski Touring Foundation and its world-respected trail system and the Mt. Washington Valley Ski Center.

Attitash is the Indian word for blueberry, and each summer, the ski area sponsors a *Blueberry Festival* for the benefit of local children's organizations that features a full day of free activities for kids, culminating in a scavenger hunt with prizes for all. Later in the summer, kids of all ages are thrilled by the wild west antics at the *Double 'R' World Championship Rodeo* with calf-roping, barrel racing and more. One highlight occurs when kids get the opportunity to try and catch the ribbon off a calf's tail during the event's *Calf Scramble.*

Also nearby is Mt. Washington, the state's highest peak, from the top of which, on a (rare) clear day, you can actually see the Atlantic Ocean. The uphill hike is too difficult for young children but there is an eight-mile drive that brings you to the summit. If you don't wish to drive, check out the Mt. Washington Cog Railway not too far away.

A short drive takes you to the bustling towns of Conway and North Conway where the outlet shopping will make you wish you left more room in your trunk for all the purchases you'd like to bring home.

THE ADVENTURES: Snowboarding is offered at both mountains. The ski area is one of those selected by *Ski Magazine* to offer its mini-rider snowboard program for kids 7 to 12. The mountain offers snowshoe rentals and holds clinics in this relatively new sport. The regularly scheduled guided trekking may feature animal tracking or backcountry exploration. You can also rent snowshoes and take lessons at the Intervale Nordic Center (356-5541) near Conway.

Take a sleigh ride over the river and through the woods in Jackson at Nestlenook Farm (383-0845) where kids can also feed the local reindeer. Families interested in dog sledding should contact the Yankee Siberian Husky Club (654-6088) in South Lyndeborough. This organization can tell you how to participate, and also where you might find a race to observe.

A wide array of outings are also sponsored regularly by Eastern Mountain Sports (356-5433) and families can take year-round rock climbing clinics at Mt. Cranmore's Sports Center, home to New England's largest indoor climbing wall, 30 x 40 feet. Rock climbing enthusiasts or wannabes need go no further than calling the International Mountain Climbing School in North Conway (356-6316) for either group or private lessons that take participants out onto the hills and ledges of the White Mountain National Forest.

The area is close to the White Mountains and is a year-round hiker's paradise, with more than 1,200 miles of hiking trails in the White Mountain National Forest. At any season, the Pinkham Notch Visitor's Center of the Appalachian Mountain Club (466-2721) offers guided excursions that welcome youngsters; some are specifically created for families. Popular summer hikes include an easy climb to Arethusa Falls (the state's highest waterfall) as well as a more challenging hike to Winniweta Falls.

Attitash Bear Peak is home to the state's longest and most unique Alpine Slide, whose Aquaboggon Water Slides are a big hit with all, especially teens. There's lots more offered at the resort, where a fleet of Proflex mountain bikes is available for rent (rentals include helmets) for both adults and kids. Big adventure is in store for more experienced bikers who can rent a Descenter, a sort of high-tech scooter with wide tires. In addition to lift-served bike paths, the resort runs a shuttle to the White Mountain National Forest where a network of challenging single track and pre-existing logging roads are open to riders. The Thorne Pond Interpretive Trail (designed as a family learning center) offers a scenic ride through the woods along the Saco River. Other trails in the system are also relatively flat. If you want to join a group trip, contact the North Conway Athletic Club (356-5774) or Eastern Mountain Sports. Scenic biking and hiking are also on tap at Echo Lake State Park where there's a one-mile hiking trail around the lake. If you're not about to try your hand at rock climbing, you might be able to catch others doing so as Cathedral Ledge, one of the area's best learning spots, is viewable from the park. Boat rentals are available at the park.

Back at Attitash you can sign up for a guided horseback ride through the Fields of Attitash (there are also pony rides for little ones) or take the one-hour hiking tour from the base of the Summit Triple Chair.

If it's fishing you fancy, you won't be disappointed. Anyone age 10 and older can take fly-fishing lessons at North Country Angler (356-6000) while younger kids can try their luck at Hills Nursery Pond in Intervale (800-640-5750), where a well-stocked pond and picnic area attract many families.

For those who prefer their adventures on the water, consider a canoe trip with Saco Bound (447-2177) in North Conway. The company provides shuttle service for its outings and also offers multi-day trips and instruction. During the spring months kayaking and whitewater rafting are possible. The Saco River is one of the few in the area that permits camping along its sandy beaches. From what we've heard, try this during the week as weekends can get very crowded. If Saco Bound is too busy, try Saco River Canoe & Kayak (207-935-2369), across the river in Fryeburg, Maine. The Downeast Whitewater Rafting Center (447-3002) in Center Conway may also be able to help. Its specialty is its kayak touring and paddling school.

BOOKED FOR TRAVEL

With the extensive amount of thought and space given to children in NATURE HIKES IN THE WHITE MOUNTAINS: An AMC Nature Walks Book, by Robert Buchsbaum, the book could just as easily have been entitled Nature Hikes With Kids in the White Mountains. Buchsbaum clearly supports taking your kids out on the trails — and gives you the tools with which to decide which jaunts will be the most successful. Moreover, he highlights all kinds of activities kids will like and provides thoughtful caveats for parents. The section on flora and fauna should definitely be read in advance as it will pique your children's interest, and give them something specific to seek out on the trail. With 44 family hikes listed, this is a real winner of a book.

FAMILY FEATURES: In winter, kids from 6 months old are accepted in the *Attitots* nursery program. Youngsters 1 year and older can take part in a snowplay option while there are several skiing programs for children between the ages of 3 and 12. There are no organized lessons for teens.

In the "other" season, the resort offers three *Summer Adventure Camps* for kids ages 5 to 12. The first runs during the entire summer season and explores a number of local adventures with each day focusing on a different theme. One night, an overnight camping/hiking trip is featured both for regular campers and outside participants. There's also an *Adventure Gymnastics Camp* for ages 6 to 13 and an *Adventure Rock Climbing Camp* (taught by staff from the International Mountain Climbing School) for beginners, ages 8 to 10 and intermediates, ages 11 to 15. Outdoor climbs include Whitehorse Ledge and Cathedral Ledge.

Little ones will find their own "adventures through tunnels and over bridges," at the 3,000 square foot *Buddy Bear's Playpool.* With maximum depths of only 18 inches, the water-filled facility was constructed especially for kids ages 2 to 7. It's a nice complement to the three waterslides older kids and adults enjoy. Attitash Mountain Village should be able to assist you in securing babysitting and arranging child care for younger children.

BEST BEDS: Attitash Mountain Village (800-786-6754) offers condominium lodging, walking distance to the lifts. Units are comprised of one- to three-bedrooms and share an indoor pool, sauna, hot tub, a game room, playground and laundry room. Blueberry Village Condos and Cathedral Trail Lodges are adjacent to the village and also walking distance, but they are not part of the same rental pool.

Christmas Farm Inn (800-443-5837) and Whitneys' Inn (see page 120), are both in Jackson, seven miles from the ski area. Also in Jackson, the Eagle Mountain House (800-966-5779) extends a warm welcome to families and has a heated outdoor pool, a small playground and game room. The Eastern Slope Inn Resort (800-258-4708) in North Conway, offers a selection of rooms, suites and townhouses and has an indoor pool, a game room and a hot tub.

SMUGGLERS' NOTCH, Vermont

Information/Reservations: 800-451-8752/802-644-8851
Unless otherwise noted, the local area code is 802.

DESCRIPTION: As you read through the vast array of offerings at Smugglers' Notch, you quickly understand why it calls itself "America's Family Resort." Family fun is guaranteed (there's even a money-back policy if you're not a believer by the time you leave). To get in the mood, be sure to request the resort video. The seven- to eight-minute tapes (there's one for summer and another for winter) are sent at no charge upon request. The tapes show a variety of activities and lodging and give a sense of the layout of the village and the mountain and what to expect.

Smugglers', by the way, was named after the bootleggers who transported contraband across the nearby Canadian border. Smugglers' celebrated its 40th Anniversary in 1996; today, you can choose to spend as much (or as little) time as you'd like as a family enjoying the vast outdoor playground of this self-contained resort. Smugglers' Notch has done its best to "create a total experience not just for mom and dad and the kids, but also for spouses traveling alone with children, one-parent families, even for blended or extended families, including grandparents and friends." Each season the resort publishes a huge, detailed brochure (almost 30 pages in winter, 50 in summer) that carefully and clearly outlines the myriad possibilities that await. Communicating with its guests is one of Smugglers' strongest assets.

The three mountain peaks, Morse, Madonna and Sterling, are the focus of both winter and summer outdoor activities. In summer, the Nordic Center is home to the tennis facility. Even the non-athletic are attracted to these mountains, because there's always something going on. *Artists in the Mountains* is just one highlight. For those who want to carry on into the evening, there's nightly family-oriented entertainment.

THE ADVENTURES: Kids of all ages are in for a treat at the resort's Family Snowmaking Learning Center, located just off the slopes at the Pump House. Accessible on skis or by car, this state-of-the-art computerized center is filled with interpretive displays. When downhill, cross-country skiing and snowboarding pall, you can head to the Nordic & Tennis Center and its more than 23 kilometers of trails. Telemark lessons and rentals, snowshoe rentals and guided walks, an all-season nature trail and a backcountry ski trip are all on tap here. One organized outing heads out in search of owls and other winter animals. Snow-sliding and tubing on Sir Henry's Hill are popular with families, as are the weekly ice-fishing excursions. The real adventure skier will be pleased to hear that the resort's *Open Trail to Open Trail* access policy has opened up 750 acres of skiing in wooded areas and in the glades between the slopes. If you are among this elite group, you might consider trying out a pair of the hourglass shaped Elan Parabolic SCX skis that were designed for skiers to more easily initiate turns and carves. Don't miss the opportunity to take a family sleigh ride or head to the Vermont Horse Farm down the road for winter horseback riding.

> GREAT VACATIONS TIP: Parabolic skis, which were introduced by the manufacturer Elan, have taken the industry by storm. The ski has a revolutionary hour-glass shaped design, visibly different from the traditional ski. Our most avid skier (and long time ski editor), David Ferber, tested the Elan SCX skis and his glowing recommendation cited their high points as superior facility in carving and quick-turning. He actually brought some along as a second pair of skis on a backcountry ski safari of the French Alps last spring. In spite of the need to travel light, David was not at all sorry to have had the Elan SCX skis with him. This upcoming ski season, you'll find lots of parabolic skis for rent across the country, many at a comparable price to standard rentals. Do yourself a favor and try them. We don't think you'll be disappointed.

Whether you enjoy hiking, biking, fishing, canoeing, horseback riding or llama trekking, you'll find them all on Smugglers' weekly summer schedule. Rum Runner's Hideaway, the 10-acre natural water playground perched on Morse Mountain, features a selection of family adventures. The more energetic can take the hour or so hike from the village; the less ambitious can drive (or take the shuttle) to the Madonna Base Lodge and hike for 15 minutes, while the truly indolent can sign on for the 30-minute hay wagon ride. Once there you can paddle a canoe, fish, hike or swim. Though most of the swimming area is pretty deep, there is a shallow beach area and an adjacent playground. There's also a vast water playground back down at the resort.

Among the more popular activities are the *Walks, Wikes and Hikes,* one- to six-hour guided hikes, ranging from easy to challenging. Some welcome entire families, others are just for adults. Paddlers might choose the *Wetlands & Wildflowers* morning canoe trip or the evening *Sunset Beaver Watch.* Once you have some experience, it's time for *CanoeCraft,* a five-hour trip that heads for the Green River Canoe Wilderness. Take a class in orienteering or opt for a fly casting clinic, which might be followed by the *Fly-fishing Stream Tour.* The end of the week brings the *Rock Climbing Social,* especially designed for beginning adventurers.

Need more? Check out the riding at the Vermont Horse Park and Stables (not owned by the resort), rent a mountain bike (helmets included), or take an off-property tour such as the *Family Funventure* in nearby Stowe or a *Discover Vermont* trip.

Fall foliage is Smugglers' third season and in recent years the nursery has remained open for youngsters while older kids and adults participate in the on-going choice of hiking, biking and canoe trips that explore the area's spectacular parade of autumn colors.

FAMILY FEATURES: As you'd expect, the kids' activities more than rival the adult and family-together fare. At Alice's Wonderland, a 7,000-square-foot facility accommodating about 100 children, kids between the ages of 6 weeks and 3 years are divided into small groups for a variety of indoor and outdoor fun. It boasts a one-acre playground and Vermont's largest sandbox. Once your child is 3 years old and toilet-trained, he or she can head for *Discovery Dynamos* (ages 3 to 4 and age 5). Older kids (ages 6 to 8 and 9 to 12) are called A*dventure Rangers* while teens (ages 13 to 14 and 15 to 17) become *Mountain Explorers.* The youngest explore the Vermont woods while the older kids can take the adventure challenge, become dirt detectives or take a class in garbology. Teens will regale you with stories of their Trapeze Plunge, High Ropes Course and more. Older kids also have an evening overnight once a week. Each age group has the opportunity to participate in the *Top of the Notch Challenge*, a program designed to help kids master skills in specific adventure-oriented areas. Kids ages 10 to 18 may also want to sign on for *Ropes & Rafts,* a three-day program of non-stop adventure for all levels of ability (limited space). Children who choose to purchase lunch (you're welcome to send lunch with your child) are treated to all-you-can-eat buffets. Three nights a week, *Parents' Night Out* (6 to 10 p.m.) feeds and entertains youngsters 3 and older. Private babysitting can be arranged for younger children.

Winter programs are centered around skiing and snowboarding. However, in the *Adventure Camp* for ages 7 to 12, kids come off the slopes in mid-afternoon and are supervised until 4 p.m. Parents with avid skiers will want to check out the *Team Smugglers* program where children receive a lesson in the morning and can ski on their own the remainder of the day. A lot of thought has gone into the resort's teen activities. The seasonal teen lessons, for example, are only offered in the afternoon (most civilized, our teens tell us) and the Outer Limits Teen Center is open from 5 p.m. to midnight. *Parents' Night Out* often operates five nights a week in the winter season.

If your kids are little, be sure that you get a copy of the *Discovery Ski Camp Coloring Book* (for ages 3 to 6) or the Adventure Journal (for ages 7 to 12) and ask your kids to share the *Kids' Trail Map and Information Guide* with you.

BEST BEDS: Lodging includes a choice of studio to five-bedroom condominiums. Week-long or mini-vacation *FamilyFest* packages are designed for a family of four in summer. They include any number of extra features such as full-day programs for everyone (including adults but not always babies) plus pools and waterslides, evening family and adult entertainment, hiking and walking tours, basketball, volleyball, Family Game Nights, Vermont Country Fair and more. Winter rates are charged per person for five or seven nights and can also be almost all-inclusive. Even baby care is free on selected dates. Some consider the Resort Village condos to be the best-located in the group. Daily maid service costs extra. Summer prices begin at about $1089/week in a studio. Winter rates for a family of four in a one-bedroom condo on the *Club Smugglers'* package (which includes daily lift and cross-county trail fees, daily group lessons in the snow sport of choice, one-day, ski-over-the-mountain to Stowe lift ticket, outdoor ice skating, bonfires with hot cocoa, family tube sliding parties, use of the indoor pool and hot tub, weekly fireworks, welcome party, showtime theater and adult evening entertainment) are $1,845/seven days, $1540/five days.

SUGARLOAF/USA, Carrabassett Valley, Maine

Information/Reservations: 800-THE LOAF/207-237- 2000
Unless otherwise noted, the local area code is 207.

DESCRIPTION: Sugarloaf/USA calls itself New England's biggest ski mountain but what truly differentiates it from other eastern ski resorts are its vast snowfields with lift-serviced above-tree-line skiing, providing a nice contrast to the more traditional narrow tree-lined trails at other resorts. Don't get us wrong, however, the mountain is big (and is part of the range that comprises three out of the four largest in the state), big enough to satisfy every level of skier with variety for all. As an example, for snowboarders, there are not just one, but two halfpipes. Similarly, in summer, there are two main entrances to the Mountain Bike Park. This is just the beginning as Sugarloaf/USA is in the middle of a great expansion.

As you might expect with a resort this size, there's lots to do year-round. With the resort's strong commitment to the family market, parents with kids of all ages will find more than enough to enjoy together combined with a number of options for kids on their own. We were not at all surprised to learn that the Western Maine Children's Museum is nearby.

What the mountain doesn't offer on-site, the Carrabassett Valley more than makes up for — whether it's family trips or a kids' day camp. Here we talk about the adventure possibilities, but golfers will want to know about the many programs for adults and kids. And, then there's always the skiing.

THE ADVENTURES: "More of everything you ever dreamed of " is Sugarloaf's wintertime slogan. Already renowned for its vast snowfields and for having the largest snowboard park in Maine (with the largest halfpipe in the country), its latest offering is *Boundary-to-Boundary* skiing, where you're encouraged to blaze your own trail and chart your own course on "the most challenging, most extreme off-trail terrain you'll find anywhere in the East."

The less proficient, however, might want to begin with a fast, just-for-fun tube ride down the Birches during the twice weekly *Turbo Tubing* sessions. Guided *Snowshoe Safaris* are offered regularly at Sugarloaf's Ski Touring Center. where there is also an Olympic-size outdoor ice-skating rink. Snowmobiling is another popular activity and there are hundreds of miles of trail in the area. In fact, you can take your snowmobile all the way to Quebec City (probably much too long a trip to do with your kids) or head for the Interstate Trail System that crisscrosses the state of Maine and connects to New Hampshire. Probably the best snowmobile trip for families would be a day trip to the Rangeley Lake Area. The quaint town of Rangeley, with its many shops and restaurants, is dominated by its large lake, and has become a winter pilgrimage for snowmobilers.

Dog sledding adventures depart right from the base of Sugarloaf's access road and welcome youngsters of all ages, even infants. (In summer, the sleds' runners are replaced by wheels and exploring is done by dog cart.) All of the above activities, plus ice-fishing, are easily arranged through Guest Services at the resort.

Mountain biking is the hallmark of summer activity; the trails are so challenging that it is recommended mainly for youngsters ages 10 years and older. The mountain maintains a fleet of bikes for rent with kids' sizes available. A mountain shuttle operates on Friday, Saturdays and Sundays and allows riders to bike downhill for most of the time and be shuttled to and from the Village Center. The Bike Shop, located in the Village Center, has a supply of trail maps. Trails are marked and rated for ability, from beginner to expert. Two kids-only mountain bike camps operate during the summer season and the local bike club sponsors a number of weekly rides on the many trails in the area. In addition to the trails in the Mountain Bike Park (that include many of the mountain's cross-country ski trails), there are 53 miles of marked bike trails in the surrounding area.

While you're at the touring center, check out the programs offered by the Edge of Maine, which runs a fly-fishing school from the facility. There is no minimum age; anyone who is interested in fishing can learn to fly-fish. There are a number of day hikes in the area and the mountain, the second tallest in the state, is located along the Appalachian Trail. Many hikes sponsored by the Appalachian Mountain Club (see page 170) are designed for parents with children of varied ages.

Guests who have booked lodging packages directly with the ski area reservations system have access to the Sugarloaf Sports and Fitness Club where lessons can be scheduled at its indoor climbing wall. Currently, the most popular weekend evening activity is the *Sugarloaf Moose Cruise.* Departing from the Inn every Saturday night, guests board the Moose Express bus and head to the touring center in search of moose in their natural habitat. The trips includes a video presentation, services of a knowledgeable tour guide and complimentary beverages and appetizers.

FAMILY FEATURES: Sugarloaf/USA has a long-standing commitment to kids. Its state-licensed Child Care Center for kids as young as 6 weeks old (up to age 5) is open both in the winter and summer seasons. In winter it provides nursing moms with beepers and takes kids as young as 3 out on the slopes. In addition to a selection of ski programs for kids up to age 16, nightly activities are offered to young vacationers, generally between the ages of 5 and 12. Avalanche (formerly Rascals) is the place for teens, who also have their own ski and snowboard school programs. The mountain's *Junior Instructors* program turns capable skiers into certified ski instructors. *Children's Weekend* is held each December, *Children's Festival Week* in January, and *Family Fling Week* in February all offer a number of discounts and specials for families.

In summer, kids join the Carrabassett Valley program *Camp Lots of Fun* (with half-day programs for kids ages 4 and 5 and full days for ages 6 to 14) or opt for one of the specialty camps that are offered on specific dates: *Soccer Camp* for children ages 5 to 14, *Mountain Bike Camp* from age 11, *Golf Camp* for any interested child. Child care for younger children from 6 weeks is also offered.

BEST BEDS: There are two lodging reservation services. For on-mountain reservations, contact the number above, 800-THE LOAF. For Sugarloaf

Area Reservations, call 800-THE AREA. In many packages, ski school and/or lift tickets are included.

At the center of this planned condominium resort development is The Sugarloaf Mountain Hotel, a hotel/motel that offers one- and two-bedroom suites (some with kitchens), in addition to individual rooms. Guests who stay at the more modest ski-in/ski-out Sugarloaf Inn have access to the Sugarloaf Sports and Fitness Club. Also at the ski area are Sugarloaf Mountain Condominiums (almost 900 of them) offering one- to five-bedroom units, most with fireplaces or wood stoves. While you can ski back to many of the units, some do not have direct lift access and require taking the area's free shuttle to get on the mountain. The best units for families are those located within Gondola Village as they are closest to the day care facility. There is also an RV park on the mountain.

ROCKIES

CRESTED BUTTE MOUNTAIN RESORT, Crested Butte, Colorado

Information/Reservations: 800-544-8448/970-349-2390
Crested Butte Chamber of Commerce: 800-545-4505/970-349-2211
No Limits Center: 888-954-6487
Unless otherwise noted, the local area code is 970.

DESCRIPTION: If you're looking for a low-key, charming environment for your explorations, head for Crested Butte, an old-fashioned Victorian town with no glitz or glamour — just spectacular adventures in store. Its latest claim to fame as an adventure destination is the opening of a No Limits Center, the first in the United States. The Center was developed by Sector Sport Watches and there are already more than a dozen centers currently operating in Europe. There, under one roof, would-be adventurers learn how they too can push the envelope and experience the region's most challenging adventure possibilities — talking to experts, watching videos, and eventually working with qualified, experienced guides and athletes. Their philosophy is simple: "The Center is not for just anyone. It is for everyone who loves life and wants to experience it at new levels."

In winter the mountain is home to the steep and the deep, offering what has been called the "best adventure skiing in the Rockies." In summer, mountain biking is the resort's claim to fame (the Mountain Bike Hall of Fame is in Crested Butte!) with *Fat Tire Bike Week*, the sport's oldest festival, held early each summer to kick off the season. The event is as much fun for novices as it is for hard-core mountain bikers.

There are many more reasons to visit this quaint, historic, old mining town. For starters, between Thanksgiving and mid-December, and for the last two weeks of the ski season, Crested Butte Mountain Resort offers free skiing. There are an unusual number of good restaurants for a town its size and a true feeling of western hospitality.

The ski area, three miles from the town, has terrain for all abilities, complimentary mountain tours, and every imaginable adventure, regardless of the season. Free shuttle service is offered till midnight in the winter and until 10 p.m. during the summer.

THE ADVENTURES: With more than 500 acres of "extreme" backcounty ski terrain it's no surprise that Crested Butte is home to both the *U.S. Extreme Skiing* and *U.S. Extreme Snowboarding Championships* nor that the ski school offers such classes as Extreme Limits and Ski the Extreme. There are even extreme skiing workshops specifically for women. We highly recommend that you take advantage of the free mountain tours that steer you to the best skiing terrain for your ability.

When we took our teens to Crested Butte, they were enthralled by the snowcat skiing at Irwin Lodge (800-2-IRWIN-2). Though 12 miles from the mountain, it's only a five-minute ride to its access trails (ride via snowcat or snowmobile only). The large cedar lodge offers some of the finest powder skiing in the country and welcomes skiers, snowboarders and snowmobilers. Some days there's so much new snow over by Irwin Lodge that conditions are not amenable to beginner powder hounds. However, at other times it can be a terrific place for novices to make their first attempt, since many of the runs terminate at the lodge where one can easily stop to rest without holding up the rest of a group. Unfortunately, as we go to print, there is a possibility that the lodge may not operate during the 1996/97 season.

Our boys absolutely loved the snowmobiling trips they took with Action Adventures (800-383-1974) — they took just about every tour offered. Located right in the mountain plaza area, Action Adventures outfitted them with snowmobile suits and boots and provided them with instruction before allowing them to blast through the powder fields of snow in Gunnison National Forest. We appreciated Action Adventures' concern for both our safety and our pocketbook; they allowed us, for example, to take only the snowmobile portion of a traditional dinner tour.

During our stay in Crested Butte, friends with younger kids took an evening backcountry excursion with Jean Pavaillard of Adventures To The Edge (800-349-5219). Jean is the father of young children and we were quite impressed with his attitude toward introducing youngsters to the many adventures his company offers: backcountry training and tours, snowshoe trips, hut-to-hut tours, avalanche courses and winter mountaineering. "Everything," says Pavaillard, can be "adapted to beginners, families and skilled alpinists." He told us that he's taken kids as young as 4 to explore and climb some of the area's ice caves.

Among the winter adventures offered by No Limits are winter mountaineering (want to learn how to build a snow cave?); ice climbing; paragliding; rescue training and dog sledding. If you're a die hard do-it-yourselfer you can contact the individual operators directly.

You can opt to dog sled at Lucky Cat Dog Farm in Gunnison (641-1636), sign up for a sleigh ride with Just Horsin' Around (349-9822), horseback ride with the folks at Fantasy Ranch (349-5425) or call Balloon Adventures (349-6712), the "highest altitude balloon company in North America."

In summer, Crested Butte is known as the Official Wildflower Capital Of Colorado, making it an especially beautiful spot from which to experience a whole host of adventures. The team at No Limits can make all the arrangements for kayaking, canoeing, whitewater rafting, mountain biking, hang gliding, rock climbing, wilderness camping, survival training, hot air ballooning, horseback riding and more. Alpine Outside is another full-service recreational activity planner (349-5011) that can set up rafting, kayaking, horseback riding, jeep tours, fishing and mountain biking.

During the annual *Wildflower Festival* in July, any number of guided hikes will stimulate your mind as well as exercise your body. Or, take the lift to the top of the mountain to the Alpine Hiking Trail (picnics are a specialty here). Don't forget to ask for the area's *Hiking, Biking & Camping Trail Map*. Alpine Express (800-822-4844), the company that provides transportation to and from Gunnison Airport, also offers a number of 4-Wheel Drive tours that explore the many surrounding ghost towns, remnants of the gold rush. Rent mountain bikes for yourself and your kids right at the ski area or take a guided fly-fishing excursion with Dragon Fly Anglers (349-1228).

BOOKED FOR TRAVEL

A fairly esoteric work, which will appeal to families where all members are experienced skiers and outdoorspeople, is COLORADO HUT TO HUT: A *Guide to Skiing and Biking Colorado's Backcountry,* by Brian Litz. There are 49 huts listed and many suggested tours, all of which include information on Difficulty, Time, Distance, Elevations, an Avalanche Note and Maps. (Westcliffe)

FAMILY FEATURES: Kids are never forgotten at Crested Butte. Day care is offered in the winter for non-skiing youngsters from 6 months to 7 years. At *Butteopia*, toilet-trained 3- to 7-year-olds are offered a nice combination of indoor and outdoor activities, including skiing. *Buttebusters* caters to the 8 to 12 age group and the *Teen Program*, for ages 13 to 17, welcomes beginners to experts. In summer, *Mountain Adventures* is specifically designed for kids ages 6 to 13. The 9:30 a.m. to

3:30 p.m. program features mountain biking, river rafting, rock climbing, horseback riding, hiking and wacky water activities, with each day highlighting a different activity. Rock climbing courses for teens ages 14 to 18 are scheduled weekly. Parents with younger children can take advantage of Annie's KiddieCare (349-9262) for children ages 1 to 8 or ask the resort for its list of local, qualified babysitters.

BEST BEDS: In general, we're firm believers that skiers should stay as close to the ski area as possible, making it easy for parents to check the kids into their appropriate programs and still get on the slopes in the morning. However, the transportation at Crested Butte is so efficient that having lodging right by the slopes is not as crucial as it usually is. It really is a snap to get around (we've been here several times and have never had a car). The area's top, the Grande Butte Hotel, is closest to the lifts and you can ski right in. Though it's not exactly posh and elegant, it offers everything you'd ever want: family-sized rooms and suites, several restaurants, a concierge floor, indoor swimming pool and outdoor hot tub/whirlpool, a game room and nightly family movies. The resort's newest hotel, the MountainLair, is also among its more moderately priced accommodations. We have also stayed at The Plaza condominiums, which we liked very much. There are a number of condominium units at the ski area. Not all are as conveniently located as The Plaza, so it's imperative that you ask about access not only to the lifts but also to the children's facilities you will need. Your choices will greatly expand in the summer season and you won't be disappointed by the options: a wide selection of B&Bs, inns, lodges and private home rentals. Many are walking-distance to town. Again, all of these lodging can be booked by calling the telephone number listed above.

> **GREAT VACATIONS TIP:** The organization **The League of American Bicyclists** (LAB) publishes the magazine *Bicycle USA*. Each November/December issue includes "Tourfinder," an impressive listing of the tours offered by any number of bicycle touring companies. Each listing should supply adequate information for you to determine if the trip is suitable for your family. The March/April issue contains the magazine's annual Almanac, a state-by-state resource guides to biking in America. Either issue can be purchased separately for $5 each. Both are automatically sent to members. Other benefits of membership ($30/individual, $35/family) include access to complimentary lodging at more than 1,600 hospitality homes, free carriage of bikes on a number of airlines (when you book your flight through LAB's travel company) and more. You can write to LAB at 190 West Ostend Street, Suite 120, Baltimore, MD 21230-3755 or phone them at 800-288-2453 or 410-539-3399.

PARK CITY, Utah

Information/Reservations:
>Park City Chamber Of Commerce:
>>800-453-1360/801-649-6100
>Deer Valley Resort:
>>Information: 800-424-3337/801-649-1000
>>Lodging: 800-424-3337
>Park City Ski Area:
>>Information: 801-649-1111
>>Lodging: Park City Ski Holidays
>>>800-222-7275/801-649-0493
>Wolf Mountain: 800-754-1636/801-649-5400
>Unless otherwise noted, the local area code is 801.

DESCRIPTION: Set in Utah's Wasatch Mountains, Park City was settled by miners in the 1870s and became a booming mining town by the turn of the century. One hundred years later, it still retains its sense of heritage as a silver mining town. A major venue for the 2002 Olympic Winter Games, Park City, with more than 4,200 acres of skiing, is home to three ski areas: Deer Valley Resort, Park City Ski Area and Wolf Mountain (formerly ParkWest) — each distinctly different in flavor. The first two resorts will host the slalom, snowboarding, aerial and mogul competitions in 2002.

The fact that town is only 35 miles from Salt Lake City International Airport is great news for parents (and kids). In many cases, you can literally board a plane in your home state after breakfast and be actively enjoying the great outdoors after lunch. Moreover, you'll discover that almost all the local outfitters offer kids' prices (or family packages) that make many activities more affordable.

With the opportunity to give your kids a first-hand preview of the winter games, there's never been a better time to travel to Park City. A visit to the Utah Winter Sport Park (see below), where the Olympic ski-jumping, bobsled and luge competitions will take place, is bound to get everyone in the family enthused. Not only will you be able to view the facility, you'll be able to take lessons and then test your newly acquired skills.

Though filled with modern conveniences, Park City will transport you back in time whether you're walking down historic Main Street (64 of its buildings are listed on the National Register of Historic Places), gazing up at the old weathered mine buildings strung along the mountainside, checking out the Park City Museum (where kids can lock themselves up in the "jail") or riding on the Heber Valley Railroad (654-5601), Utah's only historic train that chugs along the route of the Union Pacific Rail Trail.

As winter comes to a close, Park City looks forward to summer — "an excuse to play outside without a coat" — which brings an eclectic selection of adventurous fare. In spite of its relatively small size, the town has 15 reservation services for lodging and at least three representing the off-slope outfitters, that book both lodging and any number of activities: ABC Reservations Central (800-820-ABCD/649-ABCD); The Pulse of Park City (800-333-0736) and Utah Escapades (800-268-UTAH/649-9949). ABC sent us a packet chock full of outdoor choices and were the only company that knew about the dog sled tours (for all ages) at Lone Peak Mountain.

THE ADVENTURES: Year-round, families can enjoy the historic Park City Silver Mine Adventure (655-7444). You'll grab a hard hat and slicker prior to boarding the hoist that lowers you 1,500 feet below ground into the middle of the town's most prolific silver mine. As you ride the mine train through the tunnels, you'll pass archaic mining equipment, an underground horse stable and experience a simulated dynamite blast.

As we mentioned, you must visit the Utah Winter Sports Park (649-5447) in Bear Hollow, built in support of the Salt Lake City 2002 Winter Games. Not only the country's newest aerial facility (open winter and summer), it is the only ski jumping park in the U.S. open to the public. While you won't get to test out the 120 meter jump (the largest open to amateurs is only 38 meters), step-by-step instruction is offered to all ages (they say they've already taught folks from three-year-olds to grandparents) with both gentle and more challenging fare. Also on the horizon, the Olympic Bobsled/Luge track, 4,400 feet in length is set to open to the public in January 1997 — two more exciting sports for recreationers to test out personally.

Fishing is another year-round activity in the region. Both Local Waters Fly-Fishing (800-748-5329/745-2569) and Park City Fly Shop (800-324-6778/645-8382) offer outings to local rivers and streams and include casting instruction.

Winter horseback riding is also possible. Country Trails (800-876-5825/649-3423) takes riders out into the crisp mountain air, through forests and up mountains for spectacular scenic views. You can soar aloft in a hot air balloon at any season. Among the choices are Hot Air Ballooning ABC (see numbers above); Park City Balloon Adventures (800-396-UPUP/645-UPUP), Windjammer Balloon Tours (800-343-0630/649-0630) or Balloon Affaire (649-1217).

Speaking of glorious views, sign on for a *Ski Utah Interconnect Adventure Tour* (534-1907) and you won't be disappointed. This adventurous outing, open only to strong skiers, takes in five ski areas with a nice taste of backcountry for good measure. Friends who did this found it quite incredible (and unbelievably tiring).

You can get into backcountry skiing without the trekking with snowcat skiing. Both Red Pine Adventures (800-417-SNOW/649-9445) and Park City Powder Cats (800-635-4719/6459-6583) take kids 12 and older on their guided backcountry snow cat trips while snowcat skiing is also now offered at Deer Valley in Empire Canyon, its latest area of expansion.

Less rigorous backcountry incursions are also possible. The Norwegian School of Nature Life (800-649-5322/649-5322) offers several snowshoe tours, among them options that include an overnight camping trip, bunking in a snow cave or a yurt. More winter camping expeditions, guided snowshoe or telemark treks and winter wildlife tours are offered by West Wind Outdoor School (800-841-2409/649-8677). Snowshoe outings are also on the activity roster at the Homestead Resort (800-327-7220/654-1102) and at White Pine Touring Center (649-8710), where kids ages 12 and under can try out the equipment for a modest $5/full day and use its 18 kilometer of tracked/trail system for free. White Pine Touring has created a number of half-or full-day snowshoe or telemark tours that explore the local backcountry, from a "leisurely cruise (for beginners) to up and down a powder bowl for experts."

With almost a dozen snowmobile operations in the area, among them ABC's Snowmobile Tours, Park City Snowmobile Adventures (800-303-7256/645-7256) and Red Pine Adventures, it's obviously a pretty popular activity. At ABC, kids ages 10 and under sharing with parents are free. You can tour open meadows, groves of aspen or, if you prefer, blaze your own trail through the forest. If that's too much work, try a sleigh ride, perhaps with dinner. Regular sleigh rides are also offered at The Homestead.

When it's time to stow away the skis for the season, it becomes time to tune up your mountain bike and try on your hiking boots. All three Park City ski areas are open to bikers and hikers. With extensive trail options throughout the area, for those who prefer the thrill of heading downhill without the pain of the uphill climb, Deer Valley has the only lift-served biking in town; lessons and guided tours are offered by the resort. You'll definitely want to pick up a copy of the 24-page *Park City Hiking and Biking Guide* where various routes are meticulously described and local outings are listed. Guided hiking trips are organized by the Norwegian School of Nature Life, Jans Mountain Outfitters (800-745-1020/649-4949); both run fishing trips and sponsor weekly tours in conjunction with the Park City Cycling Club, and Cole Sport (800-345-2938/649-4800) offers weekly bike rides and clinics. Sport Touring Ventures (800-748-5009/649-1551) also offers guided bike trips.

Since White Pine Touring is such a major player in the winter outdoor market, we were not surprised to learn they offer free weekly Thursday evening rides with special rental rates that include a *Learn to Ride* clinic for beginners. Trips for more capable riders are also organized, including a number of overnights aimed at intermediate and better riders. Kids' trailers are available for rent as are kids' carrier packs. White Pine also offers rock climbing instruction, promising to "help you reach new heights with one of our programs or custom guided outings (including overnights) under the careful watch of our experienced guides." From basic safety and technique to stemming and flagging, options are available for all levels of climbers. *Kids Kling* classes for ages 8 to 14 are offered weekly and include shoes and harnesses. As you might expect, White Pine can also customize backpack trips.

Though you'll have to leave town, there is a choice of river rafting in the vicinity. Adrift Adventures (800-824-0150/789-3600), Dinosaur Rafting Expeditions (800-345-RAFT/649-8092) and High Country Rafting (645-7533) all offer day trips.

If being on water turns you on, rent a kayak or canoe from Peak Experience (800-361-UTAH/645-5366). Though the company does not currently offer guided trips, it may offer them in the future. Sleigh ride operators fill the hay wagon with guests in summer and once again, you can soar through the air with all of the above-referenced balloon companies.

FAMILY FEATURES: Of the ski areas, only Deer Valley offers infant care for babies (from 2-months-old). The resort's *Child Care Center* has a variety of programs in winter with private lessons on tap for kids ages 3 to 5 and group lessons for children ages 4 1/2 to 5, plus, of course, ski school for ages 6 through 12 and teens. The teen program meets at 11 a.m., something our son particularly liked when he visited there with his dad. In summer, Deer Valley offers a *Summer Adventure Camp* for ages 6 to 12.

Over at Park City Ski Area, *Kinderschule* combines indoor and outdoor fun for ages 3 to 6 (but kids must ski because it is not a day care facility), while there's a Youth School for kids ages 7 to 13. Both programs are only offered in winter.

Winter programs at Wolf Mountain take kids as young as 18 months at *Kids Central.* Ski school technically begins at age 3 but the under threes can participate in the *Skier-In-Diapers* program.

Parents of infants and preschool aged children do have other options. Creative Beginnings (645-7375) accepts drop-in visitors year-round as does Miss Billie's Kid's Kampus (649-KIDS) though at Miss Billie's the ages accepted are 3 to 8.

As for private sitters, check out Guardian Angel Babysitting (640-1229), Nanny 'n Me (483-9455), Mzz. Poppins Sitting Service (649-6463) or Professional Sitters Service Wee Care (649-0946).

If you're in need of any baby and children's equipment, contact the local branch of Baby's Away (see page 127).

BEST BEDS: For its size, Park City offers an unusually wide range of lodging options — quaint, turn-of-the-century bed and breakfast inns, full-service hotels, elegant slopeside homes and condominiums, and a range of more modest accommodations. If you head to Park City in winter and your kids are already skiing, you might consider staying in town and using the town lift to Park City Ski Area as your ride to the mountain. The Treasure Mountain Inn is both well-liked and well-priced.

The most luxurious accommodations are probably found at Deer Valley where the Stein Eriksen Lodge even has heated sidewalks to prevent guests from slipping on snow. Our visit to the Deer Valley Club was a true treat — with more amenities in our two-bedroom apartment than we have at home. Up to four-bedroom accommodations are available at Deer Valley. Snow Park Lodge sits at the base of the mountain while Silver Lake Lodge is located midway up the slopes. It's recommended that guests staying at Deer Valley make restaurant reservations at the mountain in advance of arrival.

At Park City Ski Area, Park City Ski Holidays is its "official" reservation service through which lodging, airport transfers, lift tickets and ski school can be booked. Through the middle of December, guests who stay a minimum of four nights receive free lift tickets to Park City. Among our favorites: Silver King Hotel at the hub of the town's free transportation system is a condo hotel with an indoor/outdoor swimming pool; Snow Flower Condominiums at the base both for its convenience and amenities and five-bedroom units for large family groups; Three Kings for its one-bedroom plus loft condos and its location.

Red Pine Condominiums, adjacent to the base of Wolf Mountain, feature access to a clubhouse sauna and hot tub (several deluxe units have individual hot tubs) and laundry facilities. Shuttle service takes skiers to Deer Valley and Park City Ski Area.

Central Reservations of Park City (800-243-2932/649-6606) features a number of specials, among them *Toucan,* a program offering a third night's free lodging. Other interesting lodging selections are Prospector Square for its Athletic Club & Spa, and The Yarrow as a destination hotel experience across from Park City Ski Area (too long a walk with little kids).

Farther afield, at The Homestead (800-327-7220/654-1102) in the town of Midway, 25 minutes away, winter cross-country skiing and snowmobiling are complemented by summer horseback riding and mountain biking. Its latest program is scuba diving inside a 65-foot-deep crater in 90 degree geothermal water. The resort even offers scuba certification and ski and scuba packages!

VAIL/BEAVER CREEK Vail, Colorado

Information/Reservations: 800-525-2257/970-845-5745
  Vail Valley Central Reservations: 800-525-3875
  Activities Desk of Vail: 970-476-9090
  Beaver Creek Resort Concierge: 970-845-9090
Unless otherwise noted, the local area code is 970.

DESCRIPTION: There's no doubt about it, Vail and Beaver Creek are big — and getting bigger each day. Vail Associates, the company that manages these two mountains along with Arrowhead and Bachelor Gulch, is not only in the middle of a five-year capital improvements plan, it's also in the process of a merger with three ski areas in Summit County (Keystone, Breckenridge and Arapahoe Basin). This is all good news for families, as the company has a long-standing commitment to offering a wide array of family fare.

Regardless of season, the activities you can do with your kids are restricted only by your child's ability or your own point of view. However, with so many exciting programs offered just for kids throughout the Vail Valley, you may have to cajole your children into leaving their peers and spending time with you.

Surrounded by Rocky Mountain splendor, the Vail Valley offers every conceivable outdoor adventure at your fingertips. The Recreation Departments at both Vail and Beaver Creek are happy to plan all aspects of your stay, and many of the summer lodging packages already include activities such as rafting, mountain biking, jeep tours, cattle drives and more.

As parents, we especially like the car-free pedestrian villages that are located both in Vail and Beaver Creek. When we travel with our own kids, we love being able to give them the freedom of striking off on their own without our having to worry about traffic. We admit that in winters past we preferred Beaver Creek because all of its runs terminated by the Plaza area and we were able to allow our boys to head up the chair lift on their own, knowing that they would not make a wrong turn and end up in a completely different place than that from which they left. However, with the recent expansion, skiers can now end up in Bachelor Gulch or Arrowhead (there will be a shuttle back to the Beaver Creek base for those who end up in the wrong area at day's end). Although you could easily spend an entire vacation skiing at Beaver Creek, we do encourage you to take at least one day to ski at Vail and, if your kids are capable, take a stab at its famous back bowls. Our kids loved them from when they were quite young.

The new Eagle's Nest Activity Center, "an amusement park on snow with a full menu of winter activities for guests of all ages," is bound to be a hit with skiers and non-skiers alike. It has a snowboard park with two halfpipes, a tubing hill, snowshoe trail and snowmobile tours and is open until 9 p.m. in the evening.

THE ADVENTURES: We've experienced any number of outdoor adventures with our kids but we know that the next time our winter holiday brings us to the Vail Valley, one of our first stops will be the Bobsled run on Vail Mountain (accessible only via skis or snowboard on an easy catwalk from Mid-Vail) where we'll board the four-person sled for a quick adrenaline rush. The minimum age is 8 years. This is not included in the lift ticket price; there is an additional per person charge. Ski equipment for bobsledders is transported to the bottom of the run where there's an easy ski-out to the bottom of the Avanti Express chair.

Those looking for a less hair-raising experience can rent snowshoes in any number of places in the area. For guided snowshoe trips into Colorado backcountry, contact Paragon Guides (926-5299).

Snowmobiling is always a kid-pleaser and you can't go wrong by heading over to the resort's Eagle's Nest Activity Center, where they have relocated its operation. Kids ages 14 and older can take a machine out on their own when they are accompanied by an adult. (only teens 18 years and older can go out without an adult). Both Nova Guides (888-949-6682/949-4232) and Timber Ridge Adventures (668-8349) offer guided snowmobile trips as does Timberline Tours (800-831-1414/476-1414).

Back at Beaver Creek, families with members who are intermediate level or better skiers might consider signing on for the Mountain Skills workshop, part of the ski school's Adventure Series that is operated by Paragon Guides. From navigation to winter mountaineering, you'll learn first-hand if heading out into backcountry is for you. And, if you discover that it is, ask the folks at Paragon Guides about one of its hut-to-hut trips.

With more than 4,000 acres of skiable terrain at Vail and another 1,500 plus when you also take in Beaver Creek and Arrowhead, you may be hard-pressed to have time to track virgin powder. We know first-hand just how exciting snowcat skiing can be (as well as being more comfortable and cheaper than heli-skiing). Vail Snotours (476-9090) welcomes all levels of skiers on its tours as does Nova Guides.

Lots of activities in Vail can be enjoyed year-round. Hot air ballooning is a prime example. Both the Activities Desk of Vail and the Beaver Creek Resort Concierge can provide you with information on Aero-Cruise Balloon Adventures (800-373-1243), Camelot Balloons (926-2435) or Mountain Balloon Adventures (476-2353). There's even flightseeing with Aero-Vail (800-FLY-VAIL).

For those who'd rather experience the area in a land-based vehicle, Jeep and 4-wheel drive tours are also offered year-round. A good friend of ours once hurt his leg the day before he and his family departed for Vail and he dreaded the trip. A little creativity led him to try different backcountry excursions each day, always with a knowledgeable guide.

When he returned home, he was hard pressed to say who had the best vacation — his family (which had skied all day) or himself. Outfitters to contact include Mountain Wolf Jeep Adventures (926-9653) and Nova Guides.

Rock climbing and mountaineering adventures begin in town at the Vail Athletic Club's (476-7960) indoor climbing wall where instruction is offered for all ages. According to the Club, "The wall is for everyone. We've had from 3-year-olds to a 77-year-old climb the wall successfully. Kids are a large user-group for the climbing wall." When it's time to test your newly-learned skills, contact Vail Mountaineering (476-4223), Vail Rock Climbing (476-2916), Nova Guides or Paragon Guides. For the more serious climber, Paragon has a week-long *Mountaineering Camp*.

Though more prevalent once the snows melt, horseback riding is possible year-round. A number of area outfitters offer everything from one-hour and full-day excursions to overnight trips. For the little ones, there are pony rides and mutton bustin' at the weekly rodeo at Berry Creek Ranch (summer only, 926-3679). Other outfitters include A.J. Brink Outfitters (524-9301), Beaver Creek Stables (845-7770), Black Mountain Ranch (653-4226), High Colorado Guide Service (524-7900) and Piney River Ranch (476-3941), where a number of options are offered. The ranch, which is also managed by Vail Associates, provides complimentary transportation from both Vail and Beaver Creek. The more adventurous might opt for a recreational cattle drive with Black Mountain Ranch or 4 Eagle Ranch (926-3372).

Then there are miles of mountain bike trails throughout the Vail Valley ranging from beginner to expert. Rentals are available at the top of either Vail or Beaver Creek Mountains with guides to assist in the basics of the sport. Check out Vail's most famous trail, The Grand Traverse, that crosses the top rim of the Back Bowls. Check with the Activities Desk about mountain bike tours and clinics. With the assistance of trail maps, guides and signs (available at many of the rental shops), navigation is easy. To learn about additional trails throughout the Vail Valley contact the U.S. Forest Service at 827-5715.

The Forest Service also offers a free daily hiking trip from Eagle's Nest on Vail and Spruce Saddle on Beaver Creek. If you miss these, call the Vail Nature Center (479-2291) and ask about its interpretive hiking programs. Paragon Guides offers not just guided hikes, but hiking and trekking with llamas. There are a number of popular family hiking trails out at Piney River Ranch and a hike to the Betty Ford Alpine Gardens is an absolute must. In case you don't own a pair of comfortable hiking boots, head for the Merrell Hiking Center (there's one at Beaver Creek Sports and another at Avail Adventure Outfitters) and rent a pair for the day. The $8 fee will be applied to a purchase. We absolutely swear by our summer Merrell hiking boots and have taken them far and wide, with nary a blister to be found.

Once summer arrives, a wonderful outdoor activity is rafting and the valley is close to a number of rivers: the Arkansas, Eagle, Shoshone and the Colorado. Kayaking is also popular. You can choose anything from a float trip to an expert Class V trip. Call Timberline Tours, Lakota River Guides (479-0779), Raftmeister (476-7238) or Nova Guides.

Speaking of water, we can't forget fly-fishing, truly a local highlight. As with just about all the activities in the area, more than half a dozen outfitters feature excursions and/or instruction. Nova Guides, Vail Fishing Guides (476-3296), Fly-Fshing Outfitters (476-3474) and Gorsuch Outfitters (476-2294) are just a few. Gorsuch offers free fly-fishing clinics five days a week in both Vail & Beaver Creek. You can also fish at Piney River Ranch. Be certain to inquire when Trout Unlimited and the Vail Nature Center offer their class which combines the skills of fly-fishing with an understanding of stream environment.

FAMILY FEATURES: We'll begin with kids' programs. In Vail, the children's center at Golden Peak is the larger of the two facilities (there's another at Lionshead). The capital improvement program has turned Golden Peak into a major entry point to the mountain complete with an 83,000 square foot base facility and a high speed lift up the mountain. On both mountains you'll find a *Small World Play School Nursery* for kids ages 2 months to 6 years, a *Children's Ski and Snowboard Center* for ages 3 (toilet-trained) to 6 and 6 to 13. Lessons are also designed during peak periods for intermediate or better skiing teenagers 13 to 18. Our only misgiving about these programs is that they are primarily full-day sessions. Half-days are possible but cannot be reserved in advance. On the other hand, the SKE-COLOGY environmentally-oriented program developed at Beaver Creek is such a success that it has been duplicated at a number of resorts nation-wide. After hearing their children's enthusiasm for the program and wanting to experience it themselves, parental pressure encouraged the ski schools to integrate various aspects into all of the ski classes.

In summer, the *Children's Adventure Center* programs offer a variety of day camps and child care is offered in both Vail and at Beaver Creek. Then there are the *Kids' Night Out* programs for kids ages 5 to 12 offered several nights a week. There are also on-mountain *Adventure Zones* that have been designed specifically for kids (Fort Whippersnapper at Golden Peak comprises 15 acres), kids' trail maps and more. A Family Adventure Line (479-2048) is updated weekly with a complete listing of activities. There's even a Teen Activity Line (479-4090). In summer the Vail Recreation Department sponsors *Camp Vail* for children ages 5 to 18 that includes overnights and night hikes open to youngsters ages 7 to 12. Kids will love the hands-on activities at the Children's Outdoor Construction

Museum at Beaver Creek. The Vail Youth Center is the in spot for kids from 6 to 20 (those under 13 are not permitted after 6 p.m.). Located at Lionshead, $1 admission gets kids all the pool, rocket hockey and foosball they can play, plus access to a huge music collection, movies and TV. Specialty summer camps include theater and horseback riding.

If you're in need of any baby and children's equipment, contact the local branch of Baby's Away (see page 127).

BEST BEDS: The Vail Valley offers an incredible array of accommodations, many of which are quite luxurious. Here are a few choices each for Vail and Beaver Creek. Remember, if you're taking advantage of the ski school or child care programs, there are two facilities in Vail, the larger currently at Golden Peak.

In Vail, you can't get much more upscale than The Lodge at Vail, one of the resort's original properties. Deluxe rooms and apartments (up to three bedrooms) are offered, There is an outdoor swimming pool and an outstanding restaurant. Another family favorite is the Sonnenalp Hotel. In addition to its wonderful location, the apartments and outdoor pool are big draws for families. In Lionshead, families can't go wrong at the Mountain Marriott. Though not directly in town, but with its own lifts, the Westin Resort is another family-friendly choice.

Somewhat more moderately priced recommendations are the Christiana Lodge and the Chateau Vail Holiday Inn. Condominium complexes include Manor Vail, well-priced and close to Golden Peak, and The Antlers at Vail or The Lodge at Lionshead, both located in the Lionshead area. Mountain Haus at Vail is another good choice.

In Beaver Creek, our first choice is the Hyatt Regency Beaver Creek. Hands-down, this is one of our favorite hotels anywhere. With great service, great food, great amenities and facilities (e.g., indoor pool, guest laundry), unbelievably welcoming to kids and parents, it's a winner in all categories. *Camp Hyatt* and *Family Camp* activities are always on tap.

There are many wonderful condos at Beaver Creek and the resort provides complimentary shuttle service. Our recommendation is to stay right at the resort plaza, at the Park Plaza, The Pines or The Post Montane, where you can confidently let your kids roam around without worry. Of the condos not at the Plaza, our first choice would be The Charter, although all of the properties are nice. The Beaver Creek Lodge, for example, serves a buffet breakfast.

Accommodations in Arrowhead are another more moderately-priced option for families.

WEST

LAKE TAHOE, California/Nevada

Information/Reservations:
Lake Tahoe Visitors Authority (for South Shore):
800-AT-TAHOE/916-544-5050
North Lake Tahoe Resort Association: 800-824-6348
(800-TAHOE-4-U)/916-583-3494
Individual ski area information/reservation services:
Alpine Meadows: 800-441-4423/916-583-4232
Diamond Peak: 702-832-1177/800-TAHOE-4-U
or 800-GO TAHOE
Northstar-At-Tahoe: 800-466-6784/916-562-1010
Squaw Valley: 800-545-4320/916-583-5585
Heavenly: 800-2-HEAVEN/702-586-7000
Kirkwood: 209-258-6000
Unless otherwise noted, the local area code is 916.

DESCRIPTION: The center point of this popular tourist area overlapping the state line between California and Nevada is its 12 by 22 mile pristine, Alpine lake. Surrounded by world-class skiing (there are more than a dozen downhill or cross-country ski areas) and entertainment (with gambling on the Nevada side), the combination makes the destination an exciting venue in all seasons, with incredible outdoor opportunities at each and every turn. It is a true winter wonderland, although some feel that the summer months are even more spectacular.

The Lake Tahoe region is basically divided into North and South. Each has its own tourist authority and reservations and information services. The South Shore is the more developed of the two, while the North Shore is home to the majority of the larger ski resorts. Several of the ski areas provide toll-free lodging and information services as well.

With so much to offer (literally enough to fill this entire chapter), we're limiting our descriptions purely to adventure activities. Those of you looking for the important family details on skiing, golf, tennis and other sports can check out **Great Sports Vacations With Your Kids** or research them directly using the numbers listed above.

Wherever you head in the Lake Tahoe region, you will want to spend time exploring the out-of-doors. Curiously, though there is often an abundance of snow on the mountains, the lake itself never freezes (because of its depth) and temperatures around the shore can be quite mild, even during the winter months. Lest you find yourselves in need of an indoor activity, however, both the Sierra Nevada Children's Museum (587-5437) in Truckee and Tahoe Tessie's Lake Tahoe Monster Museum in Kings Beach (546-8774) are lots of fun. Both are located on the North shore.

Tahoe is quite easy to reach. It's an hour by car from Reno, two hours from Sacramento and three-and-a-half hours from San Francisco. Although having a car is helpful (particularly in summer), it is not mandatory. Parking your car may be difficult and good public transportation operates year-round.

We hear that it's well worthwhile to take one of the scenic paddlewheel cruises on the lake, one of the most popular tours in the area. During the winter months, several decks of the M.S. Dixie II are enclosed and heated. If you visit coincides with the annual summer *Lake Tahoe Air Fest*, this is a thrilling event all ages can relish. Oasis Aviation will even take your kids out for a spin for only 5¢ per pound.

The following pages on the Lake Tahoe area are organized according to activity, not location, although we do advise you whether things are North or South. We kick off with winter and move on to warm-weather activities. Certain activities, of course (fishing, for example) are not seasonal and can be enjoyed at all times of the year.

THE ADVENTURES: We've discovered that Snowplay areas appear to be unique to Tahoe, where they ring the lake. These are facilities designated for sledding and tobogganing. Rentals are possible at some; at others you need to bring your own equipment. Parents with younger children will find them appealing as they are particularly safe for youthful frolicking. On the North shore you'll find them at North Tahoe Regional Park in Tahoe Vista (546-5043); Boreal Snowplay area in Donner Summit (426-3666); Sugar Pine Point (525-7982) in Tahoma and at Granlibakken in Tahoe City (583-9896). In the South, head for Tahoe Winter Sports Center (577-2940) in the town of Meyers.

Kids of all ages seem to love horse-drawn sleigh rides. Check out the stables at Northstar where winter horseback riding is also an option. Sleds and drivers are also waiting out back at Squaw Valley's Resort at Squaw Creek. In the South, sleigh rides offered at Camp Richardson Corral (541-3113) and from Borge Sleigh Rides (541-2952).

Snowshoe rentals are available throughout the region, including at most cross-country ski centers. Guided tours are also possible. Ranger-led tours are offered at Donner Memorial State Park (582-7892) and Sugar Pine Point in the North while at the South shore U.S. Forest Ranger Station (573-2600), guides lead treks through the woods every Saturday throughout the winter. Both rentals and lessons are offered at ski resorts also. In the North you'll find them at Diamond Peak at Incline Village and at the Nordic center at Northstar-at-Tahoe, in the South at Kirkwood's Nordic center.

Snowmobiling is another extremely popular and easily accessible outing. Most facilities not only provide rentals, they organize various types of tours. In the North, Northstar offers snowmobiling as does Mountain

Lake Adventures (702-831-4202) in Incline Village. Other options include High Sierra Snowmobiling (546-9909), TC Sno Mo's (581-3906) on the Tahoe City golf course, Eagle Ridge Snowmobile Outfitters (546-8667) in Truckee or Snowmobiling Unlimited (583-5858) at Brockway Summit, between Northstar and Kings Beach. Visitors to the South shore should try the Zephyr Cove Snowmobile Center (702-588-3833). There are also a number of snowmobile and toboggan runs at Hansen's Resort (544-3361). If you're big fans of this sport and in the area in late March or early April, check out the date of the finals in the snowmobile hillclimb competition that takes place at Kirkwood.

Though a trek to get to, a fairly unusual adventure can be had at Eagle Mountain Bike Park (800-391-2254) where on-snow mountain biking is a highlight. It is located at Donner Summit.

Speaking of mountain biking, you'd be hard pressed to find an area with more options than in Lake Tahoe. There are more than 30 miles of paved (and hundreds of miles of unpaved) bike paths open to bikers (and hikers), many more than you'll be able to cover in a visit. At Northstar, the area's premier Mountain Bike Park traverses the 2,000 acre resort. Rentals (always with helmets) are available at the Mountain Adventure Shop in the village and lessons and guided rides are always on the resort schedule. Another North shore Mecca for mountain bikers is Squaw Valley, with its extensive trail network that is open all summer long. The North shore visitor's bureau has a separate brochure on mountain biking.

There's plenty for the traditional biker as well. Baby trailers and kids bikes are widely available. Even four-person surreys can be hired. There are many relatively flat, easy trails in the area. The gentle South Lake Tahoe Bike Path starts near El Dorado Beach. The 3.4 mile Pope-Baldwin Bike Path will take you past the U.S. Forest Service Visitors Center where you can pick up a number of informative brochures on local hiking and biking. On the North shore the mostly-flat four-and-a-half mile Truckee River Bicycle Trail begins in Tahoe City. Two companies that offer guided bike tours are Cycle Paths (800-780-BIKE/581-1171) in Tahoe City and Paco's Truckee Bike and Ski (587-5561).

Hiking is a national pastime for locals with the abundance of state parks, U.S. forest land and municipal recreational areas. The trails at Sugar Pine Point State Park on the northwestern side of the lake feature several family-friendly opportunities. For example, the Dolder Trail follows the lake shore and passes the world's highest working lighthouse. Hiking around the lake can be fairly gentle and the Tahoe Rim Trail (a hiking and equestrian trail with a variety of entry points) that borders the lake and winds through the area, has almost 150 miles cleared for hikers to enjoy. If you stop by the USFS Visitor's center you'll find out about its *Woodsy Ranger* program for youngsters ages 5 to 13, its guided hikes to Desolation Wilderness and its twice daily 90-minute guided hikes. While you're in the South, you might want to try the two-mile loop at the top of

Heavenly (that is part of the Tahoe Rim Trail), accessible via the resort's tram and take one of the twice daily guided nature hikes offered. Also on the South shore, you'll find a trail designated for the physically disabled at Tahoe Meadows that is also accessible to strollers. In the North, you can take a guided nature hike at Northstar (ask about its orienteering program when you call) or catch the spectacular explosion of wildflowers at Squaw Creek Meadow at Olympic Valley.

Terrific hiking, camping and swimming are also found at D.L. Bliss State Park near Emerald Bay. Head over to Emerald Bay State Park where a one-mile hike takes you to Vikingsholm, a 38-room Scandinavian castle that was built in 1929. Families are frequent guests on the trips (by the day, by the week or combined with other adventures) offered by Katie and Rob Rice's Tahoe Trips & Trails (800-581-HIKE/583-4506) and the local summer hiking club (583-3796) sponsors a number of jaunts that will interest kids and their parents. Vertical Horizons (800-582-8644) offers a variety of outings that combine hiking with mountain biking, rock climbing, fly-fishing or outdoor survival skills.

Lake Tahoe is far from the only lake in the region and summer brings an abundance of water-based activities. Bear in mind that for the same reason Lake Tahoe doesn't freeze, it also never gets very warm so, if you want to get wet, try one of the many other water facilities where the temperature is less frigid. At D.L. Bliss and Emerald Bay State Parks and Sugar Pine Point, fishing and boating are always on tap. Lake Alpine and Pinecrest Lakes are also possibilities. Windsurfing (or boardsailing) rentals and lessons are offered at Lakeside Chalets (800-2-WINDSURF/546-5857), Carnelian Bay and Ski Run Marina, South Lake Tahoe. The only age restriction is that renters must be good swimmers.

We were terrified before we took our first parasail, but it turned out to be both exhilarating and fun (and not nearly so scary as we thought). Young children (we've met 4-year-olds who have parasailed) can harness up with parents while older kids can easily soar on their own. In the North, Lighthouse Watersports Center (583-6000) in Tahoe City can get you started (claiming to have taken folks between the ages of 2 and 95) and can also gear you up for jet skiing, canoeing and kayaking, as can Lake Tahoe Parasail (583-7245) and Sunnyside Parasail (583-6103).

Fishing, as we mentioned, is offered year-round. Mac A Tac Charter (546-2500) in Tahoe City can take you out trolling for giant Mackinaw trout; California Fly-Fishing (800-588-7688) in Truckee will teach you the basics before sending you off to fish their favorite spots; Clear Water Guides (800-354-0958) out of Tahoe City operates year round charters.

After six years of drought, rafting and tubing are once again making a comeback along the Truckee River. Kids as young as age 4 can usually participate since almost never any serious whitewater can be seen. Rent tubes or rafts from Porters Sports or Truckee River Rafting (583-RAFT) both in Tahoe City or Fanny Bridge Rafts (581-0123). For real whitewater, call Whitewater Tours (581-2441) and ask about its trips on the American and Carson Rivers. Guided kayak or canoe tours and rentals are available at Tahoe Paddle & Oar (581-3029), Kayak Tahoe (544-2011), Tahoe Water Adventures (583-3225) in Tahoe City and at Meeks Bay Marina (525-7242) on the Northwestern shore of the lake.

Climbing walls offer a safe and sensible introduction to the sport of rock climbing. At Squaw Valley, the 30-foot indoor Headwall Climbing Wall at the ski area's cable car building is open year-round. In summer, the resort also has a 45 foot outdoor wall. (Though it doesn't appeal to us, there is bungee jumping at Squaw Valley, open to children ages 10 and older.) Climbing walls can also be found at Gravity Works Rock Gym (582-4510) in Truckee, at The Sports Exchange (582-4510) in Truckee and at Northstar's Adventure Park. For instruction contact High & Wild Mountain Guides (577-2370) in Tahoe Paradise or Alpine Skills International (426-9108) in Donner Summit.

Northstar's Adventure Park also features two ropes courses and orienteering courses. The activities are open to all ages except for the ropes course which is for those 10 and older. A junior ropes course is designed specifically for kids between the ages of 4 and 9. The Granlibakken Resort (583-4242) in Tahoe City also has a ropes course.

If it's horses you fancy, check out the Northstar Stables, Squaw Valley Stables or the Tahoe Donner Equestrian Center (587-9470) in the North. You can even house your own horse at Mountain High Bed & Barn (800-231-6922) in Truckee where llama treks and hot air balloon rides are also offered. In the South, equestrians should try Camp Richardson Corral, the stables at Zephyr Cove or Sorensen's Resort (800-423-9949/694-2203), where a number of activities are offered (e.g., pack trips, llama hikes, kayaking, fishing, biking, photo workshops, etc.) and a children's program often operates.

And, if time permits, catch a birds-eye view of the Lake in a hot air balloon with Mountain High Balloons (800-231-6922/587-6922) or Lake Tahoe Balloons (800-872-9294/544-1221).

BOOKED FOR TRAVEL

Despite the sound of its subtitle, Andrew Rice's OUTSIDE MAGAZINE'S ADVENTURE GUIDE TO NORTHERN CALIFORNIA: *Hundreds Of Great Trips, Trails, And Little-Known Places For The Hard-Core Adventurer Or The Whole Family* is not really aimed at the family traveler. Here's how he answers one of the suggested questions to ask an outfitter, "Can I bring young children?" — "Most outfitters will usually answer affirmative to this. A buck is a buck, no matter who hikes or sits on the bike. However, you should take yourself and the other guests into account. Do you really want to bring the kids along? Do the other guests really want you to bring your kids along? Is this trip appropriate for children? Will they have a good time?" These are perfectly legitimate questions, but it sounds to us as though the author feels the answer will turn out to be "No, not really." Having gotten this off our chests, the rest of the book is just fine (although non-family-specific). Adventures are grouped geographically, e.g., The San Francisco Bay Area: The Peninsula, Marin County, etc. There are decent maps, convenient temperature and precipitation charts and lots and lots of adventure suggestions with all relevant details supplied. A very useful guide. (Macmillan)

FAMILY FEATURES: The selections for children almost rival the myriad activities for adults. First we'll talk about programs at the major ski areas and then consider other options. None of the ski area programs include care for children under the age of 2. Boreal's infant care is actually a well-stocked, separate area in the base lodge where parents can look after their kids. You can buy a ticket that can be utilized by both parents during the same day so that they can take turns looking after youngsters.

In the North: Alpine Meadows has only a ski school for children ages 4 to 6 and 6 to 12 in separate programs. There are no kids' summer programs.

At Diamond Peak in Incline Village half-day (morning and afternoon sessions) care is offered for children ages 3 to 6. The ski school breaks the kids into ages 4 to 6 and 7 to 12. Another option in Incline Village is Tahoe Tots (702-931-2486).

Kids need to be toilet-trained for all of the programs at Northstar-at-Tahoe. Children ages 2 to 6 (ski lessons from age 3) are taken in the winter months; a day camp atmosphere takes over in the summer for kids 2 to 10. Ski school programs are run for ages 5 to 12.

Squaw Valley accepts children ages 2 and older (diapers OK) in its child care center. Ski school begins at age 4 (to 12) and one-hour lessons are possible for 3-year-olds. In summer the area runs soccer camps for youngsters ages 8 to 18 and a series of kids' basketball camps are run by the Golden State Warriors. Right by the mountain, *Mountain Buddies* is operated for guest children ages 3 to 12 at the Resort at Squaw Creek, day and evening. A variety of activities is also offered to teens.

Down from the slopes, both the Tahoe City Parks & Recreation Department (583-3796) and North Tahoe Recreation and Parks (546-7248) offer day camps in the summer. Additionally, *Junior Ranger Programs* for children ages 6 to 12 run at D.L. Bliss and Sugar Pine Point Parks (525 7277).

Little Peoples Adventures (581-4LPA) runs an adventure camp for kids 5 to 12 and The Art of Children (800-838-ARTS) has entertaining and educational programs for kids as young as 2. Lake Forest Creative Center in Tahoe City has programs for toddlers from 18 months (583-8256)

Aimee Angel Inc. is a screened babysitting service (800-339-9541) and the *North Lake Tahoe Week* regularly publishes an updated babysitter list.

If you're in need of any baby and children's equipment, contact the local branch of Baby's Away (see page 127).

In the South: Heavenly has two learning centers for kids, beginning at age 4 (and up to 12).

Kirkwood has just built a new huge lodge to house its kids' programs (except for the day care for ages 3-toilet trained to 6 which is located in one of the resort's condominium units); Ski school is open to children ages 4 to 12. Supervised weekend evening programs are offered for children ages 6 to 12 and teenagers 13 to 18. Kirkwood says they can make arrangements for infant care. There are no summer programs at the resort.

The Lake Tahoe Children's Center (541-5887) is located in South Lake Tahoe.

All of the hotel concierge desks maintain detailed, updated babysitter lists.

If you can't find what you need, help is at hand at El Dorado County's resource center for parents, Choices for Children (541-5848). It provides referrals for babysitters and structured day-care facilities.

BEST BEDS: Two area resorts that are unusually family-friendly are: Northstar-at-Tahoe and the Resort at Squaw Creek (the most luxurious ski-in/ski out property at Squaw Valley). Both offer an array of children's activity programs, ski-in/ski-out capability and numerous other on-site amenities and services.

There are, however, definitely more choices available, several hundred in fact. Many provide free shuttle service to the various ski area. Among those that we know extend families a warm welcome are:

The luxurious Hyatt Regency Lake Tahoe Resort & Casino (located on the North shore at Incline Village) features *Camp Hyatt* for ages 3 to 12 on weekends and holidays year-round and *Family Camp* activities weekends during the summer season. The Cal-Neva Lodge offers families a choice of lodging in cabins and chalets in addition to traditional hotel rooms. On the South shore, the Embassy Suites Resort has child-proofed rooms, an indoor pool and a full cooked-to-order breakfast (which will both save you dollars and give you the needed energy for your days in the mountains.) Another popular family choice is Lakeland Village, offering hotel rooms, condos and townhouses, some right on the lake.

If you'd like to stay at or near one of the ski areas here are a few options. Closest to Alpine Meadows (where there isn't any slopeside lodging) are Alpin Place One and Two, one- to four-bedroom condominium units complete with washers and dryers, just a half mile from the area. You could walk there if you're traveling with older kids.

Granlibakken Resort in serves a complimentary breakfast even though most of their studio to three-bedroom units have kitchens.

Sunnyside Lodge, on the backside of the mountain and right on the lake, is a very popular B&B.

At Heavenly there are more than 200 area hotels and motels, including four major casinos. On-site lodging includes Ridge Tahoe on the Nevada side and Tahoe Seasons Resort on the California side. Within walking distance from the base are Heavenly North Condos and Heavenly Hideaway Casino.

Kirkwood has a condominium village at its base, comprised mostly of one- and two-bedroom units. Sun Meadows, which is the only one with three-bedroom units is where the resort's day care facility is located. All of the units are within skiing (don't take these if you or your kids don't ski) or walking distance of the chair lifts.

Northstar-at-Tahoe boasts more than 200 on-site units from hotel-type rooms to four-bedroom condos and private homes plus a terrific Recreation Center. Most have fireplaces and VCRs; not all provide daily maid service. In addition to the upscale Resort at Squaw Creek, Squaw Valley offers additional ski-in/ski-out properties, The Squaw Valley Lodge and the more basic Squaw Valley Inn. Both Christy Hill and Squaw Meadow condominium units are about a half mile from the base and the all-suite Olympic Village Inn is two blocks away.

Near Diamond Peak, in addition to the Hyatt, Incline Village offers a number of condominium and private home rentals.

For toll-free reservation services, see the beginning of this section.

> **GREAT VACATIONS TIP:** If you're thinking of taking a California river trip, call **California Outdoors** (800-552-3625). This consortium of outfitters is "dedicated to preserving, promoting and experiencing California's unique rivers." Among its list of 50 members with interesting family options are: Current Adventures Kayak School (916-642-9755); Environmental Traveling Companions (415-474-7662) specializing in trips for the disabled; Sunshine Adventures (800-829-7238); W.E.T. (916-451-3241); Access to Adventure (800-552-6284); California Canoe & Kayak (800-366-9804).

MAMMOTH MOUNTAIN SKI AREA, Mammoth Lakes, California

Information/Reservations: 888-4-MAMMOTH/619-934-0745
Mammoth Lakes Visitors Bureau:
619-934-2712/888-GO-MAMMOTH
Mammoth Reservations Bureau: 800-462-5571/619-934-2528
Unless otherwise noted, the local area code is 619.

DESCRIPTION: Mammoth Mountain, one of the nation's largest and busiest ski areas, was built around the remains of a massive volcano, the inner cone of which now features acre upon acre of fantastic bowl skiing.

Before getting on the mountain and seeing how vast the terrain is, skiers may be initially disappointed since only about 25 percent of the slopes are visible from the base.

The ski resort is located up an access road from the town of Mammoth Lakes. At the top of the road, you'll find the Mammoth Mountain Inn and a huge, sprawling base lodge, with a ski school sign-up desk, cafeteria and much more. *Woollywood*, the children's ski school, is located in an adjacent building. A second road from town will take you to Warming Hut II where there is another lodge where you can purchase lift tickets and sign up for ski school. This area also has several ski-in/ski-out condominium units adjacent to it. However, *Woollywood* and the nursery facility are both located at the Main Base area. A vast array of lodging opportunities, restaurants and shops can be found in the small but sprawling town of Mammoth Lakes.

Although there is a free bus operating between the town and the ski area, having a car is highly recommended, especially if you think you want to visit June Mountain, Mammoth's sister mountain located about a half hour away. Although June is somewhat smaller than Mammoth, it still offers interesting and challenging terrain for all levels of skiers. And, with its small old-world style village, June is considered the place for snowboarders (though both mountains permit boarders and offer lessons and rentals). Recent expansion of the snowboard park at Mammoth has added more adventurous terrain.

Year-round the entire area bustles with outdoor activity, from horseback riding and fishing in summer to dog sledding and bobsledding in winter.

THE ADVENTURES: In addition to downhill skiing (serious hard-core skiers should check out the *High Alpine Camp* program), just about every winter sport imaginable is offered at or near Mammoth. Cross-country skiing, including telemark skiing, is very popular with both Sierra Meadows Ranch Ski Touring Center (934-6161) and Tamarack Cross Country Ski Center (800-237-6879/934-2442) offering kids lessons. Reservations are required for both. Both of these facilities can get you and your team outfitted in snowshoes and take you on guided outings.

Dog sledding is also available. All ages are welcomed at Dog Sled Adventures at Sierra Meadows (934-6270) run by Paul Marvelly who encourages parents to introduce kids to his friendly huskies. Sierra Meadows is also where (934-6161) evening sleigh rides are operated. Several snowmobile companies operate in the area, including D.J.'s Snowmobile Rentals (935-4480).

One of the unusual activities in Mammoth is its bobsled facility, a designated track run by Sledz (934-7533). Sled rentals are available at Kitteredge Sports (934-7566). For those seeking a bird's-eye view of the region, even more unforgettable than the ski area's gondola ride, take a hot air balloon ride with the High Sierra Ballooning Company (934-7188) and soar through the skies.

Summer visitors looking for outdoor fare need go no further than contacting the Mammoth Adventure Connection (800-228-4947/ 934-0606) — your ticket to summer fun — that maintains an office at the Mammoth Mountain Inn. Horseback riding, guided hikes, kayaking trips, ATV tours, fishing jaunts, bicycle vacations, fly-fishing clinics, ballooning and more, all with instruction if necessary, are easily arranged with one phone call. Rock Climbing (there's a 32' climbing wall at the resort), orienteering classes and *Challenge Ropes* courses are among the summer activities of Mammoth Mountain High Adventure (924-5683). While the minimum ages for participating are 10, 14 and 14 respectively, these activities are also offered for kids as young as 4. The area's mountain bike park (accessible via the gondola) has a special area for kids, the *Li'l Rider Fun Zone*.

If hiking and backpacking appeal to you, be certain to stop in at the Forest Service Visitor Center (924-5500) where rangers are happy to fill you in on the wide range of recreational events in the area. Here you'll learn what permits you might need to fish or venture into the wilderness (the John Muir and Ansel Adams Wilderness Areas are supposed to be just spectacular) without an organized guide, hear about the many interpretive nature-oriented programs for families and pick up a copy of *Mammoth Trails*, a guide to the many hiking trails in the area.

Several packers operate pack trips into the wilderness areas specifically for families. They include McGee Creek Pack Station (935-4324) and Bob Tanner's Red Meadow Pack Station (934-2345). Be certain to sign on for a trip that is designated for families.

Canoeing, waterskiing, jet-skiing, windsurfing and horseback riding opportunities are abundant. The tourist office can give you a list of various operators. For more indoor and outdoor family activities, call the Parks and Recreation Department (934-8989).

FAMILY FEATURES: Small World Day Care, located at the Mammoth Mountain Inn, provides child care for infants on up to age 12 throughout the year, with youngsters under 2 taken care of in a separate area. They also maintain a list of babysitters for evening care (as does the town of Mammoth Lakes, call 934-2712 for details). During the summer months the *Sierra Adventure Youth Camp* operates for children ages 6 to 12 and Sierra Summer Experience for kids ages 2 to 5 at the ski area. In winter, *Woollywood Children's Ski School* gives lessons for children ages 4 to 6 and 7 to 12 throughout the ski season. On selected dates, lessons are also given to teens ages 13 to 17. Teenagers 13 to 18 also receive discounted ski lift tickets. *Big Kahuna Snowboard Club* offers lessons for kids ages 7 to 12.

Babes in the Woods is a babysitting referral service for day or evening sitters (924-2229).

BEST BEDS: Mammoth Mountain Inn, where child care is offered, is considered one of the more luxurious accommodations in the area and has condominium units, hotel rooms and a children's playground. Its *Ultimate Mountain Getaway* package is designed for active guests.

In town, Snowcreek Resort is an upscale condominium complex that has a top-notch athletic club and provides complimentary transportation to the ski area (800-544-6007).

1849 Condominiums are located right next to Warming Hut II (800-421-1849) as are Sierra Megeve, Mountainback and Aspen Creek (all can be reached at 800-227-7669). Budget-oriented visitors might consider the EconoLodge Wildwood Inn (934-6855) or Motel 6 (934-6660), both of which are located on the town's main street. There's a shuttle from town to the lifts. Two other less expensive options closer to the main base lodge are Travelodge and Thriftlodge (both located on Minaret, the road to the ski area).

WHISTLER RESORT, Whistler, British Columbia, Canada

Information/Reservations: 800-WHISTLER/604-664-5625
Whistler Activity and Information Centre:
   800-WHISTLER/604-932-2394
Unless otherwise noted, the local area code is 604.

DESCRIPTION: Flanked on either side by Whistler and Blackcomb Mountains, not only is Whistler Resort the largest ski area in North America, it is one of the continent's most popular resorts. At the base of the mountains lies Whistler Village, a pedestrians-only, European-style Alpine village with hotels, restaurants, cafes and ongoing entertainment. The gondolas that serve the mountains are located here. There is a small village area at the base of Blackcomb is referred to as Upper Village, at the center of which is sits the deluxe Chateau Whistler Resort Hotel (the area's most upscale property). A five minute walk brings you to the North Village development. We highly recommend that families seek out lodging at one of the first two both car-free villages, which will not only make getting to and from activities with youngsters easier but also much likely faster (we all know how slowly our children move!).

Though the ski areas are separately owned and managed, together they combine to offer some of the finest adventure activities around, attracting visitors from all over the world. With almost 7,000 acres of skiing it's difficult to plan to ski both mountains the same day. Some of the terrain is open year-round for skiing (summer skiing and snowboarding are operated on Blackcomb's Horstman Glacier), even though the base can often be quite mild, so if you're an avid cross-country skier or snowshoer, you'll want to check weather conditions.

For those of you who prefer warm weather adventures in, on or near water you'll be happy to note that the area boasts a total of five lakes and there are several rivers in the vicinity.

THE ADVENTURES: There really is so much available that it's difficult to know even where to begin. Your first stop should be at the Whistler Activity and Information Centre located in the front of the Conference Centre in Whistler Village. It provides details on all of the possible activities and can often make your reservations. Several of the activities are quite popular and may require making bookings prior to arrival.

Winter fare is impressive — for skiers and non-skiers alike. There's heli-skiing for those interested in untracked powder but there are also flightseeing trips that land on majestic glaciers and can include a gourmet lunch, a snowshoe outing or simply the incredible views. The Activity Centre will refer you to an outfitter that meet your needs (be specific about the ages and abilities of your kids). Year-round you can receive qualified paragliding instruction on Blackcomb with Parawest Paragliding (932-7052).

For those who don't want to take to the skies, there are a number of snowshoe options closer to the base. Canadian Snowshoeing Services (932-7877) can take you through the forest trails on Whistler Mountain. Snowmobiling also offers the option of leisurely trips or exhilarating backcountry jaunts. Instruction and tours are available for all levels of expertise and all the necessary gear is provided. Check it out with Whistler Snowmobile Guided Tours (932-4086), Blackcomb Snowmobile (932-8484) or Canadian Snowmobile Adventures (938-1616) evening fondue trips to the top of Blackcomb.

Learn to ice climb or take a private tour into backcountry powder runs with the professionals at Whistler Alpine Guides Bureau (938-9242), or call Whistler Backcountry Adventures (938-1410) for a winter fishing trip. Contact Western Adventures on Horseback (894-6155) for a true western riding experience or Whistler Outdoor Experience Company (932-3389) to arrange a sleigh ride. In summer, the company operates a number of guided canoe, biking and horseback riding trips.

In summer the options, believe it or not are even greater. Whistler's summer season runs from the beginning of June through early October. The fully-enclosed Express Gondola (up to five kids under the age of 15 ride free with an adult) whisks guests to the top of the Whistler Mountain where a complimentary guided nature walk is offered daily. If you arrive early enough in the season, you might even be able to take a guided snowshoe trek. Beginning in mid-summer, guided horseback trips head up the mountain to 7000 feet above sea level.

All summer long guided mountain biking is offered. The resort's Valley Trail system connects Whistler Village to other spots in the valley with a network of paved trails ideal for cyclists and in-line skaters. The more intrepid head for the challenging terrain of Lost Lake Park. Rentals and maps are available at a number of shops throughout the area. Parents will be happy to know that a number of rental shops offer kids trailers. A freestyle park, popular with skateboarders, is located next to Fitzsimmons Creek between the two villages and The Skate Park, a magnet for in-line skaters is located at the base of Blackcomb Mountain between the Magic and Wizard Express chair lifts.

There's all kinds of hiking and a number of four-wheel drive and ATV tours also enable you to explore backcountry terrain. Be certain to pick up a copy of the *Whistler Mountain Hiking Map* that recommends the two-mile hike to Harmon Lake for a family picnic and offers suggestions on how to react should you spot a bear in a column appropriately entitled "Bear Sense." Whistler Alpine Guides Bureau (938-9242) offers instruction in climbing or mountaineering but you first might want to test your skills on the indoor wall at the Stonewall Whistler Rock Climbing Gym (938-9858). In summer, the wall is moved outside with locations in both villages.

You can soar through the skies in a helicopter tour of the mountain glacier and don't forget Parawest Paragliding, open year-round. Blackcomb's summer season opens in mid-June and runs through Labor Day with its own long list of alpine fare. Chair lifts are open (both chairs have clear plastic bubbles to protect riders when it's cool outside), providing spectacular sightseeing en route to the mid-station where, from Rendezvous Restaurant, a guided bus tour ventures deep into the Alpine forest to the Seventh Heaven lift that heads to the top of the mountain. Hikers can skip the bus and take the 45 minute hike. With the exception of a slight rise at the beginning, most of the hiking is slightly downhill. From both the Rendezvous Restaurant (one third up Blackcomb Mountain) and the Wizard Express (at the base of Blackcomb), guided mountain bike rides and horseback rides are offered. And, as we mentioned above, both summer skiing and snowboarding are possible.

You'll find a well-marked mountain trail system atop the Solar Coaster Chair (two-thirds up Blackcomb) where signs identify local wildlife. At the base of Wizard Express, in-line skating clinics are offered. Novice and expert alike can learn circus skill from the All-Canadian Trapeze Company facility located at base of the Magic Chair.

And, yes, there's more: fishing, river rafting, jet skiing, llama treks and kayaking to name a few. If you want to learn who does what, contact the activities office. Don't forget to ask which operators pick-up in village.

FAMILY FEATURES: With so much going on that the entire family will enjoy, you'll be amazed at the activities designed just for kids. In winter, ski programs are offered to kids from 18 month at Blackcomb, from age 2 at Whistler. Children's day camps run by the municipality (932-5535) also run throughout the summer (for children as young as 2) and take the kids the width and breadth of the resort area. *Tanwood International Camps* for kids ages 8 to 17 may provide an interesting option. English lessons are offered in the mornings to non-English speaking youngsters while afternoons are just for playing.

Parents with younger children can contact Dandelion Day Care (932-1119) which is open year-round, Monday to Friday only, for kids 3 months to 5 years. Tiny Tots (938-9699) and The Nanny Network (938-2823) both accept drop-ins.

Most of the hotels maintain lists of interested sitters and can help steer you in the right direction.

If you're in need of any baby and children's equipment, contact the local branch of Baby's Away (see page 127).

BEST BEDS: Accommodations run the gamut — from B&Bs and condominiums to no-frill hotels and full-service resorts. Call 800-WHISTLER for a complete listing of the various properties. Some favorites are the following:

In Whistler Village: The Delta Whistler Resort, a full service resort located at the base of both the mountains' gondolas, has 300 guest rooms. Many have balconies, fireplaces and kitchens. Bike rentals are offered from the hotel.

The Blackcomb Lodge is a first class, 72-room hotel with studio lofts, an indoor pool and guest laundry facilities. Sheraton Suites offer studio to two-bedroom condos and is located adjacent to Whistler Village, a five minute walk from the gondola.

Westbrook Whistler is an all suite hotel in the heart of the village with 48 one- to two-bedroom suites, two of which have private hot tubs.

Holiday Inn SunSpree Resort is a nice moderately-priced option in the village center as is the Crystal Lodge where the cozy common rooms create a warm ambience.

Mountainside Lodge, adjacent to the lifts, is a condominium complex comprised of 50 studio and studio loft apartments, all with Jacuzzis.

Whistler Timberline Lodge is a rustic 42-room lodge adjacent to the Whistler Conference Centre. In addition to hotel rooms, studio to one-bedroom suites with lofts are offered.

In the Upper Village: Chateau Whistler Resort is a member of the Canadian Pacific Hotel & Resort group and has received numerous awards. It has an indoor/outdoor pool, a kids' summer tennis camp and all the amenities one expects from a property of this caliber.

Radisson Blackcomb Suites (The Aspens, Woodrun, Greystone Lodge, The Marquise and Glacier Lodge) are a collection of five properties slopeside to Blackcomb. Units range from studios to three bedrooms, some with lofts. Each property has an outdoor heated pool, indoor or outdoor hot tubs and in-suite or common area laundry facilities.

Le Chamois offers luxurious studios to three bedroom units, an outdoor heated pool, common laundry facilities and is run like a full-service hotel.

MOUNTAIN SHORTS

In the event you haven't found the mountain destination that sounds exactly right for you, here are a few more choices. In some we list a winter option, in others a warm weather choice; occasionally we list both.

From border to border, north, south, east and west, Colorado is one of our country's adventure capitals. **Aspen** (800-26-ASPEN/970-925-9000), home to four downhill ski areas is also the home base of Blazing Adventures (800-282-RAFT/970-923-4544), with a program that includes cattle drives, llama treks and river rafting in summer, and snowy adventures galore in winter. The Aspen Youth Center (970-925-7091) features a number of outings just for kids, including kayaking, rock climbing, caving and mountain biking. Guided snowshoe walks on Aspen Mountain are offered twice daily. On-mountain winter programs for kids begin at 18 months . . . Over in Summit County, **Keystone Resort** (800-222-0188/970-468-2316) has been dishing up summer fare to please all ages since its inception. Guided hiking, river rafting, llama treks, gold panning, windsurfing and more are on tap. The Children's Center is open year-round for children as young as 2 months . . . From Keystone's sister resort, **Breckenridge** (800-789-7669/800-800-BREC), you can hike the many trails that are part of the 44-acre Summit County Recreation Trail connecting the towns of Dillon, Silverthorne, Frisco, Keystone, Breckenridge, Copper Mountain and Vail. The Breckenridge Recreation Center has an outdoor skateboard park and an indoor climbing wall, where classes are offered. In addition to winter snowmobile tours (we can personally attest to the fact that these are great for families; the company even has infant carriers for the machines), Tiger Run Tours can arrange for horseback rides, bike trips and 4x4 trips in summer . . . At **Copper Mountain** (800-458-8386/970-968-2882), which will celebrate its 25th anniversary in 1997, winter brings telemark skiing, sleigh rides, horseback riding and the long-awaited lift-served extreme 700 acres of backcountry skiing in Copper Bowl. In summer, U.S. Forest Service guided nature hikes depart twice daily, free paddleboating and trout fishing for kids is on tap as are pony rides, gold panning, fly-fishing clinics and more. Horseback ride with the Copper Mountain Stables, rent a mountain bike, call Osprey Adventures (668-5573) for scenic canoe trips and check with the resort's activity desk for whitewater rafting, four-wheel-drive vehicle backcountry treks and more. The resort's children's center, the *Belly Button Bakery,* is open to children ages 2 months to 8 years, year-round; skiing programs for children ages 4 to 12 run during the winter and an *Adventue Day Camp* for ages 5 to 12 operates during the summer season . . . The **Steamboat** (800-922-2722/970-879-0880), summer brochure fills an entire page with adventures — from Airplane Scenic Flights and ATV Tours to Yampa River Park & Kayak Course. The list goes on and on "because there is really more to do per square mile than just about anyplace else." Summer packages include *Adventure Escape* and *Family Getaway* (which includes a day of *Kids Adventure Club* for children ages 3 to 12, divided by age). Additionally, a wide spectrum of cowboy and western events takes place throughout the season. The mountain is open for biking and the local rivers are open for canoers and rafters . . . In **Telluride** (800-525-3455/970-728-6900), the folks at Telluride Outside (970-728-3895) offer abundant winter and summer choices, from dog sledding to fly-fishing to jeep tours. Free mountain snowshoe tours are sponsored by the mountain three days a week. In summer, teens can take a program at the Southwest Outdoor Center while youngsters 6 to 10 head for the town-run day camp. In winter, programs and care are available for children of all ages, from 2 months through teens.

BOOKED FOR TRAVEL

Country Roads Press is a doing an **OUTDOOR ACTIVITY GUIDE** series, state by state. We've inspected *Colorado,* by Claire Walter (whose books we always like), and *Pennsylvania,* by Sally Moore. Chapters are organized according to activity and include information on where to go, who to go with, etc. Neither of the books say much about kids or families, so, while they may point the way, you'll need to do further research before embarking on any family excursions.

Of course, Colorado doesn't have a monopoly on great outdoor adventures in the Rockies. When the mountain bike clinics end at **Snowbird** (800-453-3000/801-742-2222) in Utah, try helicopter skiing by contacting Wasatch Powderbirds (801-742-2800). Hiking and rock-climbing (instruction available) are popular, as is the 115-foot climbing wall at Cliff Lodge, one of the tallest in the world. Summer and winter programs for kids (from age 6 weeks [in winter] or 3 years [in summer] to age 15) make it easy to take advantage of all of the offerings . . . Endless adventures await guests at Robert Redford's **Sundance** (800-892-1600/ 801-225-4107). Horseback riding, guided hiking, river rafting and more are easy to arrange. *Kid's Camp* is offered for ages 6 to 12 in summer, ages 4 to 12 in winter.

One of the best and most reasonably-priced snowcat skiing opportunities is at the family-friendly **Grand Targhee Resort** (800-TARGHEE) in Wyoming. In summer, the resort Activity Center (extension 1355) can set you up with a guided hike, a day of rafting or a fly-fishing expedition plus find the best activities for your kids, be they infants or teens. Don't miss the climbing wall right at the base area! Trips to Yellowstone are easy to arrange . . . Speaking of Yellowstone, guests at **Big Sky Ski & Summer Resort** (800-548-4486) are also within easy striking distance of the park. At Lone Mountain Guest Ranch, guests can take backcountry tours, head out in a dog sled or participate in winter fly-fishing or horseback riding. Snowmobiling can be found just about everywhere (West Yellowstone is considered the snowmobile capital of the world). In summer, mountain biking, guided hiking, rafting on the Gallatin River and much more are easily arranged by Adventures Big Sky at the resort. Llama treks, rock climbing excursions, and any number of guided tours are also possible.

BOOKED FOR TRAVEL

ROCKY MOUNTAIN SKIING by Claire Walter is a model guide book. It has a clear, easy-to-follow format and it's chock full of facts. It includes well written descriptions of all the major ski areas and their facilities in the six Rocky Mountain states. Cross-country facilities are always noted, as are simple but more than adequate entries on programs for children. Especially nice is the fact that summer activities are given space. No prices are given, which means the book will not be outdated next year. This is one to buy and keep. (Fulcrum)

Back east in Vermont, **Mount Snow** (800-245-7669/802-464-3333) offers one of the oldest Mountain Bike Schools, with courses for children and adults ages 12 and older. Don't worry, younger kids are well looked after at the resort's nursery and child care center . . . At **Ascutney Mountain Resort** (800-243-0011/802-484-7711) in Brownsville, guests can go dog sledding with Native Sun Scenic Tours (800-699-SLED) or snowmobiling with Vermont Snowmobile Tours (800-286-6360). In all seasons, call Ekiah Pickett at Northern Pack and Paddle (802-457-1409) in Woodstock for fly-fishing, hiking, camping, canoeing, kayaking and snowshoeing. Ekiah loves Vermont and kids — a winning combination. *Flying Ducks* day care at the resort accepts children from 6 months . . . In **Killington**, backcountry ski experiences are available to all on the mountain's *Fusion Zones*, more than 75 acres of unique wooded terrain on all five peaks that were developed in cooperation with the Vermont Department of Forests, Parks and Recreation. From cruising areas to challenging forested lanes, lessons with advanced specialized skis and boots are offered. Summer brings a Fly-Fishing School, guided hikes at the Merrell Hiking Center and 37 miles of mountain bike trails with guided tours and instruction possible. Activities for children from infancy through age 12 are possible year-round.

Loon Mountain (603-745-8111) in Lincoln, New Hampshire, is the site of Loon Mountain Park (603-745-8111), a place of "outdoor family fun and adventure." Mountain biking, guided wilderness tours, in-line skating, hiking trails, horseback riding and more, most geared to kids 8 and older.

When you visit **Ski Windham**, (800-SKI-WINDHAM/518-734-4300) in New York's Catskill Mountains, where we took our boys when they were younger, you can winter horseback ride at Silver Springs Ranch (518-589-5559), or take the fast route through this winter wonderland in a snowmobile. The more adventurous can call Rock and Snow, Inc. (914-255-1311), specialists in rock and ice climbing, mountaineering and backpacking equipment for local guide services. Kids older than 1 year can join one of the mountain kids' programs.

BOOKED FOR TRAVEL

"In June we packed the Model-A with food and clothes. We were going to spend the summer with Papa in the logging camp. I am old now, but I still remember how it was." So begins THE DAY OF THE HIGH CLIMBER, by Gary Hines, a fictional reminiscence of the world of the lumberjack several decades back. Anna Grossnickle Hines' wonderful watercolor drawings greatly enhance the book's overall merit. (Greenwillow)

Up in the Canadian province of Quebec, **Tremblant** (800-461-8711/819-681-2000) offers a variety of hiking tours, kayak and canoe trips and lessons, mountain biking, climbing and orienteering programs. In most cases, minimum age requirements are stated in Tremblant's catalog, which also lists prices for each program. Some classes are specifically designed for kids, while others welcome the entire family. The 200-kilometer linear park, Le P'tit Train du Nord (800-561-NORD), is open to bikers, hikers and skaters in summer, snowmobilers and cross-country skiers in winter. It runs through 28 communities from St. Jerome to Mont Laurier with an average incline of two percent *Kidz Club* for is open to youngsters ages 6 months to 12 years. Younger children are cared for in the nursery while those 4 and older can join the *Intrepid Adventurers* for a full (or partial) day of outdoor fun.

CHAPTER 5

TOUR OPERATORS

The companies we've talked about throughout this book tend to specialize exclusively in adventure vacations. More and more tour operators have expanded their traditional travel package offerings to include adventure holidays. Below we list 22 such organizations. All of these companies are happy to work directly with you or in cooperation with your travel agent. If there is an asterisk (*) at the start of the listing, you will find a more extensive write-up of some of the company's trips in **Great Nature Vacations With Your Kids.**

ABERCROMBIE & KENT *

This top luxury adventure travel company now has special family packages, all detailed in a separate brochure entitled *Family Holidays*. Trips take parents and kids of all ages to the far corners of the earth: Africa, Central America, North America, South America, Europe, Australia and Antarctica. On some trips, nannies travel with the group specifically to look after little ones. A domestic package at the B-Bar Ranch in Montana features horseback riding, cattle drives, mountain biking and river rafting, while the *Family Tour of Costa Rica* offers hiking through rain forests and river rafting. *(1520 Kensington Road, Oak Brook, IL 60521-2141; 800-323-7308/708-954-2944)*

BOOKED FOR TRAVEL

Vacation World's ADVENTURE HOLIDAYS 1996: *Your Complete Guide to Thousands of Active Vacations Worldwide,* edited by Victoria Pybus, is for the traveler with an international mindset. Though a British publication, the book is readily available in the U.S. Although the majority of the adventures appear to be geared to adults, many entries note the minimum age requirements and whether families participate in the trips. Organizations are grouped first by the type of adventure offered then by the area of the world where the adventures take place. This makes it easier for readers to zero in on family-friendly possibilities in a given field or region. (Peterson's)

AMERICAN WILDERNESS EXPERIENCE *

Representing a wide range of adventure travel companies, AWE offers year-round adventures — from horsepacking, canoeing, rafting and sea kayaking to dog sledding, winter camping and snowmobile trips — many of which are designated for family travelers. Additionally, its *Old West*

Dude Ranch Vacations brochure features a chart that details not only the adventures (e.g., cattle drives, pack trips, rafting) but also the ages of any supervised youth programs. *(P.O. Box 1486, Boulder, CO 80306; 800-444-0099/303-444-2622)*

APPALACHIAN MOUNTAIN CLUB *

This membership organization features a number of outings, programs and camps specifically for families with children of all ages. It also offers moderately-priced lodging facilities in mountain settings in the Northeastern section of the United States where scheduled activities include hiking, cross-country skiing, backcountry skiing, snowshoeing and dog sledding. *(5 Joy Street, Boston, MA 02108; 617-523-0636)*

BORTON OVERSEAS

Specializing in travel to Scandinavia, once considered an "exotic" travel destination, Borton Overseas offers escorted, independent and customized tours that can feature biking, dog sledding, rafting, hiking and/or fishing. General Manager Geri Eikaas says that most tours are "suitable for families; it depends on their interests." Other options include cabin rentals in Norway and Finland, farm holidays in Norway, Fishermen's Cabins on the Lofoten Islands which often include bike rentals, rowboats and fishing. The preset bicycle tours generally have a minimum age requirement, between 12 and 16 years. Hiking tours in Norway begin for children as young as age 6 while ski holidays are open to all ages (with the exception of the lodge-to-lodge trips, in which the minimum age accepted is 16). Dog sledding in Lapland also requires that children be age 16 and older. A number of unusual trips head to Africa, South & Central America and the South Pacific. *(1621 E. 79th Street, Bloomington, MN 55425; 800-843-0602/612-883-0704)*

BOTTOM TIME ADVENTURES

The company, which operates a live-aboard mini-cruise ship the *Bottom Time II,* offers a number of varied itineraries, most of which venture out into Bahamian waters. One trip has participants swimming with free-roaming dolphins, another heads out sea kayaking every day. Island bicycle trips that combine biking with various water sports and a unique whale-watching cruise are also on the company's schedule. Custom trips are also possible. *(P.O. Box 11919, Ft. Lauderdale, FL, 33339-1919; 800-234-8464/305-921-7798)*

CANYONLANDS FIELD INSTITUTE *

The intellectual focus of Canyonlands' trips is on environmentally aware recreation; the physical activities encompass hiking, rafting and camping. Family trips, workshops, intergenerational Elderhostel programs and a variety of camps and programs just for kids are among its offerings. Best for school age children. *(Box 68, Moab, UT 84532; 800-860-5262/801-259-7750)*

THE CHEWONKI FOUNDATION *

Canoeing, camping, sailing and hiking are highlights of the family fare featured by this non-profit educational organization, with instruction always included for participants. *(RR2, Box 1200, Wiscasset, ME 04578; 207-882-7323)*

ELDERHOSTEL *

Elderhostel's extensive listing of short-term, inexpensive programs designates many of their courses as intergenerational — welcoming grandparents and their grandchildren, sometimes as young as 5. Though the majority of its courses take place on college campuses, many are held in the great outdoors and feature just about every activity covered in this book. *(75 Federal Street, Boston, MA 02110-1941; 617-426-8056)*

FAMILY EXPLORATIONS, INC. *

Founded by a parent for other parents and/or grandparents traveling with kids, a number of its tours are appropriate for those seeking adventurous vacations. For the most part trips head for Central America and Europe and all trips can accommodate all ages. Currently under the label of adventure trips (there are also quite a few destinations considered discovery trips) are vacations to Costa Rica, Ireland, Italy, Canada, Jamaica and Honduras. Each trip features a daily children's program. *(343 Dartmouth Avenue, Swarthmore, PA 19081-1017; 800-WE-GO-TOO/610-543-6200)*

BOOKED FOR TRAVEL

ADVENTURING WITH CHILDREN: *An Inspirational Guide to World Travel & the Outdoors* by Nan Jeffrey is about the ways and means to achieve the freedom of family life on the road. Hers is the voice of experience since she and her husband began traveling with their twin sons while the kids were tiny. The book is aimed at independent travelers — folks who are not averse to adapting to the challenges of: "Living together in small areas (tent, boat, camper, hotel room, etc.); reducing needs to the size of a backpack, tent, canoe, car, and the like; carrying belongings in a backpack; walking good distances; handwashing laundry (including cloth diapers); cooking on a one or two burner stove ..." Jeffrey feels that if you want to travel enough, you can make it happen. This may entail taking unpaid leave from work, providing homeschooling for your children, and learning to live modestly in order to afford a trip. Obviously, such a gypsy existence is not for everyone, but for those whose wanderlust just won't quit even after they attain the dignity of parenthood, this book will be a great support and source of ideas. (Avalon House)

GRANDTRAVEL *

The first tour operation for grandparents traveling with grandchildren was founded by Helena Koenig who has put together an exciting and eclectic group of intergenerational tours. There are departures for grandparents with kids ages 7 to 11, 12 to 17 and all ages. Outdoor adventures are included in many of the itineraries, including *The American Indian Culture of the Southwest USA* (rafting, horseback riding, jeep tour), *The Grandest Canyons* (horseback riding, rafting, jeep tour), *Western Parks Western Space* (calf roping, covered wagon ride, horseback riding, float trip), *Alaska Wilderness Adventure* (gold panning, float trip, river rafting) and *Enchanting Ireland* (bicycling, horseback riding). Trips also head to Africa, Australia, China and other European destinations. Koenig is always available to arrange independent tours for this market and has recently designed a number of packages for family groups, including all three generations! *(6900 Wisconsin Avenue, Suite 706, Chevy Chase, MD 20815; 800-247-7651/301-986-0790)*

GUIDES FOR ALL SEASONS

In business for more than 20 years, this company offers hiking and other adventure trips to Japan, Switzerland, Greece, Austria, England, Thailand and Laos in addition to its main area of specialization — Nepal. Independent travelers to Nepal will be particularly interested in the Sherpa Guide Lodges that Guides For All Seasons represent. These lodges are featured in the video *A Trek With My Dad*, by Chelsea, owner Jim Wills' daughter who joined her parents on a fairly rigorous journey to Nepal when she was 8. In addition to featuring a *Family Trek in Nepal* each Christmas/New Year's season, there's also an interesting family trip, *England for Kids*, each summer. Due to the great enthusiasm for this trip, the company has just increased its offering for families. *(202 Country Road, Calpine, CA 96124; 800-457-4574/916-994-3613)*

JOURNEYS *

We're big fans of Journeys. Founders Will and Joan Weber were among the first adventure travel operators to design family departures. Among Journeys' offerings are wild animal safaris, Himalayan trekking, tropical rain forest explorations and cross cultural encounters heading to Latin America, Africa and Asia. In addition to its organized fare, customized trips are among the company's specialties. *(4011 Jackson Road, Ann Arbor, MI 48103; 800-255-8735/313-665-4407)*

OFF THE BEATEN PATH *

Pam and Bill Bryan began Off The Beaten Path in 1987 as a *Personal Itinerary Planning Service* offering unique, highly individualized itineraries for those who wanted to see more than was found in traditional tours. Their trips cover the region stretching from the Canadian Rockies to the canyons of New Mexico, and everywhere in-between — Montana, Wyoming, Idaho, Utah, Colorado and Arizona. Options are available for all, from the most intrepid adventurers to those who prefer living in the lap of luxury. In recent years, a number of pre-set tours have been added, including a few designed for families: on some you join a group, while on others you go on your own. Now, a dozen family-oriented trips in Alaska are on the roster. Trips for outdoor enthusiasts include a *Kodiak Island Bear* trip in Alaska, customized ski trips that can include snowmobiling, winter wildlife tours and dog sledding, downhill and cross-country skiing, backcountry horse-outfitted trips, "a signature travel experience of the Rocky Mountains," and much more. *(109 East Main Street, Bozeman, MT 59715; 800-445-2995/ 406-586-1311)*

OH, TO BE IN ENGLAND *

This small, personalized service run by Jennifer Dorn provides day-by-day itineraries that are individually designed. Jennie will be happy to guide your family on a quest of adventure in the British Isles and has frequently provided hiking trips for her clients. If she feels you'd be best doing the research without the benefit of her expertise, she'll steer you to the best resources to do so. She's a refreshing breath of honesty in a world usually so anxious to take advantage. *(2 Charlton Street, New York, NY 10014; 212-255-8739)*

RASCALS IN PARADISE *

Founded by veteran travel specialists Theresa Detchemendy and Deborah Baratta (who travel with their own rascals), Rascals offers a number of vacations that fall into the adventure category, as well as a number of resort-based vacation possibilities. The company's plentiful *Divers With Kids* offerings will particularly appeal to scuba divers. Biking, rafting, kayaking and ranch vacations are also featured as are excursions to the South Pacific, Australia, New Zealand, Europe, Africa and Asia. Both group and individual departures are offered to most destinations. *(650 Fifth Street, #505, San Francisco, CA 94107; 800-U-RASCAL/415-978-9800)*

BOOKED FOR TRAVEL

PARADISE FAMILY GUIDES: *Hawaii, Kauai, Maui and Lanai, Oahu.* This series always had plenty on traveling with children in the Hawaiian Islands, but it's only recently that they have designated themselves "family" guides with *Making the Most of Your Family Vacation* as a subtitle. Each of the four volumes is hefty, with lots on where to stay, eat, swim, tour, etc. (Prima Publishing)

ROYAL PALM TOURS, INC.

Royal Palm President Ron Drake tell us that although none of its specific horseback riding trips are geared to families (some are exclusively for women), the company "welcomes, invites and accommodates children." The treks, which take place in various parts of Florida, require that children be able to handle a horse and be accompanied by an adult. The treks range in length from six to eight days and include a number of visits that are certain to pique the interests of youngsters such as a visit to a dairy farm, stopping at the Seminole Reservation, swamp buggy tours and more. Trips are offered year-round. *(P.O. Box 60079, Fort Myers, FL 33906; 800-296-0924/941-368-0760)*

BOOKED FOR TRAVEL

Take a walk on the wild side with author/adventurer M. Timothy O'Keefe, whose boundless enthusiasm for embracing the exciting and unusual pervades the pages of his **GREAT ADVENTURES IN FLORIDA.** The author sets the tone on the dedication page, writing, "To my parents, who never said, 'Don't try'." Although many of his more sensational suggestions are not appropriate for young children — the chapters on Sleeping Underwater at Jules' Undersea Lodge (this Florida Keys hotel is several fathoms below water and only accepts teenagers), Cave Diving, and Spotlighting Alligators at Night; others such as Swamp Buggies and Air Boats, The Scoop on Scallops (he shared this snorkeling/fishing adventure with his 8-year-old son) or the section of Vintage Airplane Rides in Getting High Over Florida definitely are (at least for the adventurous older child). This is a lively read from cover to cover with vicarious thrills aplenty. (Menasha Ridge)

SIERRA CLUB*

The Sierra Club's Outing Department sponsors more than 300 excursions each year and a fair number of them are specifically for families. Several welcome children of all ages; others are designed for specific age groups — from toddlers to teens. Its family adventures invite you to "paddle a canoe, ride a rapid, or lead a burro" and venture from the National Parks to the shores of Hawaii and the Caribbean. Each trip includes age recommendations and there are even intergenerational trips on the agenda. *(Sierra Club Outing Department, 85 Second Street, San Francisco, CA 94105; 415-977-5630)*

The lively **SIERRA CLUB WAYFINDING BOOK,** by Vicki McVey, includes instructions, anecdotes and games. Kids will absorb a little history, a little geography and a lot of clever ideas about how to find their place in the world, wherever they may be. (Sierra Club)

SOUTHWIND ADVENTURES

Offering a variety of "nature and cultural tours" in South America (Argentina, Bolivia, Brazil, Chile, Ecuador, Peru and Venezuela), Southwind has been welcoming families on many of its excursions for several years. The trips may include trekking, climbing, river rafting or biking plus the possibility of camping for some or part of the trip. "Best suited for families with children" are its trips to Ecuador (*Wildlife Odyssey, Markets & Festivals, Cuyabeno Rainforest Workshop*), Peru (*Salcantay Sacred Mountain Trek; Southern Highlights; World of the Incas; Heart of the Amazon; Macaw Research Center*) and Argentina/Chile (*Nature Discovery Tour*). Specific age advice and children's pricing are addressed on an individual basis. *(P.O. Box 621057, Littleton, CO 80161; 800-377-WIND/303-972-0701)*

WAIRA'S FIRST JOURNEY follows the footsteps of a young Aymara Indian girl as she travels with her family and their llama herd through the Bolivian mountains to market, a trip which lasts several days. Author/illustrator Eusebio Topooco is himself an Aymara and this book is his way of recording the traditions of his people for posterity. (Lothrop)

SUPER NATURAL ADVENTURES *

This company specializes in travel to the Canadian provinces of British Columbia, Alberta and the Yukon and represents more than 200 suppliers and outfitters and their packaged and customized trips for both summer and winter. Mini-adventures, adventure touring, guest ranches, resorts and lodges are among the many options. *(626 West Pender Street, Vancouver, B.C., Canada V6B 1V9; 800-263-1600/604-683-5101)*

VISTATOURS

Though the majority of the company's moderately-priced tours are exclusively for adults, its Reno/Tahoe and Coastal California five-day/four-night *Young At Heart* tours welcome children and/or grandchildren. The Reno/Tahoe trip features a hay wagon breakfast plus enough free time to take advantage of the area's many adventures; the Coastal California trip includes a ride on the Roaring Camp Railroad. In past years selections have included trips to National Parks, rafting excursions and more. *(c/o Frontier Enterprises, Inc. Carson City, NV; 800-248-4782. Participants are encouraged to contact their travel agent to make reservations.)*

WILDERNESS SOUTHEAST *

Explore the wilderness with knowledgeable guides as you hike, camp and canoe the Southeast region of the United States. Canoe-camping (staying in comfortable cabins) is featured on some of its designated-for-family trips; others use base camps with bathhouses and cold showers on site. *(711 Sandtown Road, Savannah, GA 31410-1019; 912-897-5108)*

WILDERNESS TRAVEL

One of the first adventure tour operators to offer family trips, Wilderness Travel has severely curtailed this segment of its operation. We were disappointed to learn that their attitude is that "due to the very active nature of most of our trips, we do not have many young families traveling with us." Several trips a year welcome children as young as 6; all of the others have a minimum age of 16. Though there is absolutely no mention of kids in its extensive catalog we're told that its child-friendly options on upcoming trips include an 11-day journey to the Galapagos, a two-week trip to Costa Rica and a 17-day hiking and sailing adventure in Turkey. *(801 Allston Way, Berkeley, CA 94710; 800-368-2794/510-548-0420)*

CHAPTER 6

CAMPING

There are several things upon which all outdoor experts agree. First, camping today often bears little resemblance to what we remember from when we were young. Second, heading out for a camping trip with your kids will bring out the pioneer in all of you. And, finally, as with all forms of family travel, the more you plan in advance, the more you'll enjoy the experience.

Unlike the other chapters in this book, which focus on organized trips (where there's help on hand to set up camp, provide meals, etc.), this section is aimed at those of you who are intrepid enough to bundle up your kids and venture into the great outdoors without the benefit of someone else's expertise and/or equipment. In this chapter we include information on both tent and RV camping. Our own families, though we are far from being experts, have had many wonderful camping experiences tenting in state and national parks and during our rafting trips. Naturalist-led walks into the woods or along the coast at low tide have taught our kids a lot about nature; storytelling around the campfire at night is something they talked about all the time when they were younger.

On a camping trip, life and the world take on new aspects, both more vivid and more serene, without the intrusion of telephones, televisions and clocks. The beauty of the surroundings takes over and the stress of everyday living begins to loosen its hold on our souls. Existence becomes simpler and our sense of adventure blossoms.

If you equate sleeping under the stars with how many stars a hotel has garnered, and you fear that an independent camping trip with your kids means you'll have no choice but to rough it, think again. Nineties-style camping ranges from rustic (sleeping bags under lean-tos, tents along the Appalachian Trail, a basically-equipped state campground) to deluxe (a queen-size bed in a streamlined RV conveniently hooked up to electricity and hot and cold running water, with a grocery store, restaurant, swimming pool and other recreational facilities right on-site). While writing this book, we were both pleased and surprised to learn that outhouse-type facilities exist even in some of the more remote areas of forests and parks. Many campgrounds have wading pools, playgrounds, fishing ponds; some now even feature health clubs!

The kind of camping you choose, be it with a car, RV, canoe or while hiking, will depend on you and your family; but please, don't embark on a two-week camping vacation until you've tried it for a weekend and are sure that you like it. Your first trip should be close to home and civilization, short and simple. For those of you who'd like to try tent camping, even your own backyard will do.

The British-published Usborne series of guidebooks are really instruction manuals in which each idea and piece of information described in the text is reinforced by an accompanying full-color illustration. The aim here is to be perfectly clear and precise, leaving nothing to chance, which makes these books extremely suitable for novices and young people. **CAMPING AND WALKING** by David Watkins and Meike Dalal (illustrated by Jonathan Langley and Malcolm English) fulfills all these promises and we recommend it highly.

Another major difference in modern camping is the gear. The high-tech, lightweight equipment available today is not only easier to carry, it's also easier to use, so setting up camp takes minimal effort, leaving you more time to enjoy your surroundings. Similarly, the clothing you'll take along will keep you and your kids warm (even when you're wet), will dry more quickly and will be easier to carry.

One of the other benefits to a camping trip is cost. Regardless of which mode of camping you select, it's an extremely economical vacation. Campsites are far less costly than hotels and food costs are easily manageable. Even camping with a recreational vehicle, where the operational costs are not cheap (RVs get little more than eight miles to a gallon of gas), is still less expensive because RVers save on lodging and dining expenses without having to give up the comforts of home. RV vacations also make taking the family pet on holiday eminently doable. We'll talk more about RV travel options later in this chapter.

THE CAMPER'S COMPANION: *The Pack-Along Guide for Better Outdoor Trips,* by Rick Greenspan and Hal Kahn, is out in an updated third edition. This outstanding resource covers its subject thoroughly and in great detail, yet manages to be very readable and user-friendly. One of its new features is the *Outdoors On-line* chapter, "every camper's guide to surfing the Net." We looked in the index to see what the authors had to say about camping with children and were delighted to observe that their advice and outlook are totally in sync with ours. At the end of the book is a section of invaluable *Clip Out Lists* (including a *Kiddy List for Babies and the Very Young* and one of *Fun Games*) and *Recipes,* though, frankly, we think you'll prefer to keep the book intact. This is one companion you'll want to include on all your camping excursions. (Foghorn)

If the Boy Scout motto, "Be Prepared," was ever important, now is the time. To paraphrase the authors of *The Camper's Companion*, although the planning process takes lots of time and energy, it's worth it. The authors also believe that car or canoe camping, as well as RVing, make for the easiest travel with young children, family members with disabilities and those comforted by having modern conveniences close to hand.

A camping trip provides families some other unique opportunities: not to be in a hurry, to work as a team, and to foster a real respect and love for nature. Side-by-side, you'll be learning how to minimize human impact on the environment by seeing first-hand what you're working to preserve. Camping is also suited to people of all ages and from all walks of life. The camaraderie that is so prevalent at campgrounds, both at home and abroad, will make it easy for you and your kids to meet folks.

On most family vacations, remember you will cover less ground on a camping trip with your kids than if you were on your own. Look at this as a plus. It means that you'll pick and choose what you do with discrimination, so that chances are you'll also have more fun doing it. Always bear in mind the following three rules of thumb:

- Kids like to see and do everything — look around every tree, watch tadpoles, play for relatively long periods of time, skip rocks in the river, whatever.

- Kids don't want to be lectured and feel like they're back in school. After all, they're on vacation.

- Hunger and thirst set in much earlier and more frequently for kids than for adults. Be certain to bring along lots of snacks and drinks.

In advance of your trip, you might choose some simple books on plants and animals indigenous to the area in which you'll be and look at them together. Then, on the trip you can point out what you're seeing. It's even better if you can bring the books along with you and make a game out of finding specific flowers, trees, etc. We prefer to join an organized hike (commonly offered at many campgrounds) for the very reason that someone else is doling out the information. We've found that on subsequent hikes on our own, it's the kids who are best able to apply the knowledge they've gained and point things out to us!

Don't let bad weather spoil your outings. Nowhere is it written that you can't hike or enjoy the outdoors in the rain, especially if you've taken proper precautions. If you don't want to pack your raingear in your day pack, bring along a small supply of large garbage bags; they'll do just as well. While hiking one day in the rain, we learned that when the showers end, the birds come out and spread their plumage for the sun to dry.

What started out as a drawback quickly turned into one of the highlights of our hike.

Some things will not change on a camping vacation, or any vacation, for that matter. Our children's physical needs and habits do not magically mature when we head for the great outdoors. Diapers need to be changed. Fussy eaters remain fussy eaters. Brothers and sisters find things to argue about. Early risers and middle-of-the-night-waker-uppers continue their sleeping routines. And, there's no guarantee that one of you won't get sick. On the other hand, there are no phones ringing and (except in an RV) no television or video games to disturb your time together.

BOOKED FOR TRAVEL

AMOS CAMPS OUT is a cute story about a dog who goes on a family camping trip. At home, Amos spends all of his time on the couch, but ever since he discovered that the couch has wheels, he's able to travel anywhere he wants. His doting owners bring his couch along for him when they all head off, thus setting the scene for Amos' exciting adventures in the woods. (Little Brown)

WHY CHOOSE AN RV

For many years we've read and written about RV vacations (as opposed to tent camping) but have yet to do one ourselves. Can a middle-class New York City-reared family find happiness on the road in a motor home? We were hopeful that this summer would be our inauguration into the burgeoning group of families taking to the great outdoors in recreational vehicles. Good friends of ours with three kids head out in an RV each summer and each year they add more and more days to their vacation. Singing its praises, they convinced us that we would not just enjoy ourselves — but that we would love the experience. Imagine, they exclaimed, not having to wake our sleeping teenagers to be able to begin our day's journey. Moreover, we could avoid fast food restaurants by keeping a modest supply of healthy, easily-made lunches in our RV's refrigerator. And, to be honest, having one's own bathroom and shower on the road was appealing, as was the fact that we could avoid being bitten by bugs while we slept.

An RV is a vehicle that combines transportation and temporary living quarters for travel, recreation and camping. It isn't necessary to own an RV; one can easily rent one. Though not all RVs are motor homes (some are towables), for the purpose of this chapter we will consider an RV one where kitchen, sleeping, bathroom and dining facilities are all conveniently accessible to the driver's area from inside.

We decided to rent an RV, drive one-way and fly home. Our trip would begin in New York and terminate in Los Angeles, where we would drop our son off for his college freshman orientation. It sounded ideal and we quickly put together an itinerary that included stops we knew we would all enjoy — a few days of river rafting in West Virginia, visiting relatives and friends in Texas and New Mexico, checking out the family-friendly resorts in the desert city of Las Vegas and more. Though our initial number-crunching did not provide the main impetus for our trip (RVs are not inexpensive vehicles to operate and rentals range in price from $70 to $170/day), we truly liked the idea of having all the comforts of home (and more) on the road with us.

> GREAT VACATIONS TIP: The **Good Sam Club** provides many services for RVers, including a trip-planning service. It also publishes *Trailer Life Campground & RV Services Directory*. For more information call 805-389-0300.

Families with young children will find that RVs have additional selling points. For example, you can always warm a bottle, heat up some baby food and not have to worry about a toddler wandering off during the night — without having to give up the pleasures of being out in the wilderness. Multigenerational and intergenerational groups will also discover that grandparents might be more likely to participate in an outdoors-oriented vacation when they don't have to cope with tent camping.

Our first phone call was to the Recreational Vehicle Industry Association, RVIA, at 800-477-8669 — a sponsor of the Go Camping America™ Committee — which provided us with its 16-page *Vacation Planner* filled with information on the benefits of RV travel, rentals, purchases, campgrounds, state and regional RV associations and more. You can also write to RVIA at Dept. RK, P.O. Box 2999, Reston VA 20195-0999.

Each year millions of families claim that traveling in an RV makes getting to one's destination as much fun as being there. The thought of not having to pack and unpack during our two-week journey, not wondering what we would do with the purchases we made en route, having a VCR to help the kids pass the driving time (though this may encourage the kids to tune out instead of us all tuning into each other and take away the togetherness we like to think a long car trip involves) were all inviting. We weren't sure if our RV would have a washer/dryer or a dishwasher, but we were assured that it was possible. Though our excursion was to take place in August, RV camping is popular year-round, in both warm and cold weather venues. RVIA publishes a booklet, *Wintertime RV Use and Maintenance*, which should be helpful to both renters and owners. In addition to representing the RV industry to both the public and the government, RVIA monitors compliance for vehicles made by its members and provides a number of educational services and information on RV & Camping shows open to the public.

BOOKED FOR TRAVEL

SEARCHING FOR LAURA INGALLS: A *Reader's Journey* chronicles a modern-day visit to the world of the beloved author of the little house series. Its compilers, the Knight/Lasky family, traveled the prairies by RV, rather than covered wagon. Daughter, Meribah (who appears to be about 9 or 10), keeps a journal of the trip. Mom, Kathryn Lasky, provides supplemental historical and background data, and Dad, Christopher G. Knight, records the experience in photographs. This book is a real delight, a treasure, impeccable. (Macmillan,)

We were surprised to learn that there are 400 RV rental outlets nationwide. If you don't see a listing in your phone book (check under Recreation Vehicle — Renting and Leasing) the *Vacation Planner* mentioned above will help you begin your search or you can contact the Recreation Vehicle Rental Association (RVRA) by calling 800-336-0355/703-591-7130 or writing to 3930 University Drive, Fairfax, VA 22030. For $7.50 they'll send you the guide, *Rental Ventures*, which lists over 250 options in the U.S. and Canada. Two companies that offer RV rentals are Cruise America (800-327-7799/602-262-9611) and Go Vacations, Inc. (310-329-8999).

We also found that the *Vacation Planner* provided details on selecting campgrounds, be they on private or public land. A coupon in the booklet enables readers to contact the newest service of the National Association of RV Parks and Campgrounds and receive ($1 per state) campground directories plus information on many of the campground chains — from AAA Campbooks to Yogi Bear's Jellystone Park Campground Directory. Serious RVers will want to learn more about the ownership and member resorts that exist around North America. Though most of these facilities are only for members, several do have rental sites. The advantage of staying at this type of campground compared to those open to the public is that they cater to their member/owners and are therefore likely to provide more services and amenities.

BOOKED FOR TRAVEL

Author Bill McMillon's intention in CAMPING WITH KIDS IN CALIFORNIA: *The Complete Guide, Where to Go and What to Do for a Fun-Filled, Stress-Free Camping Vacation* is to "provide ideas for family outings that enhance family camaraderie and encourage the outdoor activities many families never experience." He points out that "family camping is one of the most fulfilling, least expensive outings available." With this in mind, he has done a superb job of compiling data on and describing in depth the very best campgrounds for kids state-wide, including recommended ages at each, plus information about camping, hiking and special activities (our favorite is the *Annual Banana Slug Derby* at Prairie Creek Redwoods State Park). Campgrounds are listed by geographical region and are sited on a map at the beginning of the chapter in which they appear. The reqisite introductory chapter on *Tips for Camping with Kids* is succinctly thorough; the reader is not overwhelmed with caveats and admonitions (though there are a few). The book culminates with names and addresses of other State and Federal Campgrounds, Army Corps of Engineer Sites, U.S. Forest Service Sites, and so on. (Prima)

Now it's time to decide where and when to plan your camping trip. Regardless of whether you've decided on an RV or car camping, the following basic advice will start you off. We highly recommend investing in one (or several) of the books we review, which go into much greater detail than we have.

> *GREAT VACATIONS TIP:* If you plan to camp abroad, consider investing in the *International Camping Carnet* available from **Family Campers And RVers**, 4804 Transit Road, Depew, New York 14043. This organization, formerly the National Campers and Hikers Association, charges a $30 annual membership fee that includes a subscription to its magazine, *Camping Today.* You can call them at 800-245-9755 or 716-668-6242.

FINDING A CAMPGROUND

Whenever possible, we recommend making advance reservations at a campground. The United States has over 16,000 campgrounds, about 8,000 of which are publicly owned. Though some are very crowded and need to be booked months in advance, especially those at many of our National Parks, others will be much easier to reserve. Additionally, there are a number of RV-only camping resorts, though many campgrounds provide hook-ups for RVs, campsites for campers, cabins for rent and even hotel rooms.

A number of good books which list campgrounds and their facilities plus booking information can be found at your local bookstore or library. Free campground information is also usually available from local and state government tourist offices and Chambers of Commerce.

Before making your reservations, prepare your list of questions. Here are some suggestions:

• Begin by checking out the site's basic facilities: water, electricity, bathrooms, showers, grocery store, and the like.

• If you're heading for a public campground, ask what, if any, activities are sponsored. Are any designed just for kids or for the entire family to enjoy together? Is anything offered in the evenings? You'd be surprised (even in this age of cost-cutting) just how much is available.

GREAT VACATIONS TIP: If you're looking to camp on public land, here are some helpful organizations:
U.S. National Parks Service, 1849 C St. NW, Washington D.C. 20240
Information: 202-208-4747
Reservations: 800-365-CAMP
US Forest Service, Office of Information,
    201 14th St. SW, Washington DC 20240
Information: 202-205-1760
Reservations: 800-280-CAMP

To learn about camping possibilities in any number of states, write to the **National Campground Owners Association** at 11307 Sunset Hill Road, Suite B-7, Reston VA 22090. Tell them which states you're interested in and enclose $1 for each state's directory.

• Ask about weather conditions. Will it be cold at night or first thing in the morning? Does morning dew cause things to get wet? This will give you guidelines on what to pack — and what to leave at home.

• What wildlife are you apt to come across? We know that anappeal of camping is that you will view animals in their natural surroundings, but you do want to talk about any dangerous critters you and your children might encounter (bears and snakes immediately come to mind here) and discuss safety strategies prior to your trip. Simple advice such as walking slowly in rocky or grassy areas and refraining from sticking little hands into crevices are both good ways not to be startled by snakes. Even cute little creatures such as chipmunks and squirrels present easily avoided health hazards for campers. Your kids should know not to feed them and, under no circumstances, touch them.

• Is there poison ivy or other poisonous vegetation in the area? If there is, ask which ones and be certain that you and your kids know how to identify these potential vacation spoilers.

- Don't forget to ask whether picnic tables, barbecues and food lockers (where you can protect your provisions when you leave camp for the day) are provided.

PICKING A CAMPSITE

How many times have you passed by a campground and seen families crowded on top of each other and wondered if this is truly the way camping is meant to be? Fortunately, not all campgrounds are crowded and right on a public highway. Even within the same campground there are choices, many of which will change as your kids grow older. You'll do less harm to the environment if you choose a site that has been used before, plus it will most likely be easier for you in the long run. Safety, of course, is paramount. Here are some things you'll want to keep in mind:

- First and foremost, you want to be absolutely certain to arrive at your destination well before sundown when there's plenty of light available.

- How close (or how far) from the common facilities do you want to be?

- If you're in an RV, what is the access? Drive-in/drive-out is highly recommended to avoid having to back out of a spot — a tricky maneuver for novice RVers.

- Though many experienced campers recommend heading for the edges of the campground, with small children this might not be the best choice. Although you'll get a better view of the river flowing by, you'll also have to be extra careful that your child doesn't fall in by accident.

- The proximity of your campsite to other campers is another factor to consider. You can be pretty certain that your kids will be noisy — that's part of being a kid. If you're next to another family with youngsters, the parents probably won't complain (though you may not love the idea of other kids' noise), but if you're next to singles or senior citizens who may not be accustomed to having active, curious children around, be careful. You don't want to have to discipline your kids all the time. Yes, you want them to be respectful of others, but the object here is to also have fun!

- Look for a campsite that's as level as possible, with ample room to move around. Avoid places that would be adversely affected by weather conditions, such as gullies.

- Don't forget to learn if campfires are permitted. If they are, be certain to discuss fire caution with your kids before you leave home.

- Above all, leave the site even more pristine than you found it.

BOOKED FOR TRAVEL

CAMPING SECRETS: *A Lexicon Of Camping Tips Only The Experts Know*, by Cliff Jacobson, comes packaged in a plain brown dust wrapper and boasts that "it details hundreds of ideas and procedures which are never found in traditional camping texts." For example: cloth diapers make the best camp towels;, dipping the tip of a knife in boiling water for 30 seconds makes it easier to sharpen; secrets to make a campfire in wet weather and keep it alight, and more. A solid book for serious campers. (ICS)

PREPARING A CAMPSITE

Once you've chosen a campsite, set specific boundaries for your kids. We like the idea of taking balls of yarn, a different color for each child, and using them to mark off the "safe" area for each. Listen to your kids. They may not be as intrepid as you think. When our boys were younger we discovered that our youngest wanted his area in front of what seemed like an inconsequential rock. Apparently he was unable to see our campsite when he ventured behind what to him was a big boulder! Next, arrange a play area for your young child to retreat to when he or she gets tired of helping to set up camp — yes, there's plenty for even the youngest to do: spreading the ground cloth, hammering in the tent posts, or filling a pot with water.

Older children may enjoy having their own tent. Not only will they think this is wonderful, think of how nice a little privacy will be for you. There's no reason RVers shouldn't bring along a tent for the kids as well.

> *GREAT VACATIONS TIP:* When it comes to food storage, we recommend that you keep all food in your car (if there are no food lockers at the campground) and seal your windows tightly. The trunk is probably the best spot. Hanging food bags from a tree is not recommended these days as the animals have caught onto this trick. If you choose not to use your car, keep the food in seal-in bags as far away from your camp as possible, on low ground. This will minimize odors that attract critters.

WHAT TO BRING ALONG
Following are basic items for camping trips:

tent(s)
ground cloth
sleeping bags or other warm bedding
extra blankets
layered clothing (avoid cotton)
change of clothing
toilet paper

raingear (cheap ponchos are good choices)
pillows
air mattress (this conducts cold; think about foam beds)
towels/washcloths

It makes good sense to consider the following:

waterproof flashlights
lots of extra batteries
lanterns
whistles
canteen
day backpack
hats

lanyard rings (good for hanging
  lanterns, flashlights, etc.)
contact cement
work gloves
rope and/or shock cords
water shoes (good for showers too)
folding chairs
all purpose tool

The following with help ensure your family's health & wellness:

toiletry kits
aspirin
bandaids
moleskin (wonderful after hiking)
ipecac
thermometer

antibiotic cream
tweezers
sunscreen
bug repellent
prescription medication
booklet with emergency medical advice

Active families might want some recreational gear:

bicycles
fishing gear
camera

binoculars
frisbee
jump rope

For feeding the crew:

food (non-perishable is best)
camp stove or portable grill
cooler
trash bags
eating utensils
pots & pans
firestarter and matches (in waterproof
  container)

extra fuel
bottle opener
sponge
biodegradable soap (for dishes and
  body)
zip lock bags
snack food (popcorn is always a winner)

TAKING PRECAUTIONS

It never hurts to prepare in advance for problems that might arise on your trip. One of the biggest concerns we've heard from parents who have camped with very young children is the need to protect them from insects and the sun. If your baby is crawling, be on the lookout for stones, sticks, kitchen utensils and other risky objects, in addition to the more evident hazards of a campfire, lake, stream, etc. And don't forget that disposable diapers do not decompose and are not environmentally sound. A packet of cotton diapers and a tightly sealed diaper bag is highly recommended.

By their very nature, kids will be lured into wandering — from the campsite or from the trail. Each child should wear a whistle and you should agree upon some signals in advance — one that will indicate to you where they are, another to alert you that they're in trouble. Children ages three years and older should be able to understand how to implement the whistle but, if you're uncertain, practice it in advance before you leave home. It's important to let the kids know that the whistle is not a toy and is to be saved for communication purposes. Some parents think that giving each child a name tag with the name of the campground and specific campsite plus relevant medical facts is also a good idea. We've taught our kids to mark their paths with small stones we've collected when setting up camp, so we can track them if they wander off.

A word about dirt seems in order. There's no doubt about it — you and your kids will get dirty. If you're not limited by space (which you will be if you are hiking and camping) then extra changes of clothes will help not only when the originals get wet (which is another given) but when you get tired of looking at the grime. Chances are that even kids' sleepwear will get dirty between the time they change into it and the time they settle in for the night.

COMBINING RVs AND ADVENTURE

If you've thought about renting an RV but aren't sure that it'll allow you to camp "in style," here are a few unusual RV vacation options that may persuade you.

Since 1993, **Alaska Highway Cruises** (AHC) has been offering a unique travel product — an RV and cruise package in which travelers get the opportunity to see the "best of Alaska, by land and by sea."

The trip begins with an Alaskan cruise on Holland America Line, followed by an RV touring package. Participants are set up with a fully equipped recreation vehicle and are given a pre-set itinerary (of choice). All campsite reservations have been made in advance and detailed driving instructions make getting there simple. There are dozens of itineraries to select from, varying in length from seven to 21 nights. Most of the routes cover only Alaska, though several explore the Canadian Yukon Territory and a few others take in portions of the Alaska Highway. Needless to say, all sorts of adventures can be sampled along the way — canoeing in Ketchikan, rafting along the Mendenhall River, or sea kayaking near Sitka. One itinerary ventures above the Arctic Circle to the famous town of Kotzebue and the city of Nome. The land packages sound so appealing that we don't know which we'd select. From Denali National Park to the Kenai Peninsula and Gold Rush Country, each is filled with wondrous opportunities for discovery and adventure. AHC founder and president Gary Odle, has personally tested many of the routes with his own two children and he, too, is hard-pressed to name a specific favorite.

In 1997, the company will offer RV-only packages for those who don't want to take the cruise portion of the program. We recommend making plans early as substantial discounts are offered prior to the prime booking season. Special prices are offered for children, even on the cruise-portion of the journey, when kids would normally pay a third or fourth person fare. To learn more, contact the company at 3805 108th Avenue NE, Suite 204, Bellevue, WA 98004, or call 206-828-0989.

If the idea of combining your RV vacation with a horseback riding experience turns you on, consider **Outdoor Resorts River Ranch** in the resort community of River Ranch, Florida, 65 miles from Orlando. The resort, 25 miles from Lake Wales, offers a wide choice of accommodations (e.g., hotel rooms, suites, cottages) in addition to 400 RV sites with full hookups. Once you're settled in on the 1,700-acre property, you'll find a long list of activities, in addition to the western-style riding. Swimming pools, golf course and a spa facility are complemented by a marina where you can rent various water craft and a bicycle rental shop. Also on-site: an archery range, a horseshoe pitch and skeet shooting. Though no activities are designed exclusively for children, there's lots to interest youngsters, including a petting zoo, hayrides, arts and craft sessions and a recreation room with video games. For information, write to P.O. Box 30030, River Ranch, FL 33867 or call 800-654-8575.

Not all campgrounds consider the entertainment of children the purview of parents. **Papoose Pond Resort & Campground** in North Waterford, Maine, claims to the "Maine's best kept secret for family fun." In the mountains of the western part of the state, RVers will discover that the most difficult part of the vacation may be securing a reservation. A staffed recreation department offers a variety of activities for families and some just for kids. The daily schedule might include a canoe trip, hayrides, a scavenger hunt, toddler story hour or teen sports. A daily *Wild Adventure Club* for kids ages 6 to 12 runs during the summer season. Activities designed for both older and younger children are offered but are not all-day affairs. To catch of glimpse of Papoose Pond and view a number of its facilities, ask for its video brochure. Write to Papoose Pond Resort and Campground, RR 1, Box 2480, North Waterford, ME 04267-9600 or call 207-583-4470.

You can add extra excitement to a Southwestern vacation by combining your RV road trip with a houseboat float trip on Lake Powell. **Lake Powell Resorts & Marinas** operates a number of facilities along the shores of the lake. At its Wahweap campground on the southern end of the lake, not far from Page, Arizona, houseboat rentals are offered in conjunction with two nights of campsite rentals. Hiking in the Glen Canyon National Recreation area is a popular family activity as are numerous water sports. To learn more about this and other camp/RV/houseboat options contact Lake Powell Resorts at Box 56909, Phoenix, AZ 85079 or call 800-528-6154.

APPENDICES

BEST BETS

While all of the organizations, outfitters and destinations found in this book make ideal family vacation possibilities, anyone who has traveled with children knows that not all places work for all family configurations. Following are our personal choices that meet the varied needs of families, listed chapter-by-chapter. No listings appear for the *Mountain Adventures, Camping* or *Tour Operators* chapters as each entry in these chapters can accommodate individual needs. The fact that your selections don't appear on these lists does not indicate that the choice is a poor one. It simply means that we are not as comfortable with this choice for your family configuration as we are those that are listed.

ALL AGES & FAMILY CONFIGURATIONS
In this section, absolutely any age child and all adults will feel welcome and accommodated.

Adventure Travel Companies
Backroads
Bear Track Outfitting
Brooks Country Cycling Tours
Ciclismo Classico
Class VI River Runners
Gunflint Lodge & Outfitters
Laredo Enterprises
Laurel Highlands River Tours
Michigan Bicycle Touring
Nantahala Outdoor Center
Towpath Treks
Trek & Trail

Wolf River Canoes

Stay & Play
Club Med
Beaverkill Valley Inn
Castle Rock Ranch
Coffee Creek Ranch
Loch Lyme Lodge & Cottages
Pinegrove Dude Ranch
Scott Valley Resort & Guest
 Ranch

BEST BETS WHEN TRAVELING WITH BABIES
If your baby is under age 2, the following can help you enjoy your quest for adventure either by assisting in child care arrangements or in welcoming your baby on the trip.

Adventure Travel Companies
Backroads
Bear Track Outfitting
Brooks Country Cycling Tours
Ciclismo Classico
Class VI River Runners
Gunflint Lodge & Outfitters
Laurel Highlands River Tours

Nantahala Outdoor Center
Trek & Trail

Stay & Play
Club Med
Castle Rock Ranch
Coffee Creek Ranch

Loch Lyme Lodge & Cottages
Pinegrove Dude Ranch

Scott Valley Resort & Guest
Ranch
The Tyler Place

BEST BETS WHEN TRAVELING WITH TODDLERS/PRESCHOOLERS

When traveling with children in this age group (best defined as youngsters between the ages of 2 and 5), it is imperative to speak directly with the organization you're interested in. Those that welcome 4-year-olds, for example, may not accept 2-year-olds.

Adventure Travel Companies

Above The Clouds Trekking
Adirondack Mountain Club
Backroads
Bear Track Outfitting
Bill Dvorak's Kayak & Rafting
 Expeditions
Brooks Country Cycling Tours
Ciclismo Classico
Class VI River Runners
Cutting Edge Adventures
Equitour
Gunflint Lodge & Outfitters
Laredo Enterprises
Laurel Highlands River Tours
Mahoosuc Guide Service
Michigan Bicycle Touring
Nantahala Outdoor Center
Outdoor Adventure River
 Specialists
Outdoor Bound Inc.
Pocono Whitewater Adventures
Sea Trek
Sheri Griffith Expeditions

Slickrock Adventures
Towpath Treks
Turtle River Rafting Company
Trek & Trail
Wolf River Canoes

Stay & Play

Club Med
Beaverkill Valley Inn
Castle Rock Ranch
Coffee Creek Ranch
The Grove Park Inn Resort
High Hampton Inn & Country
 Club
The Homestead
Loch Lyme Lodge & Cottages
Montecito-Sequoia Lodge
Pinegrove Dude Ranch
Scott Valley Resort & Guest
 Ranch
Sunriver Resort
The Tyler Place
Vista Verde Ranch

BEST BETS WHEN TRAVELING WITH SCHOOL AGE CHILDREN

Almost every listing in this book welcomes school-age children whom we define as between the ages of 5 and 12. Rather than reread the table of contents, read through each listing to determine if your child(ren) fit within the parameters of the trips that most interest you.

IF TRAVELING WITH TEENAGERS

As parents of teenagers, we've carefully chosen those organizations and places where we believe teens and their parents will all return from vacation anxious to travel with each other again. Perhaps the most important feature of these trips is that other teens will be on hand. Again, these are specific choices; many other listings welcome teenagers.

Adventure Travel Companies

Adirondack Mountain Club
Arizona Raft Adventures
Backroads
Battenkill Canoe
Bicycle Adventures
Bike Vermont
Bill Dvorak's Kayak & Rafting
  Expeditions
Boundary Country Trekking
Brooks Country Cycling Tours
Butterfield & Robinson
Class VI River Runners
Cutting Edge Adventures
ECHO
Euro-Bike Tours
Equitour
Europeds
Gerhard's Bicycle Odysseys
Headwaters River Company
James Henry River Journeys
Hiking Holidays
Hughes River Expeditions
Hurricane Creek Llama Treks
Laredo Enterprises
Le Vieux Moulin
Mahoosuc Guide Service
Mariah Wilderness Expeditions
Michigan Bicycle Touring
Nantahala Outdoor Center
New England Hiking Holidays
Northern Outdoors
Outdoor Adventures
Outdoor Adventure River
  Specialists
Outdoor Bound
Pocono Whitewater Adventures
REI Adventures
River Odysseys West
Roads Less Traveled

Rocky Mountain River Trips
Sea Trek
Sheri Griffith Expeditions
Slickrock Adventures
Sunrise County Canoe
  Expeditions
Trek & Trail
Turtle River Rafting Company
Unicorn Rafting Expeditions
Vermont Bicycle Touring
Vermont Icelandic Horse Farm
Western River Expeditions

Stay & Play

Club Med
Beaverkill Valley Inn
Castle Rock Ranch
Coffee Creek Ranch
Fir Mountain Ranch
The Grove Park Inn Resort
Loch Lyme Lodge & Cottages
The Homestead
High Hampton Inn & Country
  Club
Leon Harrel's Old West
Adventure
Montecito-Sequoia Lodge
Pinegrove Dude Ranch
Scott Valley Resort & Guest
  Ranch
Sunriver Resort
The Tyler Place
Vista Verde Ranch
Whitneys' Inn
Wild Horse/Derringer Ranch
Y. O. Ranch

BEST BETS FOR INTERGENERATIONAL GROUPS — GRANDPARENTS TRAVELING WITH GRANDCHILDREN

The key factor for this group is that both generations are able to find peers to socialize with. Soft adventures of the type in this book lend themselves well to intergenerational trips.

Adventure Travel Companies

Adirondack Mountain Club
Allagash Canoe Trips
Arizona Raft Adventures
Backroads
Bear Track Outfitting
Bike Vermont
Bill Dvorak's Kayak & Rafting
  Expeditions
Boundary Country Trekking
Brooks Country Cycling Tours
Butterfield & Robinson
Canoe Country Escapes
Ciclismo Classico
Class VI River Runners
ECHO
English Lakeland Ramblers
Euro-Bike Tours
Equitour
Europeds
Gerhard's Bicycle Odysseys
Gunflint Lodge & Outfitters
Hiking Holidays
Hughes River Expeditions
Laredo Enterprises
Laurel Highlands River Tours
Mahoosuc Guide Service
Mount Robson Adventure
  Holidays
Mariah Wilderness Expeditions
Michigan Bicycle Touring
Nantahala Outdoor Center
New England Hiking Holidays
Northern Outdoors
Outdoor Adventures
Outdoor Adventure River
  Specialists

Pocono Whitewater Adventures
River Odysseys West, Inc.
Roads Less Traveled
Rocky Mountain River Trips
Sea Trek
Sheri Griffith Expeditions
Slickrock Adventures
Sunrise County Canoe
  Expeditions
Towpath Treks
Trek & Trail
Turtle River Rafting Company
Unicorn Rafting Expeditions
Vermont Bicycle Touring
Western River Expeditions
Wolf River Canoes

Stay & Play

Club Med
Beaverkill Valley Inn
Castle Rock Ranch
Coffee Creek Ranch
Fir Mountain Ranch
The Grove Park Inn Resort
High Hampton Inn & Country
  Club
The Homestead
Loch Lyme Lodge & Cottages
Pinegrove Dude Ranch
Scott Valley Resort & Guest
  Ranch
Sunriver Resort
Vista Verde Ranch
Whitneys' Inn
Wild Horse/Derringer Ranch
Y. O. Ranch

BEST BETS WHEN TRAVELING AS A MULTIGENERATIONAL FAMILY

In the many trips we've taken with our own parents and siblings we've discovered that we rarely need the company of other folks. Yet, it's somehow more just that much more interesting when we do meet other people in our travels. As with our comments for those times when you're traveling with school-age children, we believe that every listing in this book offers something for each generation.

WHEN YOU'RE A SINGLE PARENT

We know first-hand that traveling with only our children presents a challenge. We know it's not always easy to make friends, find amenable adult company for meals or not feel guilty when we send out kids off to chldren's programs.

Adventure Travel Companies

Fortunately, the nature of adventure travel is well-suited to the single parent. We can't recall any adventure vacation we've taken where there weren't either solo travelers or other single parents along on the journey. Just ask any of the Adventure Travel Companies which trips it recommends for single parents and you won't go wrong.

Stay & Play
Club Med
Coffee Creek Ranch
The Homestead
Leon Harrel's Old West
   Adventure
Montecito-Sequoia Lodge
Pinegrove Dude Ranch
Sunriver Resort
Scott Valley Resort & Guest
   Ranch
Whitneys' Inn
Y. O. Ranch

INDEX

Other books published
by World Leisure

- Skiing America by Charles Leocha
   The most extensive and detailed guidebook to
   North America's best ski resorts now in its 9th edition $18.95

- Ski Europe by Charles Leocha
   America's most extensive and detailed guidebook to
   Europe's best ski resorts now in its 10th edition $17.95

- WomenSki by Claudia Carbone
   Award-winning breakthrough book about
   why women can't ski like men and shouldn't. $14.95

- Getting To Know You – 365 questions and activities
   to enhance relationships by Jeanne McSweeney & Charles Leocha
   A book of intimate questions that get right to the heart of
   successful relationships. $6.95

- Getting To Know Kids in Your Life
   by Jeanne McSweeney and Charles Leocha
   Interactive questions and activities to really get to know children for parents, aunts,
   uncles, grandparents and anyone who shares time with 3- to 7-year-olds
                                                                    $6.95

- A Woman's ABCs of Life – Lessons in Love, Family and Career
   from those who learned the hard way   by Beca Lewis Allen
   Inspired advice collected for her daughter helps women expand their
   lives with practical, fun and entertaining insights about life $6.95

- Travel Rights by Charles Leocha
   The book is filled with answers to travelers' difficult questions.
   It saves you money and makes travel more hassle-free. $7.95

- Great Nature Vacations With Your Kids by Dorothy Jordon
   The definitive guide to family nature vacations. $9.95

All available by calling 1-800-444-2524
or send payment plus $3.75 shipping and handling
to: World Leisure, P.O. Box 160, Hampstead, NH 03841